Religious Outsiders
and the Making of Americans

Religious Outsiders and the Making of Americans

R. LAURENCE MOORE

Oxford University Press

NEW YORK   OXFORD

Oxford University Press

Oxford   New York   Toronto
Delhi   Bombay   Calcutta   Madras   Karachi
Petaling Jaya   Singapore   Hong Kong   Tokyo
Nairobi   Dar es Salaam   Cape Town
Melbourne   Auckland

and associated companies in
Beirut   Berlin   Ibadan   Nicosia

Copyright © 1986 by Oxford University Press, Inc.

First published in 1986 by Oxford University Press, Inc.,
200 Madison Avenue, New York, New York 10016

First issued as an Oxford University Press paperback, 1987

Oxford is a registered trademark of Oxford University Press

Library of Congress Cataloging-in-Publication Data
Moore, R. Laurence (Robert Laurence), 1940-
Religious outsiders and the making of Americans.
Includes index.
1. United States—Religion.
2. Religious pluralism—United States.   I. Title.
BR515.M58   1986   291'.0973   85-8968
ISBN 0-19-503663-8
ISBN 0-19-505188-2 (pbk.)

2 4 6 8 10 9 7 5 3 1

Printed in the United States of America

In Memory of
Todd
and for
Greta, Alissa, and Patrick

Les hommes ont oublié cette vérité, dit le renard. Mais tu ne dois pas l'oublier. Tu deviens responsable pour toujours de ce que tu as apprivoisé. Tu es responsable de ta rose . . .

Saint-Exupéry, Le Petit Prince

Preface

Several years ago, more now than I care to count, I started to write a book. I have wound up with a manuscript that in form resembles a series of essays. That fact is mildly troubling to me, for I had wanted to construct a linked narrative. On the other hand if the arguments in the pages that follow are at all successful, they do suggest something of a narrative pattern. Collectively the essays aim to shake up the denominational hierarchy that governs the way in which American religious history generally gets told. This perhaps obsessive concern will become immediately apparent to the reader. Although I first prepared most of them for a number of quite separate academic occasions, the chapters are joined. They were rewritten and put together with single-minded intent during the course of a single sabbatical year. The few portions of the project that have been published previously have not been reprinted in anything like their original version.[1]

America's religious culture was and still is more Protestant than anything else, but the issue is complicated. The compulsion to stress Protestant dominance in America's past has in my mind resulted in any number of distorted impressions which, among other things, have led us to overemphasize the degree of change in the very recent past. We seem to be currently declaring the death of Protestant dominance without appreciating the fact that that sort of declaration has a rather interesting history. For as good reasons as now exist, some men and women at the very beginning of the American republic heaved a sigh of relief and stated that Protestant clergy, at least those representing the most important denominations of the colonial period, no longer set the tone for what America was all about. Similar declarations, in different contexts, were uttered periodically throughout the nineteenth century.

In truth I wonder whether we could make out from its general use in historical literature about the United States just exactly what the term "Protestant" means. Confusions abound, and they have only been multiplied by the tendency to equate Protestant culture in America with the activities of a few denominational groups labeled "mainline." In many standard religious histories of the United States, what counts as mainline begins with the Congregational and Presbyterian churches of the colonial period and eventually encompasses the nineteenth-century Baptists, Methodists, Episcopalians, and sometimes even the Unitarians. Virtually everything else in religious America, including the life habits of many people who were Protestant merely because they were not anything else, gets treated as something not quite in the American grain. Even Lutherans have been only recently noticed. What is outside the mainline churches requires special explanation as something that is not natural. Seventh-day Adventists, Mormons, Christian Scientists, Jehovah's witnesses, Pentecostals—however homegrown these sectarians might be—do not flow smoothly from the theological development that is traced always out of Puritan New England.

It requires very little digging to uncover some odd things about the pronounced and persistent habit of many historians to narrow the parameters of what constitutes significant or normal religious behavior in America. Civil libertarians have consistently insisted on America's sacred duty to make the country a place of unprecedented religious tolerance. Faced however, with the realities of religious pluralism—multiplying sects and excessive fervor for seemingly bizarre religious tenets—they have reacted with something short of enthusiasm. Thomas Jefferson did not sponsor religious freedom with the expectation, certainly not the hope, that religious Americans would long continue their religious squabbles or find pretexts to start new ones. Like most moderate deists, who viewed strongly held religious beliefs of whatever kind as superstition, Jefferson anticipated that legal tolerance would move his countrymen toward a sensible and nondividing religious center. When the results proved to be different, those who followed in Jefferson's ideological tracks argued that Americans simply had not matured enough to discover their common religious outlook. The possibility that American religious energy would necessarily expend itself with everlasting centrifugal force was one they tried to ignore.

As I shall try to show, an analogous reluctance to face up to the plain consequences of America's religious arrangements has informed the books of many of the best church historians. Although they have stressed the fact that church voluntarism was what made religious experience in America different from what it had been in Europe, they were for a long time remarkably consistent in denying that the result of religious disestablishment was a disorderly and theologically uninspiring pluralism. They maintained instead that religious divisions in America were not part of providential designs. They were therefore more apparent than real, always on their way to disappearing. Never imagining that sectarian fever was what gave energy to all American religions, they regarded an indefinitely continuing sectarian spirit as a sort of scandal. A unified church remained the ideal of both Catholic and Protestant theologians.

To be sure, some attitudes have changed. The recent attention focused on historical patterns of ethnicity has enlivened interest in religious difference. Still, I suspect that many American historians remain comfortable with Will Herberg's conclusion that American religious life has been headed for a broad and tolerant religious accommodation characterized, first, by a homogenizing of ethnic traits that has made all Protestants alike, all Catholics alike, and all Jews alike; and, second, by the development of a common faith that has bonded these three large groups together. Otherwise I find the enormous interest in Robert Bellah's article on civil religion, first published in 1967, inexplicable.[2] In an era when consensus interpretations had been challenged in all other areas of American historical research, that essay gave extended life to the view that consensus was the key to understanding religious experience in the United States. If one accepted Bellah's main point, one could distill what was important about American religious life without mentioning division at all. Above the passionate religious identifications of various denominations was a set of national symbols and rituals that transcended and effectively neutralized various oddities of individual belief and behavior. Americans, those who followed Eisenhower's advice to go to any church no matter what it was and those who went to no church at all, were one people. If cultural anthropologists could interpret the mythological cosmos of the people of Bali, why could not historians just as easily untangle the common meaning systems of religious Americans?

I am not out to prove that all views about America's religious past, other than my own, are absurdly wrong. I would not mention reservations about past historical work unless I regarded that work as valuable and important. Scholarship never eradicates, not in a field like history. It only supplements. My intention is to suggest some reasonably fresh ways to understand religious pluralism, ones that have become useful to me in analyzing what factors have made Americans so notably a church-going people. I am also concerned about emphases in past scholarship that have encouraged misinterpretations of the contemporary religious scene. It is impossible to locate a period of American history when so-called small sects were not growing at a faster clip than denominations then viewed as large and stable. That fact is crucial and central to any discussion of American religious pluralism. Yet dozens of recent books and an almost endless amount of journalistic commentary, much of it based on the work of very able sociologists, have assumed that sects and cults (usually employed as pejorative terms) began to affect religious life in this country only around 1960. Our failures in Vietnam have properly had to answer for many things, but the disruption of "normal" religious behavior is not one of them.

At the heart of my reflections is the question of what determines historical significance. Why do historians pay attention to some things in the past but ignore, or treat as sideshow events, other things that affected just as many people? Earlier, in writing a book about American spiritualism, I found myself asking why a subject that had generated so much debate in nineteenth-century America had previously received little serious or sustained historical treatment. I concluded that twentieth-century scholars with Ph.D. degrees had found it beneath their dignity to write about nineteenth-century people who avidly followed reports about alleged communications with the dead.

That disdain is admittedly less controlling these days, for everyone, and every group, named and nameless, eventually attracts the attention of a graduate student in history looking for a dissertation subject or of a young scholar worried about tenure. Perhaps my own interests began in those crucibles of anxiety. Be that as it may, a number of subjects in American religious history still need closer attention than they have received. The problem is not necessarily a lack of books, even good books, devoted to them. The problem seems rather to be that we have not found convincing ways to make them central to American experience.

They have not become important to historians in search of usable pasts.

In arguing for the significance of my own subjects, I have had to wrestle with a number of confusing problems concerning nomenclature. Those religious Americans whose stories are pursued in this book were regarded by many of their contemporaries, and by themselves, as outsiders, as people who did not share in something called dominant culture. Outsider and equivalent designations almost naturally suggest insignificance, a deviance or exoticism that by definition cannot form part of the central story. I have argued elsewhere and intend to reiterate in what follows my view that outsiderhood is a characteristic way of inventing one's Americanness.[3] Despite what Frederick Jackson Turner wrote, most people who lived in this country did not gain a sense of what it meant to be an American by going to the frontier. Far more of them gained that sense by turning aspects of a carefully nurtured sense of separate identity against a vaguely defined concept of mainstream or dominant culture.

My own search for a usable past is doubtlessly reflected in these pages. I am intrigued by the way in which the American experiment encouraged people to express their most cherished convictions in the language of dissent. New religions, which have often been linked to ethnic identifications, have served as vehicles through which people have nurtured a sense of antagonistic culture. Since the religious energy they have fostered has only sporadically fed into movements with progressive political significance, this fact has brought small comfort to political radicals. Religion has not generated class struggle in America even though class is one extremely important factor in understanding religious divisions in America. In fact the rhetoric of religious outgroups has more often than not proved compatible with a distinctly conservative politics. Established groups, whether in eighteenth-century Virginia or nineteenth- and twentieth-century America, had good reasons to worry about the disruptive influence of Separate Baptists, Mormons, or Moonies. Those groups challenged vested interests. Nonetheless, if religious outgroups were necessarily protesting groups, they usually channeled protest in ways that, from the standpoint of a contemporary progressive social reformer, contributed precious little to the general betterment of mankind.

The reader of the above paragraph and of a good bit that will follow may suspect that my quest for a usable past has turned up some fairly poor models. So be it. I remain convinced that the religious groups I have studied, however politically useless or even pernicious their dissent often was, did a great deal to expose the shabbiness and the arrogance of the culture surrounding them and contributed a fair measure to whatever success the American system has had. Besides, any past that approaches reality is never the story we might wish had happened. The very best past is usable to our very best hopes about the present and future only in the most limited and flawed ways. I should warn the reader that I am somewhat pessimistic.

Usable pasts aside, arguments about historical significance must finally come to rest on the persuasiveness of claims about how best to understand the past. We are no longer positivists, but we still aspire to know what really happened. Yet who or what is to tell us what counted, what mattered? The rhetoric of historical actors is often slippery and doubled-edged. Perhaps the battlefields of religious controversy are especially littered with the misperceptions of those who took part in the drama and even with their deliberate hypocrisies. Can we trust partisans to tell us what was important? Can we trust ourselves not to listen too intently to those who are telling us what we want to hear? If a group of people advertise themselves as outsiders, and if they really seem to be up to some silly things, like searching for golden tablets on a hillside in western New York, do we have to pay much attention to the historian who wants to move these people from the periphery to the middle?

I can attempt to answer some of these questions as we go along. However, I would like to say something about the project of counting church members which is one time-tested method for sorting out the significance of religious groups in America. Some, though by no means all, of the groups I have written about attracted relatively few dedicated adherents. Logic may suggest that they were therefore less important than the denominations that attracted the majority of Americans who formally identified with Protestant churches. Yet how can that logic explain why Joseph Smith and Mary Baker Eddy were and are names as recognizable to "average" Americans as Horace Bushnell or Henry Ward Beecher? Religious life does not easily reduce itself to church membership figures. The citation of numbers cannot tell us how to measure, compare, and interpret the different ardor with which religious belief is held. It cannot tell us how to correct our figures to take account of the fierce religious dedication of adherents of small groups. How do we measure that against the nominal piety of indifferent worshipers? Statistics relating to denominational populations are of little help when we try to analyze the enormous popular attention that was focused on religious groups which on the basis of numbers should have occasioned little public comment. If sustained controversy denotes cultural importance, then Mormons were as significant as any other religious group in nineteenth-century America. In all kinds of ways Mormons made American religious experience seem vigorous. They aroused opposition precisely because they were so profoundly a part of the American scene.

The problems of weighing significance are obviously manifold. Let me approach them with another set of suggestions. Religious struggles engage people in elaborate strategies that on each side entail affirmation and denial, advancement and repression, of a set of cultural options. Some groups champion themselves as upholders of norms, others as challengers of those norms. Despite the apparent claims being made by the antagonists, American religious culture never belonged exclusively to any side. National culture cannot be defined by reference to a set of Platonic ideals. It is created by contests between groups who revere different cultural symbols and who have different perspectives on shared cultural symbols. In many cases the contests reflect realities about social structure, about economic station, even about psychological health. Groups that presume to uphold norms often have economic power and recourse to legal sanctions to back up their claims to dominance. Their identities and sense of belonging may be relatively unproblematic when compared with the situation of people who view themselves as part of a minority. However, contests also have to do with the perceptions, even the fictions, that competitors create; and perceptions obscure and sometimes, in effect, reverse insider and outsider roles and the importance that opposing groups attach to one another. Those who play the role of outsiders can wield enormous public influence that the alleged insiders are powerless to block. They can also determine in crucial ways the outlook and behavior of the insiders. In a telling manner, insiders spend the most time asserting their dominance precisely when the values they uphold enjoy the least popular respect.

Since a good bit of the thinking underlying these essays has to do with notions of reversal, the upsetting of our usual hierarchies of significance, readers may suspect that I owe a debt to French deconstructive criticism. Actually, I have read only unsystematically in the works of Derrida and those of the other major proponents of deconstructive approaches to texts. They would scarcely recognize me as a comrade. I confess, however, that my research into the meaning of various labels attached to religious groups, and the strategic uses of those labels by both historical actors and historians, has given me considerable respect for what deconstructionists call the "heterogeneity of the text."[4] I have learned a great deal by recognizing that whatever seems to be meant or intended in a particular text takes its meaning from what the text ostensibly and explicitly denies. To note one example that is central to the ongoing argument, to call oneself an outsider depends for its effect on a meaning that is entirely opposite—to wit, everyone but the speaker and those who belong to his group are outsiders. In determining significance, the historian faces a complicated texture of fictions, and the intentions behind those fictions are not easy to decode.

Finally, I owe the reader a few words about the choice of topics that comprise the chapters. The subjects I have included should cause no controversy. They will justify themselves. However, what about the enormous range of subjects excluded? If I presume to write about religious outsiders, how can I neglect the religion of the people who were native to North American turf, or such much later groups as Shakers, the Amish, and the Mennonites? How can I omit many denominations that have recently been granted mainline status, but have nonetheless remained on the edges of general narratives of American religious history—Quakers, Lutherans, the Disciples and Churches of Christ? Why do I not emphasize more the outsider beginnings of churches that later became every historian's illustration of what was mainline—Puritans, the Baptists, the Methodists? Is their story not an essential part of the project to place outsider groups at the center of narrative?

I might try to plead a sufficient defense simply by noting that a measure of authorial eccentricity is utterly appropriate to the project. However, a better defense is my concern for the reader's patience. Although I could have written similar essays about many of the omitted groups, the multiplication of subjects would have introduced thematic repetition. I am trying to make a point, not tell the story of every religious group that has at one time or another been left outside of the "mainstream." Those stories have in most cases been well enough told. My purpose is to suggest ways that those stories may become more central to our understanding of American experience and generative of more useful historical controversy than has hitherto surrounded them.

As a corollary matter, I have deliberately excluded very small groups and very recent groups from consideration. I thought that I could better make my point about historical bias if I chose groups with a proven record of growth and expansion on American soil. Whatever else accounts for the placing of these groups outside the American Protestant mainstream, they were not hot house flowerings that were doomed to extinction once exposed for a long time to inhospitable American soil. However paradoxically, they have all maintained a sense of separation from mainstream culture while advancing a very solid claim to be typically American.

Ithaca, New York   R. Laurence Moore
May 1985

Acknowledgments

This book has been gestating in my mind for a much longer time than I spent researching and writing it. To thank everyone who gave me ideas along the way is impossible. Collectively, they include my colleagues at Cornell, my students in religious history, and participants in a National Endowment for the Humanities seminar that I organized in the summer of 1981.

The bulk of the final writing was done in the academic year 1983–84 when an administrative leave from Cornell allowed me to take my notes to Paris. I incurred special debts there. Jacques Revel gave me a place to work by inviting me to become Directeur des études associé at the École des Hautes Études en Sciences Sociales. In conjunction with that appointment, Pierre-Yves Petillon, a superb Americanist at the École Normale Supérieure, provided me with an audience for a series of lectures. I am also indebted to Caroline Kaufmann, of the Centre d'Études Nord-Américaines, who sympathetically read the entire manuscript; and to Viola Sachs, a professor of American literature at the University of Paris VIII, who listened attentively while showing me the best restaurants along the rue du Cherche Midi.

On this side of the Atlantic, I must single out the following people. Michael Kammen fed me bibliography and encouragement, and made me worry about why I was taking so long to finish a single book. Shirley Rice typed the manuscript and patiently tried to make me competent with a word processor. Catherine Albanese read the manuscript in an extraordinarily helpful way. Sheldon Meyer once again agreed to sponsor my work through the press. Glenn Altschuler continued his bad habit of reading everything that I write and managed once again to alert me to many stupid things I had done. To Jane Dieckmann, who prepared the index, I owe thanks that only authors can appreciate.

Money also helped. Without support from the Rockefeller

Foundation and the Return Jonathan Meigs research fund, I would never have reached Oral Roberts University in Tulsa, the Moody Bible Institute in Chicago, and the Southern Baptist Historical Commission in Nashville. Without those visits, I would not have discovered nearly as much as I did. And the tone of the manuscript might well have been different, and wrong.

Finally, Sydney Ahlstorm. He may or may not have liked these pages, but he made me notice many of the things that they contain.

R. L. M.

Contents

Religious Outsiders
and the Making of Americans

Protestant Unity
and the American Mission—
The Historiography of a Desire

> . . . the United States is faced with the menace of a plural society
> based on religious differences.
>
> *Christian Century*, June 13, 1951

Before getting down to specific cases, it is essential to analyze somewhat closely and somewhat skeptically the general perspectives that have determined most of the writing about American religious history. One always risks becoming tedious in talking about books that are no longer much read. However, in many cases, and certainly in the present one, a look at historiography clarifies the main issues. Until we understand what has, in the historian's eye, separated "mainline" churches from "fringe" sects, we cannot appreciate fully those aspects of dissenting religious culture in the United States that have been historically trivialized.

In virtually any field of American history the first bias to note is New England. The Puritans began writing a sort of history as soon as they disembarked from the *Mayflower*, and their New England descendants for a long time had an unchallenged hand in constructing America's national past. The intertwining of the stories of the Puritans with prophecy is well-known. What God intended for New England, including the disasters, was intimately bound up with His millennial plans. The settlers of Massachusetts Bay attempted to contain dissent within tight boundaries of orthodoxy. Although dissenters themselves, they believed that a splintered and fragmented church could not be what God wanted. Throughout the nineteenth century, American historical writing

3

proceeded under the assumption that the New England churches, shorn of their links to secular authority, provided the most attractive models of church unity and harmony.

Dissent of course was not contained, either in colonial New England or in the infant republic.[1] At the beginning of the nineteenth century a unified Protestant church was nowhere in view. Most individual states had written into their constitutions the unique American principle of "voluntary churches," or churches without government financial support. The last vestiges of ecclesiastical establishment, in Massachusetts and Connecticut, were under strong attack. Yet, the early nineteenth-century books that qualify as religious history did not give sympathetic attention to the many varieties of religious position that could be located in America. One exception was Thomas Branagan's *A Concise View of the Principal Religious Denominations in the United States of America*, which was published in Philadelphia in 1811.[2] Branagan, a prolific author, identified himself as a nonconformist, an "outdoor" preacher who had run afoul of a New York law prohibiting preaching outside of regularly established churches.

That last fact no doubt was responsible for the generous inclusiveness of Branagan's book. Although Branagan did not approve of Jews, Atheists, Deists, or Epicureans, his discussions of everything else, from Presbyterians and Congregationalists to Dunkers, Mennonites, Shakers, and Separatists, gave no particular prominence to one group over another. As an analysis of American religious experience, Branagan's account left a lot to be desired. It had no order or arrangement except an alphabetical one. Only his singular tolerance of Christian multiplicity is worth remembering. He championed Christians who like himself braved "calumny and defamation" to preach an unpopular position. Their work, he thought, represented an important part of American religious experiments.

The reasons why other chroniclers of American religion vehemently disagreed are not hard to find. They were seeking to justify church disestablishment to those who thought it was a mistake that doomed the cause of true religion. In this context of argument, Branagan's endless list of diverse sects was annoyingly and embarrassingly excessive. Parading the bewildering array of American churches only furnished ammunition to those churchgoers who wanted to maintain strong government mechanisms to enforce "respectable" religious observance and to prevent, as they saw matters, the degeneration of religion into folly and lunatic enthusiasms. The first American church histories were written in an effort to respond to that fear. The men who wrote them were genuinely concerned that the separation of church and state in America posed potential dangers to the moral health of the nation. However, they were on balance persuaded that the American principle of voluntary churches worked. It had not caused a general collapse of a properly sensible religious authority because in practice American sectarianism was not quite so wild an engine as Branagan had imagined. Many churches existed in America, but only a few were significant.

The two most important titles from the mid-nineteenth century are: Robert Baird's *Religion in America* (first published in 1844) and Philip Schaff's *America. A Sketch of Its Political, Social, and Religious Character* (published in German in 1854 and then in English in 1855). Baird's work was pioneering. It was superbly organized (especially in view of the lack of models on which to rely); and as a broadly based account of American religious attitudes and practices, it was unsurpassed for many years. Baird divided the American churches of his day into Evangelical ones (whether Calvinist or Arminian) and non-Evangelical ones (a category that swept together Catholics, Unitarians, Universalists, Swedenborgians, Jews, Shakers, Mormons, Atheists, Deists, and Socialists).[3] Unlike Branagan, Baird took sides. His preferences were clearly with the Evangelicals and moreover with those evangelical churches that eschewed the revivalistic "excesses" that had inflamed passions in many churches during the period of the Second Great Awakening in America.

Aside from his own brand of Presbyterianism, one that stressed strict standards of church membership and closed communion, Baird managed to admire the Episcopal Protestant church, the Congregational church, the Regular Baptist churches, and the Methodist Episcopal church.[4] Some of these groups had made mistakes, but Baird saved his scorn for the non-Evangelicals, especially the Universalists (who "are heard with delight chiefly by the irreligious, the profane, Sabbath-breakers, drunkards") and the Mormons ("the annals of modern times furnish few more remarkable examples of cunning in the leaders, and delusion in their dupes, than are presented by what is called Mormonism.")[5]

Except for Catholics and Unitarians, to whom Baird tried hard, without success, to be fair, he placed all the non-Evangelicals very much at the fringes of American respectability. He wrote:

> Their ministers are almost all men of little learning, and that little is almost all concentrated in specious endeavors to maintain their tenets, by perverting the Scriptures, by appealing to the prejudices of their hearers, and by misrepresenting and ridiculing the doctrines of opponents who meet their subtle arguments with the plain declarations of Scripture, as well as with unanswerable arguments drawn from sound reason.[6]

Two things convinced Baird that the system of voluntary churches was working in the United States despite the presence of churches he did not like. The first was that government had not withdrawn completely from the area of religious life. Nothing, he thought, required that it should. The religious neutrality of the Constitution had not prevented individual states and municipalities from passing laws that favored the interests of Protestant evangelical groups. Sabbath laws were enforced in many parts of the country. The King James version of the Bible was read in most public schools after they were founded. Blasphemy was punished. American jurists praised Protestant Christianity in their written court decisions. These measures did not strike Baird as parts of a religious establishment nor were they so legally defined at the time. He regarded them as reasonable compromises through which the nation sought to preserve both a genuine religious tolerance and a proper Christianity. Baird's religious view set sharp limits to pluralism. He could not have agreed more with Lyman Beecher who wrote: "The integrity of the Union demands special exertions to produce in the nation a more homogeneous character and bind us together with firmer bonds."[7] In short, Baird regarded the United States as semi-officially a Protestant nation.

The second thing responsible for Baird's sanguine tone was even more important. He believed that divine providence guided historical development. According to his understanding of providential intention, America's mission was to convert the world to Christianity through active proselytizing. That fanciful conceit has of course had many sponsors in America's past, and its consequences have often been unhappy. Here we need only concern ourselves with the effects of that belief on Baird's construction of historical narrative. They were quite important, for Baird's confidence in providential design guided his determination of whether a religious group was important or not.

At the time he wrote, as Baird well knew, Roman Catholics and Mormons were growing rapidly in numerical significance whereas Episcopalians were, comparatively speaking, declining. He professed not to be worried, however, and made no effort to give Catholics and Mormons a significant position in his story. They were doomed to the fringes of American life because, he was convinced, that was the way God had planned matters. The number of religious groups in America, Baird argued, had actually diminished as America's population had increased. His empirical evidence for that assertion was weak, but his conception of providence made it unnecessary to look too closely at the meaning of numbers. According to Baird, Christianity was going to become more and more united in American life and more and more a uniting force. Catholics, Mormons, and the many non-evangelical sects of antebellum America were curiosities of a passing and not very important phase of national growth.

Philip Schaff concluded much the same thing. He was probably the most learned Protestant theologian and scholar who worked in the United States during the nineteenth century. Educated in Germany, Schaff was lured to the United States in 1843 to teach at a small seminary in Mercersburg, Pennsylvania, an American outpost of the German Reformed church. Schaff, like almost all other Continental theologians, believed in the basic unity of the Reformed church. In the abstract, he did not approve of the voluntary principle adopted in the United States and the sect and denominational system that it had spawned. On the other hand, he was sufficiently impressed with the energy and vitality of religious life in the United States to come to its defense. He argued to his doubtful German colleagues that, unexpectedly perhaps, a fundamental framework of order had emerged from American voluntarism.

Schaff and Baird had the same view of providence. The former, no more than the latter, could bring himself to believe that God would allow many Americans to be seduced by the "abominable" Mormons (Schaff's example of the worst product of American sectarianism).[8] Schaff made his two minds clear. "The Sect System," he wrote, "is certainly a great evil. It contradicts the idea of the unity of the church. . . . The abstract separation of Church and State, I cannot regard as the perfect and ultimate condition of things."[9] Yet, he added, until such times as God chose to settle confessional controversies, the sect system as it operated in America had some great advantages. According to Schaff, "the charge that the sect system necessarily plays into the hands of infidelity on one side and of Romanism on the other has hitherto at least not proved true. . . There is in America far less open unbelief and skepticism, than in Europe."[10] The present state of American churches, "a motley sampler of all church history," did not indicate the direction in which America was headed. It "was a state of transition to something higher and better."[11] He wrote:

> It is unquestionably very probable, that the ultimate fate of the Reformation will be decided in America; . . . on the banks of the Hudson, the Susquehannah, the Mississippi, and the Sacramento; and that it will result in favor not, as the sanguine Papists think, of the Roman, but of an evangelical Catholicism.[12]

As with Baird, Schaff's sense of what God intended guided his choices of what to emphasize about American religious life and what to play down. He too attached no long-range significance to the proliferation of sects in antebellum America. For the most part they were sects that Europe had dumped on America, and Schaff anticipated for them a short life in the New World. In sketching profiles of individual churches, Schaff explicitly limited himself to the denominations he considered most important and influential. These were the Roman Catholic (which he said would become vigorous when shorn of papacy and of saint and relic worship, i.e. when it became Protestant), the English Protestant varieties, (Congregational, Presbyterian, Episcopalian, Quaker, Methodist, Baptist), and the German Protestant varieties (Lutheran, Reformed and United Churches, and the Moravian Brethren). Schaff's "mainline" churches were those that he believed would eventually restore Christian unity. Voluntarism was not the means that God had chosen in America to perpetuate a debilitating pluralism. It was the means by which God would return mankind to the one true church.

The providential view which Baird and Schaff shared remained the overwhelmingly dominant perspective in later, general histories of American religion. Three works published at the end of the nineteenth century illustrate the point. Each tried to demonstrate why quarrelsome divisiveness was not the main direction in which American churches were headed. These are Daniel Dorchester, *Christianity in the United States from the First Settlement Down to the Present Time* (1888); H. K. Carroll, *The Religious Forces of the United States Enumerated, Classified, and Described on the Basis of the Government Census of 1890* (1893); and Leonard Woolsey Bacon *A History of American Christianity* (1897). The latter two were volumes in Schaff's important American Church History Series.

Notably, these books date from a period of rapidly increasing immigration and hence one marked by strikingly different patterns of religious diversity than had marked the antebellum period. Orthodox European Jews were beginning to settle in America in significant numbers for the first time, and the Catholic mosaic grew more complex with the infusion of large populations of Italian, Polish, and Slavic people. Furthermore, contrary to what Schaff and Baird had predicted, the domestically hatched religious groups they most feared, above all the Mormons, had not dropped into oblivion. Others in fact had appeared.

These developments, accompanied as they were by other accelerating signs of cultural complexity and heterogeneity, might seem to have placed in considerable jeopardy any faith that American Protestants were coming together in one united and dominant force. It is very difficult to make out any trend in the post-Civil War period suggesting the gradual end of American religious sectarianism. Yet although our authors were aware of the "problem" of diversity, they were not about to give up easily the pattern of prophecy that had been proclaimed so convincingly by Baird and Schaff. Undaunted by apparent realities, Dorchester, Carroll, and Bacon continued to insist that God's plan was to impose a rough unity on the Protestant churches of the United States and make them a world-redeeming force. That, in fact, was their main argument.

Dorchester's large volume provided the most complete panorama of America's religious history yet published. He started with Columbus and trisected each large section of his narrative into stories about the fortunes of Protestantism, Romanism, and a variety of "divergent currents." One does not have to read very far into Dorchester's account to discover which groups he thought carried the major responsibility for American destiny. In telling his readers about the exploits of early French and Spanish colonists, he revealed his controlling biases in every other line. Columbus was a Christian saint, someone chosen specially by God to make his voyage across the Atlantic, but his Spanish successors "were men of inferior character."[13] His notion of balanced judgment produced the following paragraph:

> What striking evidences do those times afford of a superior power controlling the movement of men! . . . While thirst for gold, lust of power and love of daring adventure served the Providential purpose of opening the New World to papal Europe, and Roman Catholic colonies were successfully planted in some portions, the territory originally comprised within the United States was mysteriously guarded and reserved for another—a prepared people.[14]

English Protestants, those happily "prepared" people, brought to America "intelligence, freedom of conscience, commercial enterprise, the triumphs of inventive genius."[15] Every time Dorchester tried to compliment the pioneering enterprises of Catholic explorers and religious, he brutally undercut his effort. The attempts of the French Jesuits to convert the Indians were heroic, a fact worthy of some wonder since Jesuits were credulous, superstitious, and "shorn of some of the best attributes of real manhood under the self-mortifying processes of their peculiar discipline."[16] The excruciating torments that a few brave Jesuit fathers suffered at the hands of hostile tribes deserved sympathetic attention, but those torments were, after all, "only a little less refined . . . than those of the papal inquisitions."[17] In any case, Jesuit efforts to win over the Indians were doomed, for "these powerful tribes proved to be the bulwarks raised up by Providence, and stationed all along that long line of the State of New York, for the protection of Protestant colonies against the machinations of the papacy."[18]

Dorchester did offer a reason other than providence to explain the failure of the Jesuits. They "only slightly interfered with the native habits, wild ways and impulses of the savages," and tried to live with the Indians on easy if not equal terms. In contrast, the English Protestants tolerated no compromises with their own civilization and insisted that the Indians settle in fixed residences, become clean and improve their dress, desert their "wigwam and loathsome cookery," and conform generally to Protestant standards regarding sexual modesty.[19] Dorchester's account of the English success was accurate enough. He gave ethnocentrism a perfect description, and nothing about it troubled him.

At the conclusion of his section covering the colonial period, Dorchester had English Protestants in firm control of American destiny, so much so that Dorchester had little trouble getting through the first fifty years of the national period. He recorded one Protestant triumph after another. The leading evangelical denominations stamped out the gross infidelity of Paine and Jefferson, and kept the "divergent currents" (Unitarians, Universalists, Millerites, Swedenborgians, and Mormons) well in check.

The period after 1850 posed a trickier problem for Dorchester's interpretive powers. How was he going to fit into his story the Catholics whose numbers were each day swollen by new immigrant arrivals? What about Jews and spiritualists? What about divisions in the major denominations that had resulted from the nation's failure to resolve the slavery issue peacefully? What about the "threatening aspects . . . in our great cities . . . of vast agglomerations of men of one foreign nationality preserving almost entire their manners, language, and traditions . . . [who] have set aside the American Sabbath, opened Sunday theaters, beer gardens, infidel clubs, and communistic societies"?[20]

Although Dorchester, in discussing events in the post-Civil War period, revealed a considerable amount of nervousness, he held firmly to the party line. The difficulties were no greater than God's resources. In answer to alarmists who claimed that Catholicism had already destroyed Protestant hegemony, Dorchester presented statistics to prove that Catholicism was not growing in proportion to the number of Catholics that had been admitted into the country. Many immigrants, he correctly argued, had deserted the faith. Since the "major" Protestant denominations were growing at a rate faster than the general increase in population, a fact attributable in part to the growing fashionableness of church membership, Dorchester entertained the illusion that "this country is the biggest grave for popery ever dug on earth."[21]

Dorchester comforted himself with similarly misleading conclusions about the prospects of the "divergent currents." The proportionate number of people attracted to outgroups, he argued, was declining. Mormonism remained "a local ulcer." Spiritualism was a "delusion" on the decline.[22] All in all, although God might be putting the mainline Protestant churches through a period of hard testing, Dorchester arranged his evidence to give diversity as little narrative importance as possible. Division recurred, but it was not the central theme of the past or the present. Fragmentation of the dominant Protestant impulse was always aberration.

The useful statistics that one finds in the H. K. Carroll volume, published in 1893, were intended to confirm what Dorchester had written. Carroll's figures on church membership gave religious historians who were premising their narratives on the certainty of eventual Protestant unity legitimate cause to take heart. Carroll's presentation begged many questions, but the raw figures were impressive and no doubt roughly accurate. Out of a population of 62,622,250, Carroll tallied a Protestant population of 49,630,000 and a Catholic population of only 7,362,000. That left around 5,000,000 skeptics or disbelievers to worry about.[23] Carroll was not as confident as Dorchester had been that America would become the graveyard of Catholicism, but he was convinced that Catholicism would prosper only as it became more Protestant and emulated Protestantism's superior intellectual training. Carroll's major source of statistical comfort was the news that the five largest denominations—Catholics, Methodists, Baptists, Presbyterians, and Lutherans—comprised 60 percent of the entire number of Christian communicants. The ten largest Christian churches comprised 75 percent.[24] Christian unity in America was therefore not out of reach, and Carroll dismissed the importance of Christian Scientists, Mormons, Spiritualists, Theosophists, and Ethical Culturalists.

With these statistics in hand, and given his strong conviction that providential design governed history anyway, Leonard Bacon in his work of 1897 was not tempted to do anymore than repeat the theme that America's religious destiny was, despite appearances, to end schism, not to multiply it. The latter tendency encouraged a useless competition among churches that shamed all of them. Bacon brought to a close nineteenth-century historical writing about American religion by demonstrating exactly the same thing that Baird and Schaff had tried to demonstrate: "This least amiable characteristic of the growth of the Christian church in America [schism] is not without its compensations. The very fact of the existence, in presence of one another, of these multitudinous rival sects, all equal before the law, tends in the long run, under the influence of the Holy Spirit of peace, to a large and comprehensive fellowship."[25] Bacon was describing a pluralism where formal divisions between sectarian units had little meaning, or should have little meaning. Foreseeing an end to acrimony, Bacon concluded: "There are many indications in the recent history of the American church, pointing toward some higher manifestation of the true unity of the church. ... We hear, in one form and another, the acknowledgment that the divided and subdivided state of American Christianity is not right, but wrong."[26]

The point is not that nineteenth-century church histories ignored religious diversity in America. We are talking about desire. In regarding tightly drawn lines of religious distinctiveness as transient and superficial, historians assigned significance to groups in ways that misrepresented their importance. They were wrong about the past, the present, and the future. Some religions were given a more significant part to play in God's plan than others; those became the mainline denominations. A settled denominational life, one that maintained itself without antagonism toward other large groups and without a constant assertion of the things that rendered it distinct, was taken as a sufficient indication that a group was central to God's providential scheme and would endure. The nineteenth-century historians treated other groups condescendingly or with open contempt. They never asked why Mormonism, Spiritualism, Millerism, or Christian Science emerged in the first place and lingered so long and so prominently in public view. Nor did the historians look very closely at the schismatic origins of the churches they admired, nor at the sectional, racial, theological, and social factors that caused splits even within the largest denominations. To have placed those questions and points in the foreground would have been to suggest that God made mistakes.

Presumably church and religious historians stopped believing in providence in the twentieth century. At any rate they realized that they could not presume to write "scientific" history and make transcendent forces responsible for the things that had happened in the past. With respect to the central themes of American religious history, this important change mattered a good bit less than one might have expected. Until relatively recently, American church history continued to emphasize themes of Protestant unity rather than themes of diversity and unsettled pluralism. The groups that Dorchester had dismissed as "divergent currents" remained more or less that. The Consensus School of historical writing, which was supposed to have emerged after World War II, was in fact virtually the only school that affected American religious historians through most of the twentieth century. Evidence of social and ideological conflict, which informed other kinds of historical writing between the wars, stirred few ripples in the most successful texts that sought to summarize America's religious past.

It would serve no purpose to undertake an exhaustive review of twentieth-century historical literature about American religion. To make the general point, a look at the works of three of the best religious historians is sufficient. All three, William Warren Sweet, Winthrop Hudson, and Sidney Mead, were at one time or another associated with the University of Chicago.

Everyone who has worked in the field of American religious history is indebted to Sweet. A professor for many years at Chicago, he deserves the credit for establishing American religious history as an area of separate academic inquiry—that is, as an area of research that a secular-minded historian might tackle as appropriately as a minister or divinity school instructor. Nonetheless, the work that Sweet produced in a university environment showed strong consistencies with that of his predecessors. Nowhere was this more evident than in the way that Sweet constructed a hierarchy of significance to separate mainline from non-mainline religious groups. His much used book *The Story of Religion in America* was published in 1930 and had no rival as a survey text until the 1950s. One paragraph drawn from his section about the antebellum period says everything that needs to be said about his biases:

> Many of these strange religious movements were the unhealthy offspring of the revivals of the thirties, forties and fifties. But along with the rise of Mormonism, Adventism, Perfectionism and all the other "isms," the great Protestant churches were adding tens of thousands of sane Christians to their membership, were busily planting new churches in the ever advancing frontiers, founding colleges, expanding their missionary work.[27]

Even Baird and Schaff had not suggested that a line of sanity divided their mainline from their non-mainline denominations.

Sweet's view of American history was strongly indebted to the frontier hypothesis of Frederick Jackson Turner, a fact that makes it all the odder that he had so little enthusiasm for the sectarian fever often associated with frontier areas. What excited Sweet about the story of the frontier was its taming. In this endeavor he gave a large role to the "great" Protestant churches. It was their genius to discover cooperative ways to stamp out the "unhealthy" sects and to find ways to prevent Catholic expansion. Social and environmental conditions, in Sweet's history, replaced the providence of earlier histories, but they produced the same results. Observers of the American scene, if they followed Sweet, could safely equate national character with the work of the largest Protestant denominations.

Winthrop Hudson studied with Sweet at Chicago, and in 1953 published *The Great Tradition of the American Churches*. The great tradition that Hudson used as an organizing theme throughout his book was the principle of voluntarism.[28] Despite almost a century's worth of hindsight, which was Hudson's advantage over Baird and Schaff, Hudson proved himself to have very little quarrel with nineteenth-century historians in assessing how that tradition had worked. Hudson too believed that the voluntary principle had confounded the early critics of disestablishment who had expected it to produce a confusing pattern of socially irresponsible sects.

Hudson distinguished between denominationalism, which won his approval for practical reasons, and sectarianism, which did not.[29] The former provided for a useful competition among American religious groups, a competition that led to a general increase in church attendance, without being truly divisive. Denominational differences did not preclude cooperation, for denominations did not insist that their particular Christian beliefs were the only ones that could lead to salvation. Denominations were large and broadly encompassing, like American political parties, and entwined with the institutions of common, national life. Sects, in contrast, withdrew into a world of their own. They reached out to others, if at all, only through aggressive and obnoxious methods of proselytizing. They insisted on exclusiveness, sheltered their members from competing views, and luckily remained small.

Their influence on American life had, in Hudson's view, always been negative.

Hudson's distinction between denominationalism and sectarianism was a useful enough way to sort out tendencies in religious behavior. What got him into trouble was not his use of the terms, but ironically a set of liberal sympathies that distorted what he wanted to clarify. As a narrator of American religious history, Hudson could tolerate only those groups that were themselves tolerant. The tone of his book was upbeat when Hudson wrote about periods when he believed that all of the churches were taking on the color of the major Protestant denominations. However, when Hudson had to deal with historical epochs when the population of "disaffected" Protestants seemed to be growing, his voice became notably gloomy.

Hudson lacked a convincing analytical principle to argue that what he called denominationalism would ultimately prevail in American life. In this sense he was at a distinct disadvantage to the nineteenth-century historians who had introduced providence into their narratives. Like Daniel Dorchester, Hudson judged the years in which he lived to be a particularly troubling time of church history. Intolerant Fundamentalists were determined to make war until theological "modernists" had been driven from Protestant churches. Unlike Dorchester, the only reassurance Hudson had that things would turn out as he hoped was history itself. The meaning of American religious experience, according to his book, had always been the overcoming of sectarian fever. He could only wait for history to repeat itself.

If Hudson's book was as much about the way he thought American religious history should have happened as the way it actually did, that was not merely because he failed to control his broadly ecumenical Protestant hopes. The same thing can be said about the writing of Sidney Mead, whose work was not biased in any of the ways we have yet encountered. Mead, a Jeffersonian at heart, in his many wonderfully crafted essays never took sides in denominational controversies.[30] In principle, he was a fervent believer in the virtues of a religious pluralism that struck other observers, even liberal ones, as excessive. The very notion that the United States had sometimes been labeled a Protestant nation made him indignant. Nonetheless, one crucial link connected Mead to the others we have discussed. He was loathe to associate what he considered a cosmopolitan system of religious tolerance with acrimonious religious division.

Mead knew that many Americans had disagreed about religion and that sectarian sentiment had marked religious behavior from the time of the founding of the nation. He also knew that many religious Americans, even in the large denominations, had not come very close to embodying a cosmopolitan spirit. Nonetheless, Mead did not much interest himself in the divisive particulars of religious diversity. As a result, Mead's rational tolerance, which theoretically gave an equal place in American experience to every group, did not in the slightest raise the reputation or historical importance of what had been the religious outgroups in historical narrative. Quite the contrary. His work actually concealed the story of religious diversity in America as completely as any that had preceded it. The nineteenth-century historians at least gave attention to "divergent currents" in their narrative so that providence would have obstacles to overcome. They took a "nutty" religion seriously enough to denounce it. Mead did not bother. Denouncing a particular form of religion, indeed even noticing it, was somehow unconstitutional. For Mead, a consummate liberal, the American system of religious pluralism worked, when it worked, because it rested on consensus rather than a belligerent show of difference.

To be sure, in stressing the continuity that has marked many histories of American religion, we have neglected important counter tendencies. One can without difficulty locate a number of books written in the first part of the twentieth century that set the stage for very different interpretations of religious pluralism that have recently appeared. For example, H. Richard Niebuhr's *The Social Sources of Denominationalism*, which was published in 1929, took a fundamentally different attitude toward sectarianism than was evident in Hudson's work published several decades later. Niebuhr's book amounted to a strong defense of the splintering sects that had broken up the semblance of Christian harmony in the modern era.[31] Following an economic and somewhat Marxist line of analysis, Niebuhr argued that sects in England and America had typically been the churches of the disadvantaged. They may have been introspective and world-denying, but those attitudes were surely preferable to the religious smugness and support of privilege that one found in Europe's state-supported churches and

America's mainline denominations. Rather than harming the cause of true religion, sectarianism had become the only historical phenomenon working to keep the sparks of genuine religious fervor alive.

Niebuhr hedged his important argument with several provisos that kept sectarianism from moving into a central position in the history of American religious life. For one thing, Niebuhr believed that any particular sect had a lifetime of only one generation. Following that period of time, sectarian groups, whether Baptist or Methodist or Mormon, either went out of existence or assumed the unfortunate forms of behavior that Niebuhr associated with denominations and churches. Either way, Niebuhr's formulations left the largest denominations as the controlling force in American religious life. The second thing that restrained Niebuhr's analysis of religious pluralism was simply his belief, as a Protestant theologian, in the unity of the church. He agreed with Baird and Schaff that God's ultimate plans could not entail the splintering of churches. Even so, Niebuhr had said something that was almost unthinkable before. Sectarianism was not abberation, an inexplicable breakdown in the life of otherwise healthy churches. It was normal. It was a constant, not a disappearing factor in American religious life. It was even the necessary dynamic of progressive change.

The work of Will Herberg was also something of a landmark in shifting the emphasis of American religious history. Herberg's famous and still widely cited book, *Protestant, Catholic, Jew,* which was published in 1955, is often set down as an example of consensus history. It was undeniably a consensus book in praise of the Judeo-Christian tradition.[32] The main force at work in Herberg's historical narrative was homogenization, or the gradual and necessary loss of the ethnic and national identifications of Americans. A generalized religious identification had replaced them. Over the years, Italian and Irish Catholics had become American Catholics. Eastern European Jews and German Jews had become American Jews. Although Jews and Catholics had not merged with each other or with the dominant American cultural tradition maintained by Protestants, the former two had entered the American mainstream only after taking on a great deal of Protestant coloration. The American melting pot had thus been only slightly overrated as a device for eliminating cultural differences. Bubbling away furiously within each of the three main religious traditions, it had eradicated their most distinctive features.

The importance of Herberg's work for shaking up customary attitudes obviously derived from something other than its description of the shaping of American consensus. Rather, it grew from a central tension that pervaded the book's argument. Herberg, a Jew, was not mesmerized by ideals of Protestant unity. Although his book argued that American Jews and American Catholics had become Americans by suppressing their ethnic roots (their inferior status) and conforming whatever was left of their religious tradition to a mostly Protestant American way of life, he regarded a good bit of what had happened as unfortunate. The book was not a celebration of bland and common civil religion. It was a protest launched against the tendency of religious groups to forget their specific traditions or to merge those traditions with an uncritical nationalism. Herberg was a pluralist who liked distinctiveness. His brand of liberalism did not require treating theological difference as something without importance. What he was "really" saying was that Jews and Catholics had been most American when they had resisted the process of blending into an "American Way of Life." Herberg described and seemed to applaud their entrance into the so-called mainstream. But he also seemed to be saying that American society was most dynamic when it encouraged people to preserve, not their ethnic identities, but their genuine religious peculiarities.

Herberg's book was praised largely by people who missed the last point. Everyone, it seemed, was pleased primarily by the evidence that the book gave of cultural assimilation. Yet only a few years later, Nathan Glazer, in *Beyond the Melting Pot*, suggested that Herberg's conclusions about the disappearance of ethnic distinctiveness were wrong. Groups had not merged but had maintained a sense of distinction that was both an assertive fiction and a response to indubitable facts. The creation of a consciousness of difference, a spirit alive and well in the 1960s, involved a group in inventing a dominant culture to set itself against, for without such a notion what was the point of its own bold assertion of group pride? The rhetoric that maintained group identification thus contained a fundamental paradox. To declare the existence of a dominant culture, at the same time accepting one's status as an outgroup, was to declare that that culture did not control what one was. That was exactly the game that Herberg was playing. By positing the assimilating power of Anglo-American culture, he hoped to destroy that power and persuade his religious audience that becoming American and conforming strictly to common denominators of an imagined mainstream culture were not the same thing.

The confusions that eventually surrounded all efforts to define an American national character have in the past twenty years pushed most historians off the trail of seeking to locate a single source of national unity. Unstable pluralism had replaced stable pluralism in narrative. Conflict has replaced consensus. Contention has replaced comity.

Finally, the general trend has overtaken the writing of religious history. Martin Marty, Edwin Gaustad, and Sydney Ahlstrom have called our attention much more forcefully than earlier work did to the persistence of sectarian feelings, to the apparent permanence of division, to the everlasting ability of strange, new religions to attract a following. Catherine Albanese has written a splendidly convincing text that manages to ignore Protestants until the fourth chapter.[33] Her book suggests that if providence really had intended the sectarian patterns of the nineteenth century to die out or become less intense, it had botched the job badly. Recent histories have suggested that diversity was not just a mild competition to boost Sunday School attendance, nor a matter of small confessional differences. Diversity sometimes verged on anarchy, and those who had feared its effects on the ideal of Protestant unity had been right.

Perhaps neither Marty nor Gaustad nor Ahlstrom ever completely loses sight of an ecumenical ideal. Perhaps no one who takes Christian belief seriously can make a positive value out of the disintegration of Christian unity. Nonetheless, they and others have been able to look at the facts of religious diversity without trying to minimize them or explain them away. Consequently, they have prepared the way for the sympathetic treatment of subjects formerly regarded as merely outlandish. And they have called attention to huge areas of American religious experience, especially in the nineteenth century, that have received not nearly sufficient attention—black churches, the immigrant churches, and the uncountable number of independent churches. Their work has forced us to reconsider the whole question of Protestant dominance as it allegedly affected national development in the nineteenth century. Protestants may have monopolized the writing of religious history, but we are beginning to ask how much of what they wrote grew from the fear, never entirely suppressed in their books, that they were not in control.

The gains in our knowledge have been tremendous. What is now unclear is whether we know how to make an intelligible order out of our newly accumulated stores of information. Whatever the faults of earlier religious historians, they managed to put a purposeful order into their narratives. If we cannot count on God's plan to tell us what is or is not "mainline" in American history, and if we now recognize that the purported size of denominations does not by itself tell us which religious beliefs excited the most popular interest, then what guides do we have to tell us what was important? Are all religious groups, no matter what their size, no matter how ephemeral, equally significant in accounts of American religion? Do the concepts "normal" and "deviant" tell us nothing about how to characterize the behavior of various religious groups? Must we absolutely reverse priorities in discussing "mainline" denominational behavior versus sectarianism? Is the notion of Protestant hegemony a myth? Must we suppress the Puritans and renounce attempts to say what has been dominant or typical in America's religious past?

If American historians answer all of these questions yes, then they are back, rather pointlessly, to Thomas Branagan and the alphabetical listing of Heinz religious varieties. However, if they answer all of them no, they might as well stick with Baird and Schaff and go on writing history as if the groups they had excluded from God's preordained mainstream are of interest mainly to psychopathologists and people who for whatever bizarre reasons like to make lists of un-American things.

Perhaps we may begin wrestling with this dilemma by looking at a religious group whose historical reputation has been crazily split. It has been described by many as a fraudulent and loony sect, and by almost as many others as a quintessentially American religious creation. If we can understand how both points of view have a certain legitimacy, and why the truth of one depends on the truth of the other, then we may be on our way toward explaining why religious groups that have founded their identities on a strong sense of being outsiders have been an indispensably dynamic force in American religious history.

PART ONE

Outsider Religions, Ethnicity, and American Identity

CHAPTER ONE

How To Become a People:
The Mormon Scenario

The rapidity with which impostors gain converts in this country is indeed remarkable; witness Matthias, Swedenborg, Miller, Joe Smith, and innumerable others; with but one exception, coarse, illiterate, and vulgar impostors, whose ignorance is only equalled by their villainy. And yet, the American people have the reputation of being a very sensible people; hard, shrewd, unimaginative; little prone to enthusiasm, and perpetually inquiring into the "reason" of every thing. Such is their admitted character. These contradictions are difficult to reconcile; so much hard common sense, and so much wild credulity.

Southern Literary Messenger (1844)

The lines above, written during one peak in the early Mormon controversy, expressed a confusion that has over the years resurfaced in various versions.[1] Tolstoy no doubt compounded a problem of interpretation when he remarked during a conversation with Andrew Dickson White that the Mormons taught *the* American religion.[2] To many nineteenth-century Americans, such a judgment was outrageous. How could a church, whose leaders became fugitives from federal justice in the 1880s, teach a religion that was quintessentially American?

Foreign observers seemed less bothered by the apparent contradiction. The steady growth of the Mormon church, whose converts were largely Anglo-Saxon people commonly regarded as America's core population, struck them as natural. The story of the Latter-day Saints was closely linked to the saga of America's westward expansion. Europeans who tried to understand America clamored for interviews with Joseph Smith and, later, with

Brigham Young. The successive Mormon communities were three-star sights in European guidebooks to North America.[3] Although Mormons were publicly despised and ridiculed, visitors to the United States sought them out as if they provided vital clues to the nature of the American people.[4]

In the end neither foreign observers nor domestic critics managed in the nineteenth century to untangle mysteries that surrounded questions of Mormon identity versus American identity. Historians have done only slightly better. The problem began with the Mormons themselves. Their identity rested on a highly schizophrenic set of relations with the American experiment. On the one hand, one can find very early in Mormon speeches and public documents the sort of superpatriotic language that is common among Mormon Republican voters in our own day. Joseph Smith spoke of love of country, the "heavenly banner" of the United States Constitution, and the divine origin and destiny of the American Republic. Mormon leaders declared in 1846, two years after the vigilante slaying of Smith: "Our patriotism has not been overcome by fire, by sword, by daylight or by midnight assassinations which we have endured; neither have they alienated us from the institutions of our country."[5] On the other hand, those same leaders on many occasions defied the officials of the American government, instructed one another on the general corruption of the American nation, and prophesied a terrible destruction that was to befall the vast majority of the American people. Many of the Mormons who made the painful, forced migration out of Nauvoo in 1846 forsook the republic, like Orson Pratt, with "the greatest joy" and hoped to put a permanent distance between themselves and their fellow countrymen with whom they no longer felt any common bonds.[6]

Mormons have in the past several decades received their fair share of sensible historical treatment. The Mormon archives have for some time been open to researchers, and interest in Mormon history has sustained the not altogether parochial Mormon Historical Association as well as several scholarly journals. Despite these things, the historical connections of Mormons to other important trends in American culture have not yet been fully plotted. Some of the best historical treatments tend to interpret Mormons very much in isolation. In fact, a number of histories, written by historians who are themselves Mormon, show an understandable interest in building a case for Mormon exceptionalism.[7]

The problem of relating the rise of Mormonism to other things happening at the same time within American culture, is, like the problem of making judgments about Mormon typicality, rooted in the sources. The intention of those who wrote the documents that historians must interpret was rarely to clarify. It was to attack, to persuade, to mythify. The Mormon controversy was one of the most drawn out and highly publicized events in all of American history. It began almost as soon as the church was founded and died down, not out, only at the beginning of the twentieth century. In struggling for position, the opposing parties relied on a variety of strategies. One was violence. Another was legislation and its subversion. Yet another was rhetoric that made contradictory and competing claims. Once historians recognize that they are trying to unravel not merely what was true in some easily defined objective sense, but what people thought was true, or what they wanted others to accept as true, they have to come to grips with the fact that a lot of seemingly contrary things were simultaneously true. Perception admits, even insists on, that sort of ambiguity.

Among other things, this last statement means that few truths are absolutely obvious. The more we pick apart the things we think we know, the less certain they become. For example, we might look for a moment at the one "fact" that formed the only point of agreement in the vast nineteenth-century polemical literature about Mormons. Tolstoy aside, most everyone who wrote about Joseph Smith's church, and above all this included the Mormons themselves, asserted that Mormons were not like other Americans. We ought, then, to be able to answer a simple question. Why were they different? Was it because, as one of their enemies charged, they were guilty of "infidelity, deism, atheism, lying, deception, blasphemy, debauchery, lasciviousness, bestiality, madness, fraud, plunder, larceny, burglary, robbery, perjury, fornication, adultery, rape, incest, arson, treason, and murder."[8] Was it because they constituted a "medley of merit-making Buddhism, ancestral worship of Confucianism, social pollutions of Mohammedanism, intrigue and chicanery of Jesuitism, sublime self-conceit of Pharisaism, the coarseness of materialism, all bound together by the rites and covenants of a modified freemasonry."[9] Or was it because, as Joseph Smith claimed at the other extreme of opinion, that the Mormons were called together by God, under a new dispensation, to lead a reluctant nation towards the creation of a new heaven and a new earth.

Although these were obviously exaggerated and, if you like, subjective claims, one or the other of them sustained the case for Mormon difference in the minds of many people. Can we do better? Do we have more "objective" measures of difference that improve on the rhetoric just quoted. If one could have polled Americans at the end of the nineteenth century and asked them what made Mormons different, the most common response would surely have been polygamy, or the Mormon system of plural wives. Washington politicians, spurred on by evangelical leaders, regarded it as a dangerous departure from American norms regarding family life. Beginning in 1862, they began to enact increasingly severe legislative measures to suppress it. In response, Mormon leaders described plural marriage as a precious and distinctive feature of their church and sought protection for its practice under the provisions of the First Amendment. The longer and more tenaciously the Mormons fought to retain it, the more everyone regarded it as the principal feature of Mormon deviance.

So far so good. These are indeed facts. Yet there are some competing facts. First, the vast majority of nineteenth-century Mormons did not practice polygamy, and many of them found it distasteful, at least as a way of conducting their own lives. Second, those who did practice plural marriage scarcely exhibited the lascivious behavior made familiar in anti-Mormon literature. Plural wives were commonly the widowed or unmarried sisters of the original wife.[10] Third, a strongly perceived difference between Mormons and non-Mormons existed well before a belief in plural marriage became a badge of Mormon identification. A probably unresolvable controversy surrounds the question of when Joseph Smith first hit upon the doctrine of plural wives. Yet neither the doctrine nor its practice played any significant role in anti-Mormon literature or the persecution it sought to justify until late in the Nauvoo period, or over a decade after the founding of the Church of Latter-day Saints. "Polygamy" was not the reason for the troubles that the Mormons encountered in Missouri and in Illinois. Interestingly, other American religious groups that adopted distinct sexual practices and followed them consistently, the Shakers and the Oneida "perfectionists," for example, were far less persecuted than the Mormons.[11]

In assembling a historical reality, one need not abandon the reasonable proposition that the practice of plural marriage constituted one difference between Mormons and other Americans. The problem is that this difference took on rather greater significance, and led to far greater conflict, than any objective difference in value system would have warranted. After all, on issues affecting the sanctity of the permanently joined family unit and of sexual role differentiation, Mormons squarely fit the patterns that historians have established as normal for middle-class Victorian Americans. They have always been strong proponents of the family and did not argue, as John Humphrey Noyes did at Oneida, that the sexual exclusiveness of married people was a form of selfishness.

With somewhat more success, one can attempt to "objectify" a difference between Mormons and other Americans by referring to the sum total of the peculiarities of the Mormon faith. There were any number of them, including Joseph Smith's claims about his discovery of the golden tablets, the importance assigned to the Book of Mormon and Smith's other revelations at the expense of traditional Christian scripture, the theocratic government established by Mormon leaders, and the secret Temple rituals. Governor Ford of Illinois, who tried unsuccessfully to mediate the conflict that developed between the Nauvoo Mormons and their neighbors, wrote to Brigham Young that anyone who tried to introduce novelties in religious practice was bound to stir up resentment.[12]

Governor Ford's judgment and all the hypotheses that may be constructed upon it flatter common sense, but they duck the very tricky question of just why a particular practice seems novel, in this case dangerously and treacherously novel. Mormonism was born in an era fecund in religious inventiveness; and in the competition for establishing a particular practice as novel, Joseph Smith's innovations had a good bit of formidable competition. A generation that read almost daily about the claims of various men and women to new religious revelation might have been expected to greet Joseph Smith's Book of Mormon more calmly than one vociferous part of it did. Ministers in the churches of the largest Protestant denominations had no trouble spotting doctrinal peculiarities in Mormon teaching. But it is highly problematic whether those evangelicals either commanded the intellectual allegiance of most Americans or represented what was typical American religious belief. In strictly theological terms, one may argue that Mormonism, which placed little emphasis on predestination, sin, and the experience of conversion, was generally in line with other liberalizing trends that provoked religious controversy in the nineteenth century but not the scandalized outcry that frequently greeted Mormonism. Theologically, in fact, Mormonism was in its beginnings a dull affair.

The question of what makes something seem novel takes on considerable importance when we remember that a number of Americans, despite what Governor Ford wrote to Young, did not initially judge Mormon practices to be bizarre, certainly not bizarre enough to set Mormonism apart from what was judged to be respectable American life. The polemical nature of the documents has not quite buried that fact. Even after the violent turmoil of the Mormon experience in Missouri, most of the politicians and newspapers in Illinois, where Mormons went next, warmly welcomed them and extended to them some striking favors in praising their efforts to found a city at Nauvoo. One editor in Quincy, whose sympathetic reactions reflected the attitude of much of the nation's press, noted the compatibility of their religion with the times: "The signal success which everywhere attends their exertion, proves how well their religious system is adapted to give expression to the various forms of enthusiasm that pervaded the religious sentiment of the day."[13] That assessment has been endorsed by at least one later historian who wrote that Mormonism "brought together various impulses and ideas of the emerging American *Weltanschauung.*"[14] The reason many people in Illinois just a few years later sharply reversed their words of greeting was not because they had suddenly discovered differences in Mormon religion that pushed Mormons outside the norms of antebellum American culture. Rather, for reasons having little to do with religion or with normal and abnormal value systems, they had decided to give any distinctive practice followed by the Mormons a heightened and negative significance. Expulsion required a pretext.

Mormonism's enemies tried hard to validate a claim that Mormons were morally and ethically peculiar. Mormons, they

charged, lied, stole, swore, and fornicated. No doubt they did, just
like many other antebellum Americans. Mormons were frequently
aggressive in their dealings with their perceived enemies; and a
number of charges accusing them of crimes of theft and murder
dealt against their non-Mormon neighbors appear to have a substantial basis in fact. Nevertheless, any case for Mormon difference that rests on a purported Mormon rejection of middle-class
standards of virtue is bound to fail. If inculcation in the work ethic
was the hallmark of true Americanism in the nineteenth century,
then Mormons were the super Americans of that century. Like
the Puritans before them, the Mormons linked disciplined labor
with religious duty. Mormon culture promoted all of the virtues
usually associated with the formation of middle-class consciousness—thrift, the denial of immediate gratification, and strict control over one's passions. Thomas Kane, a long-time and long-suf-
fering friend of the Mormons, delivered honest witness to a plain
fact: to an unusual degree Mormons were honest, frugal, self-sac-
rificing, humane, and decorous.[15]

One can argue about how well the close cooperation and control of Mormon group life fit with the individualistic ethic of
Jacksonian America. Some historians have maintained that Mormonism, because it recalled John Winthrop's Massachusetts Bay
Colony, was anachronistic in antebellum America. That is perhaps
so. On the other hand, as corporate as they were, the Mormons
strongly emphasized self-reliance, a trait that many interpreters
have counted as typically American. Despite the concentration of
church power in the First Presidency and Council of Twelve,
Mormon society was in the context of nineteenth-century America exceedingly egalitarian. Mormons had no professional clergy
and made every man a priest on his way to becoming a god.
Women, although subordinate in social status to men, were not
mere ornaments; they too had essential roles to play in the community and in the church.[16]

In noting these problems that beset efforts to make out an
"objective" case for Mormon difference, we arrive finally at a less
complex proposition: Mormons were different because they said
they were different and because their claims, frequently advanced
in the most obnoxious way possible, prompted others to agree and
to treat them as such. The notion of Mormon difference, that is,
was a deliberate invention elaborated over time. It was both cause

and result of a conflict in which all parties discovered reasons to stress not what Mormons had in common with other Americans, which was a great deal, but what they did not have in common. One result of the conflict was an ideology that sought to turn the self-advertised differences of the Mormons into a conspiracy against the American republic.

This simply stated formula by no means solves all of the problems. Not all conflict can be explained by the distances created by rhetoric. Not every fight in the Mormon controversy was rooted in mere words. Mormon leaders did establish a secret Council of Fifty and sought in other ways to subvert regularly constituted channels of legal authority.[17] The Mormon community did arguably seek to divert the economic resources of the areas where they became numerous to their own exclusive use. The actions destroyed the relations between Mormons and their neighbors. What is important, however, is that these actions represented conflicts about power, not about values. They created the context in which the notion of a separate Mormon culture became believable. They did not necessarily give "objective" status to that separateness. Mormons had to invent an identity for themselves and that required them to maintain certain fictions of cultural apartness. Their enemies acquiesced in the fictions, but they twisted them to justify their charge that Mormons were disloyal and unAmerican. The problem for historians is not that they lack hard facts. The problem lies in explaining why some facts assumed disproportionate importance in the minds of those who lived with them.

The line of analysis that we are pursuing comes close, perhaps too close, to saying that Mormons deserved what they got. After all what is being suggested is that Mormon efforts at self-definition, which aggressively and systematically gave importance to practices and beliefs that might with as much reason have been trivialized, brought down upon them the brutal persecution that they suffered. Furthermore, as their opponents charged again and again, they fed on their persecution. They memorialized it in ways that seemed to invite more of it. In exaggerating what they had suffered, and in ignoring the reasons for it, attributing it solely to the fact that God's chosen people always suffered persecution, they turned away people who might have helped them. They carelessly lost allies because of their insistence on rhetorically casting all "gentiles" indiscriminately into the same category.[18] The trait most commonly cited to denounce the Mormons, the one that clearly rankled anti-Mormons the most, was arrogance. Smith called God his "right hand man" and taught his followers all too well to regard themselves as superior to others. When God smote the nation for its unrighteousness, the Mormons as a people would be spared.

Religious persecution is nasty business, and no one in the free pursuit of a religious belief deserves ridicule, physical attack, and murder. Nonetheless, it takes two sides to maintain this liberal piety. The history of religion is so filled with martyrs that one must wonder whether religion could exist without them. One may bemoan the way people treat one another in a less than perfect world without ignoring the fact that people often make choices fully aware of unpleasant consequences, indeed even with the intention of hurrying those consequences along. We have spoken of deliberate strategies of differentiation. In the matters under discussion, the line between what is deliberate and what is not deliberate is indistinct to the point of invisibility. We may well imagine that Joseph Smith in his early religious career innocently crossed some conventional boundaries of belief that, without any elaboration on his part, aroused feelings of hostility against him. He did not mean in every thing that he did to make himself a target of abuse. Even so, if we write all of our histories based on the innocent stigmatization of Joseph Smith, we will in our sympathy miss a good bit of his cleverness.

We need to look more closely at the ways Joseph Smith employed a rhetoric of deviance to describe himself and to elaborate the institutions of his church. His strategies were already evident in the story that he told about reactions to his first vision of an angelic visitor, purported to have occurred in 1820. Although it was penned some years after the fact and embellished in imaginative re-creation, Smith surely did not lie when he said that he encountered scoffers. According to Smith, when he reported the vision to his friends, his words "excited a great deal of prejudice against me among professors of religion, and was the cause of great persecution, which continued to increase."[19] If we take Smith at his word, the interesting question becomes why did young Joseph Smith persist in a kind of behavior that proved so troubling to him. Unless one accepts the view that Smith was a prophet of God and had no choice except to obey the divine voice that spoke to him, one has got to pause with puzzlement over a pattern of behavior that courted notoriety by spreading claims that struck others as outrageous. An irreverent thought is unavoidable. Joseph Smith eventually learned that he had something at stake in making his claims appear as outrageous as he possibly could. He recognized that reproach was one way of being noticed and taken seriously.

Biographers of Joseph Smith disagree as to whether Smith was an utter ne'er-do-well prior to 1830, but they agree that no one paid much attention to him before he found his religious vocation. His mission had no chance of going anywhere without opposition, both real and imagined. Very early in the 1830s Smith had determined to cast himself in a martyr's role, and a considerable part of what he wrote and said was designed to further that image. By the last years of his life, his statements had become numbingly formulaic. In 1842 he wrote: "I am at this time persecuted the worst of any man on the earth." A year later he elaborated: "It always has been when a man was sent of God with the Priesthood and he begins to preach the fulness of the gospel then was thrust out by his friends—and they are ready to butcher him if he teach things which they had imagined to be wrong." Finally in the year of his death, 1844, when reality decisively overtook his rhetoric, he stated: "I, like Paul, have been in perils, and oftener than anyone in this generation. . . . I should be like a fish out of water if I were out of persecutors. . . . The Lord has constituted me so curiously that I glory in persecutions."[20]

The Mormon church collectively nurtured a similar identity. Early in the 1830s, carefully noting any instance of the ill treatment of Smith's followers, the first Mormon newspapers began to give persecution a dominant place in the printed Mormon word. Bearing persecution became the distinctive badge of membership in the church; it was the test of faith and of one's chosenness. By the end of their stay in Missouri, Mormons had accumulated a long list of trials to commemorate. They lost few occasions to do so. Persecution was the chief theme of virtually every political speech. It was by and large what was celebrated on Founder's Day each July 24 in Utah. It formed the major lesson of every Mormon autobiography and biography, of everything written to instruct children in the faith.

A good bit of evidence about the early history of the Mormon church bears out something that Luther Gerlach and Virginia Hine concluded in their study of several twentieth-century religious movements: oppositional movements often perceive more opposition to their cause than seems to exist objectively. Opposition gives value to struggle and inculcates self-confidence.[21] However ungenerous it may seem to suggest that elaboration distorted what the Mormons in fact suffered, one can hardly ignore the habitual, even casual, ways that Mormons talked about their troubles in connection with describing feelings of elation. Martha Hall, who had accepted Joseph Smith's invitation to "come and partake of the poverty of Nauvoo," thought it natural to write to her parents back in New England that Nauvoo was at once a place of enjoyment and a place to "try people."[22] The one thing depended upon the other. At a later date, William Hepworth Dixon, an Englishman, reported with entire plausibility that he had heard Brigham Young tell missionaries departing from Utah that they were not to suggest "the beauty of their mountain home, but to dwell on the idea of persecution, and to call the poor into a persecuted church."[23] Another reporter observed that songs and hymns about their persecution had stimulated the enthusiasm of the Mormon men, women, and children during their forced departure from Nauvoo.[24] It is difficult to imagine a successful Mormon church without suffering, without the encouragement of it, without the memory of it. Persecution arguably was the only possible force that would have allowed the infant church to prosper.

This is an old story. The trials of ancient Israel and of the primitive Christian church provided examples, well known to the Mormons, of the growth and survival of religious beliefs because of adversity. With respect to the nineteenth century, what the Mormons managed to accomplish is quite singularly striking. The amazing part of the story, the thing that won a grudging admiration even from those who continued to regard Joseph Smith as an utter fraud, is how much the Mormons were willing to risk, how long they belligerently maintained their sense of apartness when external circumstances suggested that they had succeeded and could afford to maintain their sense of difference in ways that would have aroused less opposition.

A fundamental contradiction pervaded Smith's career. He said that he founded the Mormon church to put an end to the theological bickering that divided religious denominations. His professed aim was to restore the universal church. Yet, throughout his career, he constantly searched for new ways to distinguish his church from every other church. When Smith led his followers into Nauvoo, one may argue that Smith had done all he needed to do. His followers had memories of persecution to nurture. They had created distinct forms of worship organized around an unusual concept of priesthood and had gathered a community. Smith entered Nauvoo with a political welcome and a generous city charter that allowed Mormons a considerable amount of autonomy. Yet, precisely at that point, he embarked on a course of new departures, introduced in politically maladroit ways, that threatened to destroy everything he had created. Most of the distinctive features of Mormon theology, the plurality of Gods, the baptism for the dead, marriage for eternity, and plural marriage, all date from the Nauvoo period.[25] In Nauvoo, Smith created the controversial Council of Fifty, permitted the establishment of a Masonic Temple (a secret organization banned in the Book of Mormon), and borrowed from Masonic rituals to establish the secret rituals of the Mormon temple.

Before they came to Nauvoo, Mormons had been accused of doing things secretly in ways that offended the openness of American democracy. In Missouri, the charge had centered on the notorious Band of Danites, an alleged organization of Mormon men who swore to tell nothing about their membership or about the various terrorist acts of revenge that they carried out against known enemies of Mormons. Smith always claimed that the Danites did not exist, or if they did, that they existed with the express disapproval of the church. Those disavowals gained little credibility from his conduct of Mormon business in Nauvoo. Much of what he did in Illinois was shrouded in secrecy, secret not only to the "gentiles" in the communities surrounding Nauvoo, but secret also to many Mormons whom Smith did not fully trust.

Secrecy, as Georg Simmel suggested many years ago, can serve a variety of purposes.[26] It can protect infant, half-formulated ideas from persecution by keeping them hidden from public knowledge. That purpose would not seem to apply to the situation in Nauvoo, for the general outlines of most of what Smith wanted to keep secret were well enough known. Moreover, Smith made no secret of the fact that he maintained secrets, and the state of Illinois was awash with lurid rumors about Mormon conspiracies to disrupt its economic and political life. Rather than warding off the persecution of his ideas, Smith's strategy of secrecy only intensified it and gave total license to the imaginations of those who wrote anti-Mormon propaganda. Smith, therefore, appears to have used secrecy for another reason, as part of his effort to give his followers a sense of distinct identity. Those who knew the secret, or those to whom it was promised, were joined together. Those who were excluded from the secret were invited to regard the Mormons as mysteriously different.

Smith's flurry of innovative practices during the Nauvoo years and his selective, some would say capricious, disclosure of them almost did not work. Not only did Smith's actions turn public opinion in Illinois against the Mormons, but they created serious dissension within the Mormon community. In particular, many people in Nauvoo reacted negatively to the initial stories about Smith's plural wives. In the last months of his life Smith found himself in the center of a storm of controversy that badly shook the foundations of Mormon solidarity. Only after Smith's assassination was the effectiveness of what he had done apparent. Then, the innovations clearly worked to reinforce Mormon identity and prepared veteran Mormons and the many new recruits for their next taxing enterprise, the journey to the basin of the Great Salt Lake. Completing the Nauvoo Temple, even after it was clear the Mormons would have to leave Nauvoo, and sharing what quickly became the sacred rites of the Temple, provided an essential bond for Mormons during the months between Smith's death and their forced departure. Controversial or not, Smith had created the mechanisms through which his church maintained its sense of continuity and endured.

A certain poetic truth attaches to the notion that Smith glimpsed the necessity of his own death. Although one may confidently state that Smith did not plan his death, he knowingly courted it and did not forget to prepare his followers for it. Scholars have marveled that a comparatively young religious sect, founded on the flimsiest of religious claims, managed to survive once its charismatic founder had died. Yet, to entertain whimsically a counterfactual proposition, suppose that Smith had not died a martyr. What else would have confirmed so dramatically the correctness of the Mormon endeavors? What else would have proved so convincingly what before had been merely a rhetorical boast, that Mormons were a separate and holy people? What would have maintained a community that was on the verge of flying apart? Everything in Mormon prophecy prepared the Mormons not merely to survive the severe rupture of the founder's death, but to find renewed dedication in it.

When Smith was killed, only two of the Quorum of Twelve Apostles, Willard Richards and John Taylor, were present in Nauvoo. They wrote calmly to saints abroad: "Proceed onward with your labors as though nothing had happened, only, preach Joseph martyred for his religion, instead of living."[27] Fortunately for them, and for those who now had to control the potential for fratricidal division among the Mormons in Nauvoo, the rhetoric to preach a martyred Joseph was readily available and utterly familiar.

Whether the Mormon voyage to Utah would have happened in quite the triumphant way that it did without the leadership of Brigham Young is a moot point. All one can say is that most of the Nauvoo Mormons were mentally prepared to follow any leader who could reinforce their sense of distinctiveness. Young proceeded to do just that in even more aggressive ways than those employed by Smith. For the rest of the nineteenth century, the Mormon strategy for survival continued to risk destruction by straining to advertise Mormon deviance.

Other strategies were available. For comparative purposes, that point is important. One group that broke away from the main body of Mormons after Smith's death—the group that became the Reorganized Church of Latter Day Saints—in effect gave up the rhetoric of deviance.[28] They stayed faithful to the claims that Smith had made in behalf of the Book of Mormon, but they took a number of steps to make peace with hostile public opinion. They repudiated most of the things that Smith had instituted to create the idea of a separate Mormon culture—the insistence on gathering, the secret temple rituals, and the doctrine of plural marriage. Interestingly, with respect to our analysis, although this group survived as a church (it was the only one of the breakaway Nauvoo groups that did), it did not prosper to the same degree as the Mormons who went to Utah. That fact alone sets one to doubting whether the latter were so far from an American religious mainstream as reports tried to suggest.

The strategy of the Utah Mormons put their outspoken enemies in a troubling quandary. Anti-Mormons knew very well that their attacks, verbal and physical, had often proved counterproductive. Abuse seemed to give Mormons what they most needed. Yet, especially after the battle lines became joined mainly over the issue of polygamy, they were afraid to leave the Mormons alone. Like America's first religious historians who confidently predicted that the Mormons could not survive, they fell into strident modes of argument that suggested an opposite fear. One thing was incomprehensible to them. Although they appreciated well enough, after bitter experience, how their attacks upon Mormons served to increase the militance and determination of those already in the Mormon fold, they could not understand how the movement was able to attract a significant number of new converts. Logically, it seemed, few people would elect to join a group when the consequences of affiliation were so dire.

One can appreciate their puzzlement. The record leaves no doubt about the success of Mormon recruitment. The return from their proselytizing efforts in America and England must have surprised the Mormon leaders themselves. Even in retrospect, it is by no means obvious why they did so well. To say that Mormons used effective missionary techniques only begs the question. Successful proselytizing is not possible unless social and cultural factors render the appeals made by a religious group plausible and seductive. And indeed, many aspects of nineteenth-century American culture worked to make Mormonism a believable religion. As noted earlier, we are talking about a period in American history when claims advanced to prove one new divine revelation or another were not unusual. There was room for Mormonism, and not merely in the sense of territorial space. Most nineteenth-century Americans were probably familiar and comfortable with generalized principles of a Protestant Christian faith, but in 1830 the vast majority neither belonged to a church nor had a strong denominational tie. To religious seekers tired of spiritual drifting, Mormonism offered something authoritative. It was one version of a millennial idea that appeared in many guises in the period between 1830 and 1850. God was introducing a new dispensation that would change the course of history. The new era would put an end to the quarreling among Christians and restore the unity of the primitive church.

While unity is not exactly what Joseph Smith accomplished, he did, despite the many distinctive features that he introduced into Mormon practice, offer a simplified faith that suppressed many familiar and divisive theological controversies. If one likes, one can attach the labels Arminian, Antinomian, and Universalist to Mormonism. However, Mormons spent little time debating controversial points of religious doctrine. The labels that had divided America's Calvinist churches had a much reduced meaning in Mormon culture. The authority that Mormonism promised rested not on the subtlety of its theology. It rested on an appeal to fresh experience—a set of witnessed golden tablets that had been translated into a book whose language sounded biblical. Joseph Smith instinctively knew what all other founders of new American religions in the nineteenth century instinctively knew. Many Americans of that period, in part because of popular enthusiasm for science, were ready to listen to any claim that appealed to something that could be interpreted as empirical evidence.[29]

The intellectual plausibility of Mormonism needs to be stressed much more strongly than many accounts have done. Doing so, however, is only one step of analysis. Well-established Protestant denominations also gave authoritative answers to disputed questions and offered a religious perspective at least as plausible as Mormonism. The puzzling thing about conversion to Mormonism, as contrasted, for example, with a decision to become a Presbyterian, was that converts remembered it as something that separated them painfully from friends and family. Mormonism boasted not of the peace that it brought, but the trouble. History has repeatedly demonstrated that people are willing to sever significant attachments for the sake of religion, but such actions of religious sacrifice remain hard to explain. A faith, once accepted, may prompt, as Mormonism did, a fervent readiness to die for one's belief. However, we are looking for the reasons why the faith was embraced in the first place.

With varying degrees of reluctance, historians have sought part of their answer to questions of religious motivation in sociologically grounded deprivation theories. They have good reasons to be careful in using this approach. Deprivation theory often seems to demean the integrity of people's actions by suggesting that their choices arose from a need to compensate for low self-esteem or for economic poverty. Moreover, deprivation, whatever the hard scientific ring of the word, is often used to refer to nothing more particular than universal human experience. It does little good to describe Mormon converts as deprived people if their social deprivation was no greater than that of the vast majority of ordinary people. We can of course talk about "severe" deprivation, but that is hard to prove about Mormons. Elaborate frameworks of psychopathology or deviance theory rarely get us far in explaining, in one sociologist's terms, why people depart from a widely held religious perspective to accept "an unknown, obscure and often, socially devalued one."[30] Joseph Smith needs explaining, but anything resembling insanity is not a helpful start.

We shall return to this problem of explanation in subsequent chapters. Deprivation theory is always relevant. In the Mormon case, it suggests the common sense proposition that people who were content with their lives were not in the nineteenth century the most promising targets for Mormon proselytizing. Nor were they likely to find themselves in places where they encountered a strong Mormon influence. People who join new religious groups generally bear, or think that they bear, marks of social or cultural disadvantage. We do not have enough information to provide a fully satisfactory portrait of the typical Mormon convert. They do not seem to have been unusually poor with respect to material things.[31] Yet for a variety of personal reasons, they did not think of themselves as "fitting in." They came to their new religion, which guaranteed them a life that provoked opposition, already thinking of themselves as outsiders. What Mormonism had to provide, if its appeal was to be successful, was a meaningful content for that outsider role. Mormonism, as most of the other religious groups we shall consider, gave its converts an identity that worked.

Without doubt, Mormonism in its early history conformed to what is generally characterized as sect-like behavior. That fact frames our whole problem of interpretation. Physically and rhetorically Mormons set themselves off from a society which they regarded as corrupt. One can easily characterize that action as disfunctional. Yet in many crucial ways it was, in a strictly secular sense, redemptive. Mormons in any case remained typical products of their culture.

We are driven back to one more look at values before we attempt to conclude. Mark Leone has suggested that the distinctiveness of the early culture of the Mormons rested on a communal way of life that furnished a critical perspective on capitalism.[32] Opposing the atomistic individualism of a society that thrived on competition and conflict, Mormonism projected a utopian vision that challenged the political, economic, and social values of antebellum America.

Unfortunately, according to Leone, the first stage was succeeded by other stages, and in time Mormon culture became something altogether different from what it had been in its origins. A culture once hostile to capitalism changed eventually into one that provided strong and reliable support for the conservative wing of the Republican party. Sectarian separation from the world gave way to denominational accommodation to ordinary Americanism. Mormon culture, Leone argues, failed to provide a collective memory. Despite the pioneer lore that survived, Mormons did not accumulate "a coherent, systematic interpretation of the relationship between past and present."[33] In effect, Mormons forgot their history. They remembered that they were supposed to be different, but they did not remember why.

Leone's argument is a sophisticated variation on a generally accepted view that Mormon values changed dramatically in the twentieth century. The stringent enforcement of federal antipolygamy laws, beginning in the 1880s, put the survival of the church at stake. As a result, the options that had been available to Mormon leaders earlier were no longer viable. Further risks were bound to bring disaster. Consequently, Mormon leaders sought divine revelation and revised the practices of their church. They renounced plural marriage, broke up the theocratic structure of Utah's political life (dividing Mormons among the two large American parties), and ceased to isolate themselves economically from their neighbors. Those things done, they were no longer so clearly distinguishable from other Americans. As part of a state finally freed from dependent territorial status, Utah's Mormons elected Reed Smoot senator and gained a spokesman for their new commitment to conservative American values. Mormon patrio-

tism and Mormon belief in the doctrine of competitive individualism became fervent. According to one excellent historical
account: "By the end of World War I in America, if not before,
the Mormons were more American than most Americans. Patriotism, respect for the law, love of the Constitution, and obedience
to political authority reigned as principles of the faith."[34] However deviantly Mormons had begun, they had become, according
to George Will, a syndicated columnist noted for his politically
conservative views, "quintessentially American."[35]

The point of view that insists on two Mormon cultures, one
for the nineteenth century and another for the twentieth century,
is appealing because it furnishes an explanation of why the fric-
tion between Mormons and other Americans declined sharply
once Utah became a state. Mormons simply jettisoned those
beliefs and practices which had made their culture deviant, and
their neighbors stopped worrying about them. However, in light
of everything that has been argued, we cannot be completely
happy with this explanation. In making their peace with the federal government, Mormons did cast off those features of the
church that had become the central bones of contention—polygamy and the control of church leaders over Utah's political life.
Yet, and this fact is equally important, rhetoric changed as much
as any reality. In the political struggles that led Utah to statehood,
an important goal for Mormon leaders who resented territorial
dependence, Mormons learned to mute their rhetoric of deviance.
They talked much less aggressively about the distinctiveness of
their culture. Whether that meant that they had suddenly abandoned one value system in favor of another is a question that has
no easy answer.

We are not done yet with ambiguity. Interpretations that seek
to make early Mormonism a distinct subculture, one even with
radical economic overtones, are correct in many ways. On the
other hand Mormons were always in many ways, save in an imaginative space created by rhetoric, just like non-Mormon Americans. Their religious subculture was a deliberate invention whose
distance from the values of an American mainstream cannot be
measured in strictly objective terms. If we assume that an adherence to certain economic values, a cooperative ethic for example,
once separated Mormons from an American mainstream of dog-
eat-dog capitalism, we must immediately confront the perfectly

tenable proposition that present-day Mormons, despite the flourish with which some have welcomed them into the mainstream, have not abandoned those values. In fact some of those values are now pointed to as evidence to support the case for Mormons as quintessential Americans. What, after all, were the principles of cooperation that explained the success of Mormon communities in the nineteenth century? A short list includes an emphasis on self-help and self-reliance, a deference to authority, a strong preference for local control, an insistence on privately administered charity based on traditional group ties, and an aversion to any sort of social legislation engineered in Washington. These are the very principles that form the core of Mormonism's alleged conservatism in the present day. What has changed arguably are not the deep-seated values of Mormon culture but the political label that many people want to attach to them.

Moreover, to keep matters complicated, a tension persists in the United States between Mormons and non-Mormons. Newspaper editorials about Mormons being super-Americans do not change everything. The Mormons have retained the main quality of sect-like behavior, which is insistence on a difference that *matters* between themselves and everyone else. They have shown little enthusiasm for ecumenicalism. Many non-Mormon Americans living in western states continue to believe that present-day Mormons in secret councils hatch conspiratorial schemes against other Americans. Objective differences persist of the very same sort that laid the basis for the Mormon controversy in the nineteenth century. Mormons are gathered. Their empire has spread, but geographically they are a singularly concentrated group. Mormons have not abandoned the Book of Mormon; they give a great deal of deference to their church authorities; and they proselytize aggressively. A sense of difference has persisted so strongly among Mormons that they have probably gained an ethnic as well as a religious identity, thus becoming like the Jewish people they have always emulated. As in the nineteenth century, the mere fact of difference or the lack of difference does not explain conflict or the lack of it. The explanation lies in what people, because of particular contexts of living in proximity to one another, will choose to make of difference.

As a group, Mormons have been prosperous and successful for a long time. In 1943, Edward Thorndike noted that Utah ranked among the highest states as the birthplace of distinguished men of science and letters.[36] Clearly, the persistence of the Mormon habit of seeing itself in opposition has nothing any longer to do with deprivation. The first Mormons had gone to a good bit of trouble to distinguish themselves from other people and had gained some substantial benefits for their pains. Despite the changes made at the end of the nineteenth century, later Mormons did not allow that work to come easily undone.

Mormon identity, then, continues to contain a central paradox. Mormons regard themselves, as they always had, as good and typical Americans. At the same time, they do not regard themselves as being like other Americans. The paradox was always most sharply expressed in Mormon expressions of patriotism. Their Fourth of July declarations of loyalty in the nineteenth century were fervent, even during periods of persecution; but they invariably contained an element, expressed with varying degrees of subtlety, that called into question the patriotism of everyone else. The early Mormons thought of themselves as trying to hold the country to its highest ideals but made it clear that they did not regard other Americans as having much use for those ideals.

What then can we conclude about typicalness? Were Baird and Shaff right to regard nineteenth-century Mormons as a bizarre aberration, a marginal and fringe group that deserved treatment in American religious histories only after Presbyterians, Methodists, Baptists, and Congregationalists had been thoroughly dealt with? Was their success an accident, something that happened under unrepeatable circumstances that were only marginally related to conditions of American experience? Or was there something of central and crucial importance about Mormon history, something that can stand for a great many other things that happened in the American past and that helps explain both the strengths and shortcomings of American culture?

We come back to Tolstoy. He knew what he was talking about. Mormons taught *the* American religion, or at least a vital aspect of it, but not because their doctrines somehow sprouted naturally out of the American frontier and provided a domestic alternative to faiths imported from Europe. Mormons followed a lesson, already by their time well established in American experience, that one way of becoming American was to invent oneself out of a sense of opposition. This was perhaps the most useful consequence of America's voluntary system of church formation. The American mainstream, certainly its religious mainstream, never meant anything except what competing parties chose to make of it. It was not anything fixed. It was an area of conflict. In defining themselves as being apart from the mainstream, Mormons were in fact laying their claim to it. By declaring themselves outsiders, they were moving to the center.

Granted, nineteenth-century Mormons were a relatively small religious group when placed aside the five or so largest church denominations. It was the impulse which the Mormons represented that made their story important. Nineteenth-century historians, and many who followed them, got the meaning of American religious experience almost exactly backwards. The trend was never toward unity. American religious experience began as dissent, and invented oppositions remained the major source of liveliness in American religion both in the nineteenth and twentieth centuries.

That has not necessarily resulted in anything wonderful. As we shall reiterate in future chapters, American religious dissent has rarely been theologically sophisticated. It has only intermittently provided the smug, self-assured enclaves of American power with the criticism they deserved. And yet over the years sectarian dissent has provided an extraordinary number of people with strategies of success when others were lacking. In conscious and unconscious ways, they built a usable social identity for themselves by stressing the degree to which polite society called them the scum of the earth and the filth of creation. In those charges, they found their badges of respectability and, at least sometimes, a path to upward social mobility and greatly enhanced power in the social and political world around them.

Unquestionably the strategy worked best, was more reliable, for those who had the greatest leeway in inventing and controlling the fictions necessary to the strategy. The first Mormons, although they did not emerge from the most privileged strata of society, enjoyed some advantages when compared to many others who had to play outsider roles in American society. They were not stigmatized because of race, or because they could not speak English, or because they could not claim Protestant ancestors. Many other religious groups had to do what they could with outsider strategies after strong and demeaning fictions were, through no choice of their own, thrust upon them. In the next chapters we shall consider two important cases where immigrant and ethnic churches managed, despite the difficulties, to turn demeaning stereotypes into successful outsider roles. As they made themselves, they made America.

CHAPTER TWO

Managing Catholic Success in a Protestant Empire

If our religion fails in this country, true Americanism will fail with it; and we believe that those are the only true American Catholics who, while they maintain the rights and liberties which our constitution guarantees to us, are obedient to the divine voice which speaks to man through the Catholic Church.

Thomas Preston (1891)

Until recently, American Catholic history has largely been a story about how the Catholic faithful, who suffered a double stigma on account of their religion and their recent arrival from Europe, gradually overcame an instinctive hatred of American Protestants, accommodated themselves to American institutions, and finally gained, after World War II, social status and economic prosperity. The razor thin victory of John F. Kennedy in 1960 marked the final passage of American Catholics out of their nineteenth-century ghettos. Not every one has agreed with Daniel Boorstin that the postwar advances of American Catholics represented "a peculiarly significant and inspiring chapter in the growth and fulfillment of American institutions."[1] As we shall shortly see, some American Catholics have worried that, in the act of accommodating, they forgot that their religion was supposed to be something more than simply another faith among many others. However, whatever the reaction to the process, Philip Gleason was correct in noting the degree to which "Americanization is the grand theme in the history of the Catholic Church in the United States."[2]

Gleason was also right in saying that most histories of the Catholic church have made heroes of the so-called Americanizers,

48

also referred to as "liberals," who wanted to strip away as quickly as possible every feature of the church that suggested foreignness or an ideological antipathy to American institutions. This point of view, which was most convincingly argued in the work of Thomas McAvoy, required the scapegoating of nineteenth-century "conservative clerics" who, it was alleged, viewed American democracy and its active, melioristic spirit with grave suspicion. They unwisely insisted on treating certain "foreign" elements in the church as integral parts of the universal faith rather than as anachronistic survivals from a past better forgotten.[3] The criticism of the "conservatives" has gone rather far, even so far as to suggest that the anti-modernism of Catholic priests was more responsible for the delayed upward mobility of American Catholic immigrants than the anti-Catholic campaigns waged by American nativists. According to a number of accounts, the welcome that sections of the American Catholic clergy accorded to Pope Leo XIII's famous strictures against "Americanism" made in a papal letter of 1899 set back the intellectual and social progress of the church by fifty years.

The recent interest that historians have taken in "ethnicity" has quite abruptly begun to change attitudes toward a number of the issues that gave rise to the Americanist controversy within the nineteenth-century Catholic church. For example, Catholic "liberals" are now commonly pilloried for having equated "Americanness" with Anglo-American culture, and for thus pinning a label of "foreignness" on many things that clearly did not deserve that name. Andrew Greeley, who once championed the Catholic clergy who had pushed for the rapid denationalization of Catholic immigrants, changed his mind when he concluded that a strongly maintained ethnic or national identity, which in the Catholic case was closely linked to religious identity, had not retarded the social advance of immigrant groups. Greeley has joined others in viewing ethnicity as "a way for the immigrant population to look at its present and future in America rather than its past in the Old World." Ethnic feeling was "not a way of withdrawing from the rest of society so much as an institution for dealing oneself into it."[4]

David O'Brien has made the most effective criticism of what the "liberal" Catholic clergy attempted under the name of accommodation. Their Americanization schemes were irrelevant

because they were "trying to reform to their model of an American church men and institutions already quite at home in the
United States." Moreover, they introduced into the mentality of
the church an unthinking and uncritical view of "the American
way of life" that has in recent years brought the church close to
"losing its soul, surrendering its historical claims and betraying its
most basic functions."[5]

The downward reevaluation of the Catholic strategies that carried the label "Americanist" in the nineteenth century has not
necessarily redounded, as one might have expected, to the credit
of those who opposed them. Quite pointedly, O'Brien in his criticisms of Catholic liberals has not tried to rescue the reputation
of the Catholic clerics who have borne the stigmatized designa-
tion "conservative." Their dim and medieval social vision may
have provided an alternative to the fatuous optimism of the liberals, but it was a useless and unproductive one. Even John
Hughes, the militant archbishop of New York City who became
one of the most famous American Catholics in the nineteenth century, gets little credit for insisting that Catholics needed to maintain a distinct point of view, one that sought something more than
a merger with status quo American life. His militance, according
to many accounts, unwisely legitimized a parochial-minded program of ghettoization that led American Catholics to seek their
identity in nothing more important or socially valuable than saints'
days and meatless Fridays.[6]

In the present chapter, we mean to provide a somewhat sympathetic account of what nineteenth-century conservative clerics,
the alleged non-Americanizers, tried to accomplish. Doing so
requires linking their oppositional strategies to those of other religious leaders we are discussing in this book. At the same time, we
must keep in mind distinctive features of Catholic history. The
first and most obvious of these has to do with unshakable realities
about number and political power. By 1850, the Catholic church
was the largest denomination in America. Despite important ethnic rivalries and divisions within the Catholic community,
Catholicism was a formidable political force in key American cities and states during the last half of the nineteenth century. Catholics suffered persecution and predictably cultivated a myth of
group powerlessness, but Catholics had many allies outside the
Catholic community. After the Civil War, virulent anti-Catholi-

cism was a weaker force in American life than Catholicism. That fact explains among other things why there was a significant debate in the Catholic community about strategy. Catholics encountered hatred, but Catholic leaders had the relative luxury of being able to imagine more than one way to press their collective fortunes in America.

A second factor, which differentiated the Catholic experience from that of some other outsider religious groups in America, was the immigrant nature of the church. Despite Columbus, despite the French Jesuits, despite Lord Baltimore and John Carroll, despite the relatively high social and economic position of American Catholics in the early national period, the typical American Catholic in the middle of the nineteenth-century began life in the United States as a foreigner. Unlike the Mormons, Catholic leaders did not have to invent a sense of difference between a native culture and something else. Immigrant Catholics brought with them not only their strong sense of the cultural differences between Catholicism and Protestantism but also their sense of the differences between their own national identification and that of other nineteenth-century immigrants to America. The important disputes within the American church, despite the labels that were pinned to the various positions, were never over the question of whether immigrant Catholics should become American. The quarrels were about how. Indeed they were about what it meant to be an American.

Since a public dispute between the Irish-born archbishop of New York City, John Hughes, and the American-born Catholic convert, Orestes Brownson, was seminal in drawing lines between purported "Americanizers" and purported "non-Americanizers" in the nineteenth-century Catholic Church, we may as well begin with a review of their disagreement. Brownson and Hughes started finding fault with each other's position in the 1850s. Much of their argument reflected the wild inconsistencies that then marked the many estimates made about the future of Catholicism in America. Evangelical Protestants coupled their predictions that Catholicism had no future in the United States with the contradictory claim that, because of the merely nominal Protestant attachment of most Americans, the Catholic church effectively controlled the nation's secular press and a major part of its politics.[7] For their part, the Catholic clergy complained about their lack of influence in a hostile country while simultaneously boasting about the "splendid" progress of their church. The Papal Nuncio, Cardinal Bedini, after a tour of the United States in 1850, estimated that the population of twenty-four million was split between two million Catholics, five million badly divided Protestants, and seventeen million "indifferent people or quasi-pagans."[8] The only apparent statistical agreement fostered by American realities was that America's religious future was up for grabs.

Orestes Brownson came to Catholicism by way of a long religious odyssey. Even after his conversion he remained an individual of profoundly unsettled mind. He had learned too well from Emerson not to value consistency. His own estimates concerning the likely success of Catholicism in America underwent a sharp reversal between the time of his entrance into the church and the end of his career. At the moment of his clash with Hughes, the estimates were highly optimistic. In the decade before the Civil War, Brownson used the pages of his *Quarterly Review* to convince American Catholics that because of "the natural relation" of concord between "our religion and the government," Americans would soon recognize that "it is only through Catholicity that the country can fulfill its mission."[9] He expected nothing less dramatic than a national conversion.

Brownson linked this extraordinary expectation to one proviso: Catholics had to follow a strategy of conformity to "Anglo-Saxon" manners. He wrote to his friend Isaac Hecker, who believed even more strongly in the possibility of a Catholic America, that the progress of the church faced serious obstacles unless "a large portion of our bishops and clergy" got over their "real dislike of the American people and character."[10] In the following passage, Brownson summarized his ideas about what constituted Americanization:

> If Catholics choose to separate themselves from the great current of American nationality, and to assume the position in political and social life of an inferior, a distinct, or an alien people, or of a foreign colony planted in the midst of a people with whom they have no sympathies, they will be permitted to do so, and will be treated by the country at large according to their own estimate of themselves. But if they quietly take their position as free and equal American citizens, with American interests and sympathies, Amer-

ican sentiments and affections, and throw themselves fearlessly into the great current of American national life, ready to co-operate with any and every class of their fellow-citizens for the true interests and glory of a common country, their religion will not be in their way, and they will gain that weight and influence in the country to which their real merit entitles them. All depends on ourselves.[11]

In matters of strategy, Brownson was not the wisest of men. One of his detractors remarked after Brownson's switch to Catholicism: "We cannot too sincerely congratulate the Protestants on the fact, for if the doctor should render his new friends the same sort of service that he has his old friends, Catholicism will soon be at an end."[12] With good reason, many Catholic leaders were not enthusiastic about Brownson's advice. Archbishop Hughes issued the most direct challenge to Brownson's apparent belief that Americans would all become Catholics if only Catholics would stop acting like immigrants. He sharply rebuked Brownson publicly when the latter in 1856 delivered a commencement address at St. John's College (later Fordham University). Although we do not have the precise words that Hughes or Brownson used that night, a subsequent exchange of letters between them makes their differences clear enough. Hughes cautioned Brownson not to "say anything calculated to represent the Catholic religion as especially adapted to the genius of the American people as such." Moreover, he did not concur in what he took to be the drift of Brownson's commencement remarks—"to the effect that if the Catholic religion had been or could now be presented to the American people through mediums and under auspices more congenial with the national feelings and habits, the progress of the Church and the conversion of Protestants would have been far greater."[13]

Hughes obviously did not want an equation drawn between Catholicism and America. However, neither his remarks to Brownson nor those on any other public occasion furnish evidence for the surprisingly dominant judgment among historians that Hughes "simply could not penetrate the American mind and the country's Protestant heritage."[14] Hughes intended many of his words and actions to shape a Catholic outgroup mentality, a mentality that had more to do with social identification than with religious piety. If that was a fault, the one charge against him is fairly

made. It is the various related charges that are wrong. Saying that
Hughes did not like American society, that he encouraged a totally
defensive mentality among American Catholics, that he failed "to
provide a working alternative in precisely the time and the place
where such an alternative could have been of critical importance,"
misrepresents Hughes's attitudes as well as the issues at stake in
quarrels about the Americanization of the Church.[15]

The flare-up between Brownson and Hughes had virtually
nothing to do with points of Catholic doctrine. On issues of doctrine and theology, Brownson was obedient and conservative.
What irritated Hughes was the equation Brownson drew between
being native-born and being American. He resented Brownson's
suggestion that the foreign-born (i.e. Irish) American Catholic
clergy, in retaining "their foreign habits and manners," were not
doing an adequate job of promoting the faith or of turning Catholic immigrants into Americans. Brownson's frequent references
to the quasi-foreign character of the church reflected a nativist
disdain for the Irish immigrant.[16] Brownson quoted approvingly
the opinion that naturalized citizens should not become "violent
partisans" in American elections. He agreed with the counsel: "A
certain moderation, a prudent reserve in the exercise of their fran-
chises is expected of them."[17]

Hughes's anger at Brownson for suggesting that native-born
citizens had more of a role to play in shaping America's destiny
than foreign-born citizens was not the reaction of an Irish nationalist. It was the reaction of an American patriot. This is the point
that is often forgotten. Hughes had a great deal of affection for
Ireland and was proud to be Irish. At the same time he had no
wish to go back. He was no friend to the young Irish patriots who
spent their time in New York working exclusively to free Ireland
from English rule. When Hughes ascribed to Providential plan
the discovery of this "great unpeopled hemisphere" at precisely
the "period when it could serve as a refuge and an asylum for the
persecuted of every name, and of every creed," he meant it.[18]
American nativism was bad, but Hughes did not believe that it was
the worst form of anti-Catholicism in the world.

These considerations are extremely important for understanding Hughes's role in the New York City school controversy that
began in 1839, several years before the beginning of the so-called
"famine-wave" immigration that dramatically increased New

York City's Irish Catholic population. Hughes's actions in that affair were not, as his critics have claimed, needlessly inflammatory efforts to reject the American way of public education. That way was still undetermined. At the time of the controversy, public education was in its infancy in most areas of the nation. The patterns of financing the developing educational systems varied. Since one pattern that had been used in New York and elsewhere included state aid to the schools maintained by most Protestant denominations, Hughes, in challenging the refusal of New York City's Public School Society to fund Catholic school education, was not attacking a firmly rooted tradition of secular public education.[19] All nineteenth-century sponsors of public education, at least up to 1850, saw some sort of religious instruction as an essential part of a school curriculum. Far from questioning that perspective, Hughes was trying to sustain it by promoting the then constitutional practice of publicly funding denominational schools. He was also contesting a peculiarly Protestant definition of what constituted appropriate religious instruction.[20]

From the perspective of American Catholics, the results of the Great School War in New York City were mixed. Hughes rallied a political force strong enough to crush his *bête noire*, the Public School Society. It was replaced by a decentralized system of school control that proved to be more responsive to pressures from Catholic neighborhoods. In addition, New York City school officials grew genuinely concerned with eliminating blatant anti-Catholic references in school textbooks. Hughes even was partially able to challenge the Protestant view of what constituted non-denominational religious instruction (e.g. the reading from the King James Bible without comment).

On the major issue Hughes lost, and he lost in part because he was unwilling to compromise.[21] Despite help from Governor Seward, a Republican, he failed utterly to win concessions on public financing for parochial schools. One may argue whether the particular tactics adopted by Hughes constituted skillful politics, for when the battle was over, a system of secular public schools, one that Hughes believed Catholic children could not accept, was well on its way to becoming *the* tradition. Hughes then had to turn his attention away from public education to building a system of church-financed parochial schools.

However, political ineptness, if that is the charge against Hughes in this affair, does not make one un-American. Nor does it make the cause a stupid one. Hughes wrote to the archbishop of New Orleans that a defeat could be a gain, and he had good reason to say so.[22] In his stubbornness, Hughes accomplished some things of considerable importance. He convincingly argued to Irish American Catholics that the essence of Americanness did not reside in accepting norms created for them by native-born Protestants. Further, he demonstrated that American institutions could be made to work to their advantage. Far from encouraging anti-American feelings, or from advising his flock to remain "separate from and adverse to the principles of the country to which they belong," Hughes waged his fight in the most familiar cadences of American political patriotic rhetoric: "I am not disposed to waive either my rights as a citizen, or sacrifice my principles as a patriot and a man, simply because the tide of American public opinion may be turned against me."[23] Hughes criticized Brownson because well before Brownson developed his plan to Americanize the church, Hughes had developed one of his own. His plan stressed the theme that Catholics did not have to become American. They already were.

Hughes's clannish appeals to Irish Catholics, appeals that encouraged a minority consciousness and discouraged mingling with Protestants, helped perpetuate a belief among American Catholics that Protestants held the upper hand. Yet when Hughes talked about Protestant dominance in the United States, he did so in ways that were calculated to call that dominance into question. He appealed to parochial and isolationist sentiments in the Catholic minority in an effort to break down the feelings of inferiority that attached inevitably to the experience of being an immigrant. In responding to nativist attacks on the church, Hughes contested the notions that "Catholics are necessarily strangers," or that "this is a Protestant Republic."[24] He wrote: "That the great majority of the inhabitants of this country are *not* Catholic, I admit; but that it is a Protestant country, or a Catholic country, or a Jewish country, or a Christian country in a sense that would give any sect or combination of sects the right to oppress any other sect, I utterly deny."[25] With respect to the claim that Hughes's attitude reflected dislike of America, it is instructive to remember that Brownson, not Hughes, ended his life bitterly disappointed with Catholicism's progress in the United States.[26]

Brownson and Hughes failed to settle their quarrel, and so did the Catholic leaders who followed them. The dispute was echoed in many ways in what became known at the end of the nineteenth century as the "Americanist controversy." In his influential book, *The Emergence of Liberal Catholicism in America*, Robert Cross described two clerical parties in the late nineteenth-century American church, one liberal and one conservative. He associated the latter with clergy who were deeply hostile to America.[27] Members of this conservative party were suspicious of the foundations of American government, especially the emphasis on democracy and the separation of church and state. They viewed Protestants as irredeemably lost and were pessimistic about America's future. They wanted no contacts between Catholics and Protestants and promoted Catholic neighborhoods, parochial schools, and foreign language parishes. Finally, they believed that Catholics would remain a stigmatized minority in America, and they paid more attention to what was going on in Rome than to what happened in Washington. The conservative leaders most frequently cited in Cross's book are Michael Corrigan, Bernard McQuaid, and Anton Walburg. Their principal opponents, men who supposedly held the opposite view on each of the above points, were John Ireland, Denis O'Connell, James Gibbons, and John Lancaster Spalding. This party of liberals, according to Cross, waged a useful campaign to establish harmony between American institutions and Catholic ideology. Unfortunately, when Pope Leo XIII in 1899 sharply reproved those who praised American institutions too unreservedly, the liberals lost their credibility both within and without the church. As a result, American Catholics were left stranded outside the American mainstream for two more generations.

Recent scholarship has recognized that Cross's divisions were too simple. An interpretation that depicts one party of Catholic clergy (so-called non-Americanizers) who despaired of America's present and future pitted against another party (so-called Americanizers) who loved and understood America simply does not square with the facts. There was more than one dimension to the "Americanist controversy." Various issues split the clergy in var-

ious ways. Moreover on many points affecting the Catholic attitude toward America the voice of the Church was virtually unan-
imous. Catholic leaders, for example, despite the reputation that
some of them gained for being conciliatory toward non-Catholics,
expressed little respect for American Protestantism. John Ireland,
the archbishop of St. Paul who seized for himself the label "Americanizer," described Protestantism as "a religious system ... in
process of dissolution; it is without value as a doctrinal or moral
power, and it is no longer a foe with which we need to reckon."[28]

Ireland, like Brownson in his optimistic years, ardently
believed that America's future was Catholic. Many of his opponents in the Catholic hierarchy understandably regarded him as
naive and therefore seemed to place less emphasis upon America
as a promised land. Their tempered expectations, however, did
not mean they had given up on America. They took second place
to no one in boasting about the progress of the American church.
In an article written for the *American Ecclesiastical Review*, a journal noted for its conservative theological posture, Edward
McSweeny argued that "God means our great Republic, the greatest that has yet appeared, to be an apostle, not of the rights of man
alone, but of the rights of God's Church."[29] This point of view,
which had grown tiresomely familiar in Rome by the end of the
century, did not define a party of American clerics.

The unanimity with which American Catholic leaders claimed
the major part of America's future for their church joined them in
a project, equally noncontroversial for them, of reclaiming the
same portion of America's past. All Catholic writers, not merely
"liberals" and "Americanizers," wished to revise the telling of
American history to remind Americans that "it was a Catholic
monk who inspired Columbus with hope; it was a Columbus and
Catholic crew that first crossed the trackless main; that it was a
Catholic queen who rendered the expedition possible; and that it
was a Catholic whose name has been given to the entire
continent."[30]

The enterprise of recovering America's Catholic past produced
one nineteenth-century historian of real merit, John Gilmary
Shea, and a well-argued literature that sought to shift the center
of colonial America from New England to Maryland. Catholic
writers emphasized again and again that Protestants, and especially the Puritans, had not authored American religious liberty.

Shea debunked the founders of Massachusetts Bay with a relish that has not been surpassed. He wrote:[31]

> For writers to claim for the Fathers of New England the high honor of establishing liberty of conscience ... is a farce too contemptible for consideration ... the Separatists and Puritans of New England were narrow-minded, tyrannical, and intolerant in religious thought; cruel and unmerciful to white or red men who refused to submit to their ruling; grasping and avaricious in their intercourse with the Indians; full of superstition and easily led by it into any excess.

James Corcoran added a thought that hit Protestant leaders in their most vulnerable spot. The true legatee of the Puritans' irascible provincialism was not, he said, George Washington or Thomas Jefferson, but Joseph Smith.[32]

Accommodating American and Catholic traditions, then, was a general Catholic concern, not the hobby horse of one party. No important Catholic writer in the late nineteenth-century sought to unite Catholics in a rejection of America. The common task was to describe the proper fit between American and Catholic ideals. Disputes rarely arose over the question of whether European systems of governments worked better than the American system. When they did, comparisons normally ran in America's favor. The Catholic clergy agreed with Bernard McQuaid, the bishop of Rochester, New York, who was often attacked as a "non-Americanizer," that American Catholics were well rid of Europe.[33] The several disagreements that made up the Americanist controversy stemmed from questions about which stereotypes of American belief and behavior should serve as models for Catholic accommodation.

It is perfectly true that American Catholic writers who were conservative on matters of church doctrine had greater difficulty describing the proper fit between American and Catholic ideals than others who were less conservative. The popes of the first part of the nineteenth century were, from a democratic point of view, political reactionaries who maintained a despotic rule over the Papal States. That fact created difficulties. Even Leo XIII, who many regarded as more progressive than his predecessors, was no particular friend of republican notions. Moreover, Rome in 1870 insisted on its infallibility in a way that made it hard to sort out what a Catholic had to accept as part of his religion and what he was free to choose as part of his politics. On the issue of church-state separation, American Catholics seemed to be caught in a dilemma where their religion required them to view the American system as just plain wrong. In contrast to self-styled Americanizers, like John Ireland and Isaac Hecker, who spoke as if American institutions were expressly invented to serve Catholicism's needs, a number of Catholic writers expressed their beliefs concerning the compatibility of American and Catholic institutions in cautious, even negative terms. According to one less than exuberant formula, there was "no fundamental hostility."[34]

Before reading an un-American spirit into this last phrase, we should recall the case of Hughes. An expression of complaint is not the same as rejection. Catholic conservatives stated any number of complaints: America was a heathen country, dangerous territory for the Catholic conscience; too many Americans believed that the power to create government came from the people and not from God; Americans stressed social equality to the point that it encouraged social turbulence; they confused liberty with an individualism that undermined duly constituted authority. However, in criticizing, most Catholic conservatives were not turning their backs on America. They were rather presenting their own version of the genius of American politics. According to them, the church had first revealed the "true and noblest form" of American republican institutions. They defined their task not as undermining institutions but as saving them from Protestant corruptions.[35] Without trying to prove the impossible thesis that the American Constitution was a perfect form of government, they managed to conclude just as often as their opponents did, that in the less than perfect world, the American government was the best government for the American people and for the American Catholic church. Whatever the present problems, the burden of their argument was to disprove any notion of an ultimate clash between an ideal America and an ideal form of Catholic practice.

The thorniest issue that Catholic writers had to address was the issue of church-state separation. Rome clearly did not regard American arrangements as a model to copy elsewhere, and no American Catholic leader expected Rome to put a definitive blessing on the First Amendment. On the other hand, American Catholic writers all endorsed freedom of conscience, and the theological conservatives had no trouble coming up with arguments to challenge Protestants who viewed themselves as the sole guardians of religious liberty. Perhaps, conservatives said, when a distant day put American Catholics in the overwhelming majority, the state might appropriately, without disturbing freedom of conscience, encourage the one true church. In the meantime, the significant threat to free religious practice in America came not from Catholic priests, but from Protestant evangelicals.[36] It had been the Protestants in Massachusetts and Connecticut who had created state-supported churches in America and who had clung longest to them. It was Protestants who sponsored legislation that took the education of children away from families, that dictated standards of Sabbath behavior, and that sought to inject Protestant forms of worship into public ceremonies. In one of the small ironies surrounding Protestant-Catholic clashes in the United States, religiously conservative Catholics, supposedly hostile to everything begotten by the descendants of John Locke, wound up presenting their version of what America should be in unmistakably libertarian language.[37]

One risks only slight exaggeration in claiming that the sort of patriotic feeling, so apparent in the anti-Communist rhetoric of Catholic leaders in the early part of the Cold War, was shaped as much by nineteenth-century Catholic leaders who were falsely accused of harboring anti-American feelings as by anyone else. Church conservatives tried not to confuse love of country with love of God. They warned of the dangers of needlessly flaunting the American flag and of promoting a false nationalism at the expense of a respect for religion.[38] Nonetheless the patriotism expressed by archbishop Michael Corrigan was common fare among the entire wing of the American clergy who are commonly remembered as non-Americanizers: "We who are born in this Land of the Free, regard our country, not only with love and affection, but as the dearest spot on all the earth."[39]

How, then, did nineteenth-century Catholic leaders who fought for parochial schools, who refused to say the United States was perfect, and who sharply warned their parishioners to stay clear of Protestants gain the reputation of harboring strongly negative feelings toward America? William Purcell, the editor of a Democratic newspaper in Rochester, placed the blame on John Keane, a clerical ally of John Ireland, rather than on the Protestant press. Keane, according to Purcell, had invented the "absurd notion" that there was a party of non-Americanists and Ultramontanists within the American church.[40] He, like Ireland, had done so with polemical intent in pressing his own recommendations about the proper course of the church. Writing about the church in a later era, Gary Wills noted that the "Catholic liberal . . . opposed the American Church because it was too American. Its bishops had been shaped more by the ethos of the local Chamber of Commerce than by the American Academy in Rome. The pastor was obnoxious, not for his theology and transnational ties, but for his lack of theology and parochialism. He was Babbitt in a biretta."[41] Wills was not looking at anything new. The so-called liberals in the nineteenth century, not the conservatives, ran most frequently to Rome. What bothered Ireland about his New York colleagues McQuaid and Corrigan was not their un-Americanness. It was their comfortable acquiescence in the marriage of many Irish Catholics with the very American institution of Tammany Hall. Ireland's misgivings about the uses of the Irish Catholic vote reflected his staunch ties to the Republican party. They also recalled the attitudes of Brownson.

Doctrinal conservatives eventually prevailed in Rome, at least with respect to the issues addressed by Pope Leo in his letter of 1899. This was not because they appealed to rampant anti-American feelings. Quite the contrary. They won because they depicted the strength of the American church with greater accuracy than their opponents. The party of "Americanists" seemed to lose confidence in their country whenever they traveled to the Vatican. Arguing there for a compromise plan to finance Catholic education at Faribault, Minnesota, John Ireland emphasized the fragility of the American church and the dangers of doing anything to stir up Protestant opposition. His friend, Denis O'Connell, in opposing the idea of installing a permanent Papal delegate in Washington, told his Vatican contacts that a "Culturkampf was as possible in America as in Germany."[42] It was left to the conservative McQuaid to brand these attempts to raise fears about nativism "as a libel on the character of the American people."[43] And, in fact, Leo XIII's controversial letter on America, written just after the Spanish American War when Catholic loyalties were vulnerable to attack, stirred little anti-Catholic feeling among Protestants.

One may suggest a further point. It is doubtful whether a so-called Americanizer like John Ireland had a better strategy for appealing to Protestant Americans than a so-called non-Americanizer like Michael Corrigan. Anti-Catholic Protestant writers reacted no more favorably to the former than to the latter. Cross, in his book, argued that Father Edward McGlynn, a social radical who supported Henry George as well as Ireland's brand of Americanization, became a "hero to Americans."[44] In fact, although some anti-Catholics used the disciplining of McGlynn by the Catholic hierarchy to attack Catholic "authoritarianism," the majority of American Protestant leaders had little use for Henry George and his friends. Corrigan, who was the alleged villain in this authoritarian silencing, enjoyed the editorial support of most of New York's newspapers.[45] In contrast, Ireland was at about the same time the American Protective Association's favorite target of abuse.[46] This nativist organization, which was active in the last decades of the nineteenth century, interpreted Ireland's friendly overtures to Protestant America as an example of Catholic duplicity. The APA wanted nothing to do with people who aimed to make America Catholic; and if the choice was between Catholics who did not mince words in stating their goals and those who tried to make their aim palatable by extending a hand of ecumenical friendship, they preferred the former.

In addition to resolving questions about the fit between American practices and belief and Catholic practices and belief, the Americanist controversy also involved disputes over ways and means for the church to adjust the steady stream of Catholic immigrants to the manners and mores of the people who were already here. As a practical matter, the most critical issue in the controversy was whether the church should insist on a territorial, i.e. a geographical, organization of its parishes, thus mixing recent immigrants with "older" American Catholics, or whether it should encourage or allow ethnic and national parishes. Everyone agreed that if the church chose the latter path, immigrants would take longer to learn about other American communities outside of their own. They would also find it easier to preserve the use of a native tongue other than English.

What American Catholics disagreed about was whether the preservation of ethnic and national identities in America was a good or a bad thing. The bulk of the Irish clergy, including those classified as conservative or non-Americanist on other issues, insisted that it was a bad idea. They after all spoke English and were an "older" group of immigrants by the end of the century. They never could quite understand why other immigrant groups would want to make a distinction between being Irish and being Catholic. Arrayed against them were Germans, Poles, Slovaks, and Italians who viewed the establishment of national parishes not only as their defense against Protestant America, but as their defense against the dominance of the Irish clergy in the American Catholic church. To them, the Irish insistence that they "Americanize" themselves by learning English was simply a command to put a "Mc" before their name.

Parish organization became a particularly contentious point within the American church following the Cahensly Memorial of 1890. Peter Cahensly, a member of the German Reichstag and a wealthy Catholic layman, feared that conditions in America led millions of Catholic immigrants to abandon the church. Brutally uprooted from their culture and their traditions, they found the church in America as strange to them as everything else in their new environment. Since, in addition, their religion often got them in trouble with Protestants, they were sorely tempted to shed it along with their ethnic identification. The only way to prevent this "leakage," according to Cahensly and other observers in Europe, was to provide means for the immigrants to re-create their national cultures in the new world. Cahensly's plan to insist on the ethnic organization of Catholic worship not only raised cries of alarm among Protestants who feared that the flow of immigration already threatened the nation with fragmentation, but from most Irish Catholic leaders as well.[47]

Among Cahensly's backers in America was Anton Walburg, the German-born pastor of St. Augustine's Church in Cincinnati. His controversial pamphlet *The Question of Nationality in Its Relation to the Catholic Church in America*, published in 1889, gained for him a reputation as a non-Americanizer. His detractors argued that in it he unwisely said many unflattering things about native-born Americans and compared their manners and their intelligence unfavorably with those of recently arrived German immigrants. One recent historian remarked that Walburg "denounced 'Americans' as fanatic, intolerant, radical, dissimulating hyprocrites."[48]

America, Walburg most certainly did say, was overcome by
Mammon worship. He pointed to money as the supreme power.
Moreover, he ridiculed the many Americans who measured the
worth of their country by size alone, the bigness of its rivers, the
tallness of its trees, the grandness of its scenery. They lacked a
sophisticated sense of culture.[49] Yet despite the criticisms that his
pamphlet contained, Walburg was trying to do something more
than add to the pile of negative European literature on the subject
of the United States. If one reads him through, one discovers that
his intention was almost exactly the opposite. He sought to distinguish a "true Americanism" from a "false Americanism," and
in so doing to project an exceedingly flattering image of America's
destiny. To Walburg, "true Americanism," like true Catholicism,
made "no distinction of color, rank, condition, or nationality."[50]
It was the opposite of Bismarck's program of cultural homogenization that had driven so many German Catholics to America in
the first place. Walburg was not casting a nostalgic glance back-
ward toward Germany. He was predicting a great future for cultural pluralism in the United States. He was encouraging what
another Catholic writer called "marked and multiplied diversities
in matters not essential."

Interestingly, in view of his alleged hostility toward the United
States, Walburg's pamphlet assigned no importance to American
nativism. The strategy of the argument he was making to American Catholics required him to say that nativism was dead, at least
in respectable circles. By making the bold assumption that "the
foreigner is considered as good an American as a native," Walburg concluded that the foreigner was free to make his own claims
about what America should become. "Here," he said, "where the
people are sovereign, they can change the official language as well
as they can change political parties."[51] Immigrants who spoke
German with their neighbors and who restricted most of their
social intercourse to a German-speaking community were not
deviating from behavior that the founding fathers had intended.
They were exercising a fundamental right that the Constitution
had meant to protect and that made America special.

As a statement endorsing cultural pluralism, Walburg's position now seems both moderate and conciliatory. He did not urge
a permanent isolation of immigrant cultures in foreign enclaves.
"No foreign nationality," he concluded, "can permanently main-

tain itself in this country . . . The American nationality will finally prevail." He noted that when pressed too far, "nationalism in the Church has always proved disastrous."[52] What Walburg feared was that most so-called programs of "Americanization" wound up wedding cultural factors of the lowest common denominator. Immigrants, Walburg believed, had two choices. Either they could seek a quick and superficial entry into American society by adopting the worst vices of the native-born. (Vice was easy to imitate whereas the virtues of another culture took many years to emulate.) Or they could maintain a proud sense of who they were, seeking their virtue within their own heritage, and thus contribute to the cultural enrichment of their adopted homeland. Walburg no doubt would have agreed with Arthur Preuss, another German Catholic who wrote at the height of the anti-German agitation during World War I: "The man or woman who would tamely submit to a large part of what goes on under the name of 'Americanization' is not fit to be in America."[53]

With respect to this dimension of the Americanist controversy, it is not easy to say which side won. The purported Americanizers, since they represented the strongly positioned Irish clergy, won most of the skirmishes. The papacy gave no support to Cahensly's Memorial, and Leo XIII did not address this aspect of the Americanist issue at all in his letter of 1899. Walburg himself felt that the American church ignored his arguments.[54] In the middle of the 1950s, Will Herberg was able to convince himself that ethnic and national divisions among American Catholics had virtually disappeared. Yet he was wrong. National and ethnic parishes remained important. After World War I, their importance, at least in numerical terms, declined; but despite the lack of widespread hierarchical enthusiasm for maintaining them, the ethnic identifications of Polish, Irish, Italian, and Puerto Rican Catholics did not disappear in urban areas. National parishes survived in de facto form, and nurtured identities that in some cases have grown stronger rather than weaker in recent years.[55]

Arguably, of course, the phenomenon of ethnic distinction was bad for the American church, and not just in the sense of upsetting its theoretical unity. Many American Catholics, particularly German Catholic immigrants who fought hard to preserve a national identity in the first generation, did very well and soon passed most other Americans on the scale of economic and professional attainments.[56] However, many other ethnic Catholics climbed relatively slowly up social and economic ladders. Ethnic consciousness, it has been suggested, worked to keep Catholics content with their second-class status.

Obviously, the question of whether it would have been better for the church if those who appropriated the label "Americanist" had won victories on all disputed points has no definitive answer. However the range of possible responses is not unlimited. The "Americanists" were certainly correct in maintaining that it made a difference how Catholics learned to perceive themselves. Defining themselves as apart from Anglo-American culture carried costs. If the American church had gone along with the public school system, had it proclaimed the American government as God's only government, had it threatened any member who refused to learn English with excommunication, many individual Catholics might have found their way to economic prosperity more quickly than they did. One can say with equal assurance that if a Polish Catholic, newly arrived in America in 1880, had somehow been able to stop being Polish and Catholic, he would have had a considerably easier time in his new environment than he did.

The point is that such expectations were unrealistic. The so-called non-Americanizers recognized that immigrants did not have the option of becoming quite anything they wanted. They also recognized better than their opponents that certain ways of becoming American were not compatible with remaining Catholic. They argued that their immigrant church had to plot its strategies taking into account the following realities about life in the United States: 1) Most native-born Americans in the nineteenth century were not Catholic; and although they were not all actively hostile toward Catholicism, they did not comprise a particularly fertile field for mass conversions; 2) Most immigrants could not in their lifetime shed the accents and manners that made them seem foreign to a native-born, English-speaking American; 3) American public schools as they developed were strongly Protestant in their cultural orientation, and Catholic children schooled among Protestant children were more likely to move in the Protestant direction than vice versa; 4) Catholic immigrants were quite often accustomed to do without material things and did not immediately have strong aspirations of upward social mobility. Many had no goal other than to earn enough money to go home again; 5) American experience was the experience of immigrants, and the claim of Protestant evangelicals that American culture and their culture were synonymous was open to challenge. The list was perceptive. The most aggressive programs of cultural assimilation urged on the church in the nineteenth century were wrong to the extent that they were out of touch with these facts.

In saying that, we have by no means made out a fully sympathetic hearing for those Catholic leaders who followed Hughes in insisting that Catholics, just as much as Mormons, had to become Americans by insisting on differences which separated them from other Americans. The clerics who directed the Catholic outsider strategies that prevailed until very recently probably did accomplish what they did at the expense of social mobility of many individual Catholics. Moreover, their concentration on retaining the immigrants' faith by constructing a strong and vigorous Catholic subculture, while potentially more interesting and creative than a plan that sought to surrender Catholicism to the inadequacies of nineteenth-century American life, rested on an anti-modernist perspective that committed the church to intellectual mediocrity and gave it no very compelling vision of an alternate America.[57] We shall have more to say about outsider religious identities and political stances in later chapters. We shall only note with respect to American Catholics that the nineteenth-century church, although it criticized American materialism, was not notable for fostering a progressive social vision or very interesting social thought. That remained true despite the example of Dorothy Day and the Catholic Workers Movement for most of the twentieth century.[58] Rather than furnishing a critical perspective on American life, the Catholic church became a patriotic vehicle for reinforcing many of the least interesting and least sophisticated aspects of American life.[59]

The best defense of Catholic leaders rests on two considerations. First, they were in a difficult position that would have taxed anyone's wisdom. Second, what they failed to do represented general failures of American culture, not particular failures of the Catholic minority. Philip Gleason has written about the dilemma faced by the nineteenth-century Catholic clergy with great understanding.[60] On the one hand, they were wary that efforts to make the major mission of the church one of purifying the larger American society might reduce the church to something not distinctly

Catholic. That concern was one reason they rejected Brownson's advice. At the same time, an excessive concern to preserve the distinctive flavor of Catholicism could drive the church into an artificially maintained sense of opposition that was useful for maintaining Catholic identity but useless for anything else. The strongest part of Ireland's argument was the warning against this possibility.

The purported non-Americanizers saw one important thing clearly. They knew that in the long run the difficulty the church faced was not in fitting Catholic immigrants comfortably into American society; the difficulty was in preserving a tension between the things that God demanded and a regard for a continent that was too easily loved. They tried hard to distinguish a proper patriotism from state worship. They told Catholics to wave the American flag, but repeatedly cautioned them not to mistake it for the image of Christ. Ethnic Catholic communities during the McCarthy period often forgot the caution. That is only to say, however, that the Americanization program of the purported non-Americanizers worked too well. The alternatives held up to the nineteenth-century church scarcely constituted a remedy for excessive patriotism.

An increasing number of observers have suggested that Brownson has finally prevailed over Hughes. Since World War II, a sense of difference has grown less acute in American Catholic consciousness. If that is so, then, as Brownson hoped, the Catholic church may enormously have increased its influence on Protestant America. What it may have lost, as Hughes feared it might, was its best chance to make a difference in American life. Meaningful activity in history usually involves exchanging one dilemma for another. As was the case with the Mormons, perceptions and reality are difficult to separate. If most American Catholics no longer think of themselves as different from other Americans, that is an important fact. Nevertheless, one can not therefore conclude that Catholics only recently became a significant part of the American religious landscape.

H. Richard Niebuhr thought that "both history and the religious census support the statement that Protestantism is America's only national religion and to ignore that fact is to view the country from a false angle."[61] Surely he was wrong. The religious census of the nineteenth century as well as that of the twentieth proves that the majority of Americans were not Catholic, but nothing more than that. As a statistical matter Catholics were as well off in the nineteenth century as now, since as late as 1890 over 67 percent of all Americans were not reported as members of any church. In that year Catholics probably constituted close to one third the number of church-affiliated Americans, a somewhat larger proportion than in these days of supposed mainstream acceptance. Surely its size has for a long time given Catholicism standing as one of America's national religions. [62]

The false angle from which to view national experience is the one that compels us to talk about everything in Catholic history, from the burning of the Ursaline Convent in Charlestown to the defeat of Al Smith, as evidence of Catholic powerlessness. In American histories told from this perspective, "real" Americans set the national norms and encouraged aggressive attacks on Catholic communities. Catholics reacted, usually ineffectually and with a sense of inferiority, to those attacks. In fact the most famous clashes between Protestants and Catholics are best understood as evidence of Catholic power and should be analyzed in that way. While feelings of insecurity and of inferiority are relevant factors in describing immigrant Catholic communities, those feelings are just as relevant for discussing those who attacked and burned Catholic churches.

In the end, what strikes one with the greatest force is the realization that the United States would be vastly different today, that it would have been vastly different one hundred years ago, if the Catholic church had not been a part of the American experience. Nothing was more important in shaping political party divisions, the character of those parties, and the way they worked, than the presence of a large Catholic population. Given the extent to which the politics of anti-Catholicism became linked to anti-slavery feeling in the antebellum period, one is inclined to agree with those who argue that the most important cause of the Civil War was the Irish potato famine.

One may argue that these particular items do not constitute positive contributions. Noting them, however, has the virtue of forcing us to recognize that nineteenth-century American culture was not a monolith that required Catholics to react to the actions of other Americans. That culture, scarcely a monolith, was just as much an arena in which other Americans had to respond to the actions of Catholics. Knowing that, we can transport American Catholics to the center of American religious history where they belong and appreciate the fact that if Catholic culture did not transform Protestant culture, it profoundly affected the myth of what American Protestant culture was supposed to be. Moreover, Catholicism shaped the way in which millions of immigrants became American and provided a definition of Americanization that was vastly more "real" in American experience than the formula suggested by Orestes Brownson. Only Protestant historians who refused to yield to the logic of pluralism, joined by Catholic historians who did not necessarily want to disturb the minority consciousness of American Catholics, could have ignored that fact for so long.

CHAPTER THREE

American Jews
as an Ordinary Minority

Not a Polish Jew fresh from Warsaw or Cracow—not a furtive
Yacoob or Ysaac still reeking of the Ghetto, snarling a weird Yiddish to the officers of the customs—but had a keener instinct, an
intenser energy, and a freer hand than he—American of Americans, with Heaven knew how many Puritans and Patriots behind
him. . .   Henry Adams, *The Education of Henry Adams*

The first chapters of Jewish outsiderhood commenced long
before Jews arrived in the United States. Irving Howe has noted
that the immigrant Jews who disembarked at Ellis Island, sometimes only weeks after they had left the shtetls of the Russian pale,
knew little about their collective history.[1] However, a vast historical memory was not necessary to structure what was fundamental
to Jewish consciousness: Jews were chosen, and because they
were chosen they suffered. Their experience in the Diaspora had
for centuries been one of uprooting, of expulsion, of forced con-
tainment within ghettos. New York was just another point in a
long flight; and Jews did not, as many of the other immigrant
groups who came to America, have to adjust suddenly to minority
status.[2] They had survived both despite and because of barriers
between themselves and others that they themselves had struggled
to perpetuate. The knowledge that had accumulated from their
struggles, the consciousness of being different, proved useful in
the United States, but useful in ways that changed the meaning of
Jewish apartness from what it had been in Europe.

The exceptional part of the American Jewish story lay not in
American anti-Semitism, which, after all, had parallels in every
country where Jews had lived. It lay in the fact that Jews in the

United States found themselves sharing a great deal with the majority of other Americans who could not either aspire to a place in the Social Register, the Daughters of the American Revolution, or the Junior League. Most immigrant Jews came to America without an experienced connection to a homeland, but something similar was true of many other immigrants of the late nineteenth century. They were in the main village people who lacked a sense of nationalism. A European homeland was a concept they invented for themselves after they got to America. Moreover, not only did other immigrants often have bitter memories of European persecution to nurture, they also encountered discrimination in America. The United States even offered Jews an opportunity to witness Christians being treated more shabbily than they were. Anti-Semitism was at no point in the nation's past the most vicious form of American prejudice.

Saying these things is merely to reiterate what has long been recognized: Louis Hartz's analysis of America's freely inherited liberal tradition has a special importance in explaining the history of American Jews.[3] For immigrant Jews, the United States was born free not merely because there was no feudalism in its past but also no legally established ghetto. The Jews who came to America, even the vast numbers who arrived in the difficult period between 1880 and 1917, were not legally distinguishable from the other immigrants who were eligible for citizenship. Many within America's other immigrant groups returned home and in large numbers. By and large Jews stayed.[4] Not because America was paradise. Jews watched plenty of human lives and dreams crumble on the Lower East Side of Manhattan. Yet whatever the homesickness they felt for communities they had left behind, the United States seemed to offer something that most of them had not had before. In America they could pursue opportunities believing that what they gained would not later be stripped from them. The initial conditions of life in the United States exacted a high price for that security. Jews paid it because everywhere else before the beginning of Jewish emancipation and for a long time thereafter in Eastern Europe, security for them was not for sale at any price. Well before the Holocaust increased transcendentally the value of what had been achieved through immigration, American Jews were among the strongest subscribers to the view that America was different.

So many European Jews came to America before World War I (perhaps a third of the Jewish population of Eastern Europe) that we forget that most stayed behind. Jews who remained in Europe saw plainly enough that Jews advanced both economically and socially in the United States. The doubt was whether, in advancing, American Jews could or would remain Jews. If, as Karl Marx thought, American opportunities threatened to tame the radicalism of European political activists who fled to North America following the struggles of 1848, they posed significantly greater dangers to the religious component of what was Europe's most conservative, rule-bound way of life. The fears that European Catholics entertained about America were as nothing when compared with those of Europe's leading rabbis. To the latter the United States remained "this trefa (ritually impure) land," a place that destroyed the force of Jewish law. How were Jews to maintain a meaning for their belief in being God's particularly chosen people in a country whose competing version of that myth turned Jews into nothing special? David Levinsky, Abraham Cahan's famous fictional immigrant, learned on his first day in New York that "Judaism has not much of a chance here."[5] For Levinsky that assessment proved true enough. For most others, it depended on how you defined Judaism.

We know the end of the story, and the outcome therefore seems deceptively preordained. Jewish identification survived through successive generations of American Jews, some of them many times removed from the immigrant generation; and it never lost an important religious component. To all but the strictly Orthodox, who regard the identification of most American Jews as insubstantial, that fact constitutes one of the great success stories of American outsider strategy. Jews after all did more than merely survive as a group. Never more than 4 percent of the American population, they became early in the twentieth century a major intellectual force in the United States, and arguably the dominant force in shaping the popular culture spread through journalism, radio, and the movies. How Europe's most particularist people managed, some without learning more than a broken, thickly accented English, to supply mass entertainment to Americans more effectively than people judged in conventional terms to be more typically American is a subject closely linked to the major themes of this study.

Henry Adams could be intelligent even when he was being anti-Semitic. His bitter remark quoted at the beginning of this chapter indicates that Adams was at least aware of the feebleness of the Brahmin complaint that only people of old British birth qualified as genuine Americans. His despair over the energy of the "furtive Yacoob or Ysaac" was only partially mock. How strange, then, that Carl Bridenbaugh would tell assembled members of the American Historical Association in 1962:

> Many of the younger practitioners of our craft. . . are products of lower middle-class or foreign origins and. . . find themselves in a very real sense outsiders on our past and feel themselves shut out. This is certainly not their fault, but it is true.[6]

No doubt Bridenbaugh's phrase "younger practitioners" had targets other than Jews who had risen so rapidly in academic circles once American universities stopped discriminating. But it certainly did include them. Had Bridenbaugh recognized what Adams had already realized a long time before, he might have understood that the "young practitioners" he mentioned were not sitting in his audience because they felt "shut out." They were there to challenge what Bridenbaugh apparently thought American history was all about.

As we have seen, American Mormons tried to appropriate Jewish experience, particularly its beginnings, in building their own communities. In their determination to found Zion, they separated themselves as much as they possibly could from their less divinely favored "gentile" neighbors. Striking parallels exist between the charges that were used to justify anti-Mormon activity in the nineteenth century and those that Jews had confronted during a good part of their European history. Mormons were accused of trying to construct a nation within a nation; of using privileged forms of self-government to protect the exclusiveness of their community; of practicing economic isolation and of treating their neighbors differently in commercial relations than they treated one another; of conspiring secretly with the blessing of their religious leaders to kill "gentiles." American politicians cited the millennial teachings of Joseph Smith and Brigham Young to question Mormon loyalty to the American Constitution just as European rulers had periodically used the messianic teachings of the Jews to cast doubt on the firmness of Jewish allegiances to their Christian "protectors."

The Mormons succeeded so strikingly well in fastening upon themselves the stereotypes associated with an ideological anti-Semitism that America's Jews did not have to worry about an anti-Semitism directed at them until the end of the nineteenth century. The first Jews in America, Sephardics who had been forced out of Portugal and who eventually arrived in New Amsterdam and Newport during the colonial period, found themselves close to a religious culture that had been strongly influenced by the stories and symbols of the Old Testament. New England Calvinists were religiously opposed to the greater parts, both Protestant and Catholic, of Christian Europe. They interpreted their voyage to America typologically as the flight of chosen, covenanted people from Egypt or Babylon. Puritan law did not endorse much of the behavior prescribed by the Torah, but it did command religious observance. Setting themselves firmly against Antinomian tendencies found in many other forms of Christianity, the elected officials of Massachusetts Bay and Connecticut made it part of their responsibility to enforce the commandments given to Moses. If they failed in this task, they knew that their avenging God had ways to show His displeasure.

The Old Testament influences on American Puritanism were not sufficient to guarantee America's first arriving Jews an unreservedly warm embrace. Since the contracting parties involved in the covenant theology of Massachusetts Bay and Connecticut included Christ as well as Abraham, America's first Jewish communities grew up in New York, Newport, and Philadelphia, areas beyond the reach of the colonial, Calvinist theocracies.[7] However, Jews in the colonial period were not perceived anywhere as a primary threat to Christian practices. In this respect, their small numbers, perhaps 2000 by the time of the American Revolution, helped. From the standpoint of the Puritan colonials who taught a strict Calvinism, it was better to be a Jew (whom God had not entirely forgotten) than to be a pernicious Christian attracted to Quakerism or Catholicism. Although Jews in many localities suffered under a number of civil disabilities, disabilities that lingered into the nineteenth century, they were not the primary or original targets of discriminatory measures. Others shared their disabilities.

Compared then with the situation they had left in Europe, America's first Jews stepped onto North American shores as almost fully emancipated. The main problem which they faced was one that European Jews encountered only after Napoleon's Emancipation decrees: how were Jews to perpetuate themselves in circumstances where one gained nothing or lost nothing by being a Jew. The disestablishment of churches in the United States, which led eventually to complete civil and religious liberty for Jews, compounded the problem. Pre-emancipation Jews in Europe had suffered, but their sufferings had been made supportable by one large compensating factor, semi-autonomy. Jewish leaders had been able to enforce a normative Jewish life within the ghetto. Even in the nineteenth century, in areas where emancipation was fully achieved, European states and principalities usually recognized an official Jewish leadership which had the authority to maintain orthodox standards of Jewish belief and ritual.

Arguably, no brand of Christianity, not even Catholicism, was as ill-prepared to survive the American practice of church voluntarism as was European Judaism. The problem of maintaining some semblance of orthodoxy was surmountable so long as the number of American Jews remained small. The arrival of approximately 200,000 Jews, mostly Ashkenazi and mostly German-speaking, in the first two-thirds of the nineteenth century changed matters. They turned the question of Jewish survival into the most interesting test of America's religious experiment in church disestablishment. Any hope for a normative Judaism was impossible. No one had the authority to declare what normative Judaism was unless ordinary Jews conferred it. They never did, and American Judaism had to make its way following a model of extreme democratic congregationalism. It had no national organization until 1885 when a Rabbinical conference in Pittsburgh managed to agree on a platform of Reform belief. Even that event only underlined how split the American Jewish community had become in its religious practices. Not all Reform leaders agreed to the Pittsburgh Platform, and Reform itself was by that time rapidly becoming a minority movement among American Jews as a result of new patterns of immigration that had begun in the 1870s.

One has to keep these difficulties in mind to appreciate what the Jewish Reform movement managed to accomplish between

1825, the date of the first Reform society founded in Charlestown, and 1880, when all but eight of the two hundred major synagogues in the United States showed the strong influence of Reform practices. Without any clear guidelines for transferring Judaism from a European to an American context, without assurance that remaining Jewish was uppermost in the minds of Jews who crossed the Atlantic, and with only a handful of well-trained religious leaders, American Jews settled affirmatively the question of whether a Jewish identification could survive in the American environment.

The manner of the Reform solution did not of course please all Jews nor was it perhaps the only possible solution. In some important senses Reform Judaism constituted a rapid program of Americanization which left Jewish worship looking much more like a form of liberal Protestantism than what had been practiced in the shtetl. Aside from their congregational organization, Reform Jews accepted the laws of the Torah and Talmudic commentary "only as far as they can be adapted to the institutions of the Society in which they live and enjoy the blessings of liberty."[8] That phrase in effect invited Jews to discard the most distinctive Jewish rites of worship and daily life. Services in most Reform temples, highlighted now with a sermon, were far more ordered and decorous than they had been in traditional Jewish societies. American Jews began to accept aesthetic embellishments in their temples, including stained glass and organ music. Family seating during Sabbath services became normal. Amid these changes, the rabbi inevitably lost his position as a feared and authoritative teacher, a scholar whose command over a community was second to none. He was merely a pastor, whose status as a religious leader depended in almost all cases on his being hired and subsequently tolerated by a congregation of worshipers.

Traditionalists quite naturally interpreted these changes as an abandonment of the essential aspects of Judaism. In their minds, the practices introduced by the Reform leaders in America led directly to Felix Adler's Ethical Culture Society, founded in the 1880s. As Ethical Culturalists, Jews stopped calling themselves Jews, spoke piously of universal ethical duties and public service as the essence of religion, and disappeared into Christian America. The apparent wish to acculturate seemed to require Jews in all things to conform "to the feelings, sentiments, and opinions of

Americans."[9] Messianic hopes, a restored Israel, a nationalistic basis for Jewish identity—Reform Jewish Americans rejected all of them. In a famous phrase attributed to Gustavus Poznanski, a Polish-born, German-educated rabbi, "America is our Zion and Washington our Jerusalem."[10]

Without question, Reform leaders in the United States wanted Jews to have a strong American identity. Much later, in the twentieth century, when most Reform rabbis decided that it was appropriate for American Jews to express loyalty to a Jewish homeland in Palestine, they were not expressing disenchantment with the United States. They were reacting to tragic events in Europe that reinforced their conviction that America was different, and wonderful. However, if a different and praiseworthy America was the perceived context in which a nontraditional form of Judaism flourished, one needs to recognize that nineteenth-century Reform was also considerably more than a narrowly conceived program of Americanization. In the beginning the connection between Reform practice and acculturation to the United States was incidental.

This last fact serves to modify any tendency to interpret the Reform movement in the nineteenth century as a one-sided compromise in which frightened American Jews traded their birthright for status in a Christian society. In fact, Reform Judaism was a carefully considered strategy for Jewish survival in the modern world. Judaism had a hard adjustment to make in reacting to American liberal institutions, but that was the easy part of a larger task. The harder adjustment lay in responding to several centuries of accumulated scientific knowledge that in the seventeenth and eighteenth centuries had revolutionized most of the intellectual elites in Europe except the rabbis living in the Jewish ghettos. Reform, a movement begun in Germany, intended to deal with the very real possibility that no one could live outside the ghetto and take seriously the normative Judaism that was practiced there. Reform Judaism was the intellectual child of Europe. Although it had, as a separate movement, less impact on European Jewish practices than on American Jewish practices, that was only because a normative Judaism was more easily enforced in Europe. In neither Europe nor America did Judaism remain exactly what it had been. In all cases, citizenship, when it arrived, forced changes.

Even if one sticks with the particular circumstances of the American case, one cannot avoid concluding that Reform leaders were as concerned with Jews staying Jewish as with their becoming American. American conditions made the latter process relatively unproblematic, at least for the German Jewish arrivals in the antebellum period. The former issue was more worrisome. David Einhorn, Isaac Wise, and the other American Reform leaders in the middle part of the nineteenth century rarely talked about Americanization in specific terms. It did not become an issue to them in quite the same way that it was forced on the antebellum Catholic community. The arrival of immigrant Jews from Eastern Europe made the cases more parallel, but in the formative period of American Reform Judaism, Einhorn spoke to his congregation in German. To Einhorn, switching to Reform practices had nothing to do with becoming American, and becoming American had little to do with a narrow cultural conformity. In urging changes from traditional practices, he was not concerned with what American Protestants thought about Judaism, but what Jews thought about Judaism.

Two other points are important in understanding the motives that prompted most of the German Jewish immigrants to accept Reform practices. The most extreme forms of Reform Judaism, that is, those which pushed Judaism in the direction of a nondistinctive adherence to purported universally-recognized ethical standards, borrowed styles from Protestant church services. For all that, Reform Judaism had little in common with the majority forms of American Protestant thought. The fact that some types of liberal Protestantism were headed in roughly the same intellectual direction as Reform Judaism scarcely placed the latter close to most Protestant evangelical churches. American Christians and American Jews had little trouble making distinctions between their religions. Second, the Reform practices that German American Jews embraced were not always as blandly ritual-less as some accounts have suggested. The case of Louis Spanier, who in 1850 punched Isaac Wise in the nose when the Reform leader reached to take the Torah from the ark during Sabbath services, reminds us that most German American Jews, however ready to depart from tradition, retained forms of Jewish identification more distinctive than an allegiance to free thought or ethical service.[11] As already noted, a number of rabbis, who had previously accepted many changes in traditional Jewish practice, walked out of the 1885 meeting in Pittsburgh. They objected to a platform that abandoned virtually all observance of Jewish law. Their protest, and especially the work of the German-born Isaac Leeser, laid the basis for what emerged in the twentieth century as Conservative Judaism.[12]

The Reform movement cannot be blamed for the uncountable number of Jewish families who stopped being Jewish in nineteenth-century America. Orthodox practice did not save Newport's population of colonial Jews from extinction. The temptation to Christianize, to shed traditional forms of Jewish dress, or to seek marriages with America's Christian gentry, was a part of the process of climbing the social ladder no matter how many laws of the Torah one tried to keep. Although one can appreciate the argument that the Reform movement, in lowering considerably the barriers that Jews had maintained between themselves and gentiles, was a long step toward assimilation, one must also recognize that as a strategy to *prevent* assimilation, the American Reform movement fared rather well. From a comparative perspective, one can plausibly argue that at the end of the nineteenth century Jews in Germany and France were more acculturated with respect to gentile society than the German Jews in the United States.[13] That was precisely because the Jewish leadership in those countries failed to provide well-educated and economically prosperous Jews with a comfortable form of religious identification.

One can easily exaggerate the ease of the entry of German American Jews into middle-class respectability. By and large the German Jewish immigrants in the first part of the nineteenth century were poor and uneducated. Their shabby dress, their "pushiness" in seizing opportunities, their lack of social polish marked them in the eyes of Americans who controlled entry into Social Registries as a people apart.[14] General Grant banned Jewish peddlers from circulating among troops in the Union army. And yet at perhaps no moment in history did a group of Jewish people have a freer option to give up being Jewish. Most of them ignored the chance because the choice was not appealing. Besides, remaining Jewish proved an effective way to find an acceptable niche in American society. As outsiders, Reform-minded Jews found ways to prosper. At the same time, their determination to remain Jewish eventually made them the first victims of the institutional anti-Semitism that arose in the United States during the last fifteen years of the nineteenth century. That was not something they had entirely expected to avoid.

American Jews of German ancestry were to later Jewish immigrants what American Catholics of Irish ancestry were to later Catholic ethnics. Neither the Germans nor the Irish were the first of their religious group to arrive in America, but in 1870 they were overwhelmingly the dominant influence. That fact made for strained relations within their respective communities. Both the German Jews and the Irish Catholics had found formulas to remain loyal to their non-Protestant religions and at the same time make themselves at home in their adopted country. Naturally they believed that their formulas were good enough for those who started arriving in the last quarter of the nineteenth century. The Irish Catholics, as we have seen, only got part of their way. Other Catholic ethnics saw the Irish resistance to American nativism as militant only insofar as it touched on issues of Irish identity. The German Jews of America fared even less well. The newcomers not only challenged them with their own ideas about how to be Jewish in America, they also usurped the dominant position that the German Jews had gained over American Judaism.

In 1877, slightly more than a quarter of a million Jews lived in the United States. That population was scattered around the country since German Jews had dispersed with the rest of America's German immigrant population. Probably the most important center of Jewish culture then was Cincinnati, where Isaac Wise had in 1875 founded the Hebrew Union College. Less than twenty-five years later, at the turn of the century, the number of American Jews had quadrupled to one million. On the eve of America's entrance into World War I the figure had trebeled again—to three million.[15] The great majority of this new population remained clustered in the urban areas of the Northeast, indeed most of it within a few miles of the point of entry at Ellis Island. These "new" immigrants stood out not only because they huddled together, but because they were poor, because they spoke Yiddish, and because they were people who had been uprooted from the rural Middle Ages and placed in the modern industrial world almost without transition. When they moved beyond their own settlements in urban America, they neither looked like nor spoke like nor acted like any other group of Americans.

Whatever were the free choices that life in the United States theoretically afforded, these immigrant Jews were clearly going to remain Jews for the foreseeable future. They had no alternate form of primary identification. Aggressive programs of cultural conformity were as meaningless to them as they were to many Catholic ethnics. They learned instead that they could become American and be Jewish on terms they set largely for themselves. On the other hand, if free and liberal institutions did not threaten the Jews of Eastern Europe with extinction, as they arguably had America's earlier and smaller Jewish population, they did leave the new arrivals confused and divided in opinion. Where, after all, were they to turn for help in deciding what it meant to be a Jew? Outside the Russian pale, the question had a number of possible answers.

One place that held no answer for them was the Reform temple. The Eastern European Jews instinctively rejected the norms of existing American Judaism. Nothing in Reform practice was recognizable to them. Yet, although Reform was impossible, "Orthodox" synagogues furnished only slightly better guides for being a good Jew in America. Until after World War I the so-called Orthodox synagogues were even more congregational in their ways than the Reform temples. Eastern European Jews, in the absence of authoritative teachers, founded their synagogues around their *Landsmien*, the people who came from the same town in Europe. It was a practice that spawned more synagogues than strict piety. America made it easy to neglect religious observance and almost seemed to require the abandonment of important parts of Jewish life, the Saturday Sabbath for example, that got in the way of earning a living. The fact that Jews were going to remain Jews in America still left them with an identity to create. In reality, the Eastern European Jewish population, although everyone in it might look equally strange to a native-born American, was not yet in the 1890s a community. It was a group of people split by class, nationality, and religious practice.

Irving Howe, in his magnificent account of Eastern European Jews in the United States, only rarely in some seven hundred pages of richly detailed text found it necessary to discuss religious life.[16] Whether or not, as it is commonly asserted, only the least pious of Europe's Jews came to the United States, the most pious certainly stayed home. Secularism and the economic struggle for survival altered the way most immigrant Jews treated their religion. Orthodoxy could not by itself provide them with what Howe terms a "sense of collective worth."[17] Some Jews managed to ignore the changed context of Jewish existence in New York City and continued to observe strictly all laws of the Torah. Among the possibilities open in New York City was the possibility of not changing. However, the moment Jews began to pay attention to the world beyond the *Shul*, they encountered activities that inexorably drew them away from observance of Jewish Law.

. The secular forces that loom the largest in Howe's book are *Yiddishkeit*, an enthusiasm for Yiddish culture, and labor radicalism. The former provided immigrant Jews with a substitute for the intellectual stimulation of yeshiva study. Split as they were in other ways, the immigrants shared books, newspapers, and a theatre written in a language that was their exclusive property. Labor radicalism was a different matter. In its most extreme version it was hostile to all religious practice and to all versions of Jewish particularity. It nonetheless drew the immigrant community together because it too provided a substitute, in this case a nonreligious equivalent for the idea of Jewish chosenness and mission. According to one source quoted by Howe: "It's my idea that the Jewish community in the United States was not really a Jewish community, it was just something in fermentation until the labor movement came along. That gave the Jewish community its character, its face."[18]

Even though Howe devotes the bulk of his pages to secular influences that joined together the immigrant community, he never loses sight of another fact: the synagogue "remained the single institution everyone took for granted."[19] In analyzing the first generation of East European Jewish immigrants in America, one should be careful not to draw too firm a line between the sacred and the secular. Jews were only beginning to learn about that particular dualism in Western thought. Thus they did not necessarily make distinctions that other Americans, particularly Protestant Americans, saw as logical. Having a sense that one was Jewish, even if one had stopped believing in God, was somehow according to much testimony, a religious feeling. The labor radicals in the Eastern European Jewish communities in America, including the ones who held balls on Yom Kippur night, felt more comfortable among the Orthodox than among the Reform Jews. It was almost as if the seriousness with which some Jews took the Torah excused others to find surrogate forms of Jewish identity. The Jewish labor movement, no matter what its belief in a united world proletariat, grew strong in the United States only because it served the needs of Jewish particularity. And after both it and *Yiddishkeit* had been nearly obliterated by the vertical and horizontal mobility of the second and the third generations of American Eastern European Jews, the synagogue remained the single institution that most American Jews took for granted.

Abraham Cahan probably understood the world of the Yiddish-speaking American Jew, including the ways that religion worked on his mind, as well as anyone who belonged to that first generation. His novel *The Rise of David Levinsky* was published in 1917. We have already quoted the opinion of one of Cahan's characters that Judaism did not have much of a chance in America, but we might now consider that observation in connection with the entire book. The plot is not complicated. Levinsky, a Russian-born Jew and a Talmudic student of talent, immigrates to New York after his mother is murdered by Christians. In New York he aspires to become a scholar. In scraping together money to attend City College, he almost immediately begins to neglect synagogue attendance and his study of the Talmud. Impressed by the financial success of many of the immigrants who came to the United States only shortly before he did, he devotes his time to learning to act like other Americans. He never leaves the Jewish community, in part because the gentiles will not have him; but he remains Jewish without any clear sense of what that means. Abandoning his plans to become a scholar, Levinsky rises economically to become a wealthy but terribly lonely clothing manufacturer.

We can be certain that Cahan, who was himself a socialist and not an observant Jew, was not in his novel making a plea for Orthodox religious practice. On the other hand, he was not making fun of it. For Cahan, throwing Orthodoxy out as something that was impossible in the modern world did not guarantee a meaningful liberation for the Jewish spirit. Levinsky's utter emptiness at the end of the novel was proof of that point. Presumably Levinsky would have done better had he remained poor and joined the labor movement. Yet Cahan, socialist though he was, seems to have sensed that it was not the lot of the Jew in America to remain poor. Unlike the immigrant characters in Upton Sinclair's *The Jungle*, which predated Cahan's book, and in Michael Gold's *Jews Without Money*, which followed it, Levinsky's rise into prosperity was incredibly easy. Cahan's book is not primarily about economic hardship. Like Howells's book *The Rise of Silas Lapham*, which it consciously echoes, it takes for granted the possibility of economic advance in the United States. What it means to question is whether economic advance is worth the spiritual price that it exacts.

Taken as a parable about Jewish religion, Cahan's novel contains a fundamental irony. The intellectual rigor that Levinsky developed as a youth in puzzling over the intricacies of the Talmud prepared him to master what he needed to learn in order to succeed in business in the United States. The transition from the medieval world of the Talmud to the modern world of clothing manufacturing proved easier than one might have guessed because the same habits of mental agility worked in both. Cahan's point seems to be something like this. The religious studies that had occupied the early years and leisure hours of many Eastern European Jews had prepared them all too well for the opportunities offered by America. Jews would succeed in America, not merely because of commercial skills already learned, but because of the discipline of Jewish religious study and practice. However, unless they found some substitute for the religion that their success threatened to bury, they would not, any more than Levinsky, gain anything important.

Most scholars have accepted, along with Cahan, the premise that Jewish religious culture was crucial in shaping the lives of Eastern European immigrants even when they were consciously trying to throw it off. (Most of course were not.) Shirley Gorelick has recently raised an argument with scholars who have attempted to explain Jewish economic success in America by Jewish traditional respect for "the book."[20] The usual argument is that Jewish immigrants, steeped in years of Talmudic study and shaped by an enormous and competitive drive for learning, arrived at just the right moment to seize the opportunities afforded by free university education in New York City. How could that argument be correct, Gorelick asks, when Talmudic education was passive, rote learning that had nothing in common with the academic skills requisite for success at City College? Moreover, many of the immigrant Jews from Eastern Europe were illiterate; many of them did not rise; and those who did rise most quickly did so, like the German Jews before them and like David Levinsky, without the benefit of a college education. Gorelick would seem to agree with Cahan in only one particular. Those Jews who advanced through City College abandoned with perhaps undue haste their Talmudic study. Lured by the false promise of an education into universal values, they abandoned themselves to an education into the narrow culture of American capitalism.

Although the relation between the values shaped by the Orthodox Jewish communities of Eastern Europe and the economic success of both European and American Jews will remain controversial, one scarcely knows where to look for answers other than culture. Eastern European Jews were not quite a one generation proletariat as some American folklore suggests; but compared with other immigrant groups, their swift rise into the professions and into general economic security was astounding. The questions raised by Gorelick about the compatibility of the intellectual skills nourished in traditional Jewish settlements and those required for economic and professional success in America are difficult to assess. As one study has convincingly demonstrated, non-religious Jewish academics have been somewhat more successful in their fields than Jewish academics who are very religious.[21] Yet in all the fields in which Jews advanced, intellectual inventiveness was important. A cultural explanation for the prominence of that trait among Jews may beg a lot of questions. Yet without it, we seem left with the genetic argument advanced by James Russell Lowell who referred to "this race in which ability seems as natural and hereditary as the curve of their noses."[22]

Stephan Thernstrom, who pioneered the study of the social mobility of American immigrant groups, made essentially a cultural argument in explaining differential rates of advance.[23] Since Thernstrom's argument rests on a comparison between Protestant, Jewish, and Catholic Bostonians, it looks like a variation on the famous thesis advanced by Max Weber. Never mind whether Jewish religious culture had prepared many Jewish immigrants for City College and a few for Harvard. What is more important is that it prepared them, like the first New England Protestants but unlike the first New York Irish, to work hard without demanding initially very much in return. Judaism did not have a doctrine of the calling, but it was a religion of deed rather than faith. One served God by what one did as an individual Jew, and without anyone's mediation. Rabbis were teachers, not dispensers of divine grace. Although the intricate behavior prescribed by Jewish ritual life was not very useful for making one's way in the junk business, it accustomed Jews to a disciplined and ordered life. God demanded rest on the Sabbath, but that left six days for work. Jewish religion did not equate financial success with moral goodness any more than Calvinism did. Yet as Jews moved up the social scale in America, how could they regard their mobility as anything other than a sign that God after all had not forgotten his people?

We are saying here that in a community where lines between the sacred and the secular were not clearly drawn, religiously acquired habits could remain a decisive influence on behavior that was no longer primarily religious. Moreover, those habits could be passed along from generation to generation in forms that either were explicitly religious or that could be rediscovered as religious. The flight from religion of the first generation of Eastern European Jews was precipitate only if measured by strict standards of Orthodox observance. God was present on the Lower East Side to confirm Jews in their role apart. God's favor explained why they succeeded and encouraged them to seek every possible avenue to success. God was also there to explain why they suffered as a result of their success.

Unlike the case of the Catholics or the Mormons, the particular forms of Jewish religious observance, strange as they seemed to many Christian Americans, were not used to justify anti-Semitism. Jews in colonial America were Orthodox in their ritual observance, but that fact did not mark them as an especially important target of persecution. One suspects that the German-speaking Jews who came to the United States in the first part of the nineteenth century could have remained Orthodox without having increased perceptibly the low level of anti-Semitism that existed in America prior to the 1870s. Two things accounted for the rise of anti-Semitism in America. First, Jews became the victims of the negative stereotypes that attached generally to the immigrants who arrived in the United States at the end of the nineteenth century from parts of the world that had not before contributed substantial numbers to the American population. Second, they became the victims of their own rise up the economic ladder, a rise that seemed to threaten the stability of established social hierarchies in several American cities.[24] In the end, the Eastern European Jew who refused to shed his beard and caftan and who faithfully followed the way of the Torah did not bear the brunt of anti-Semitism in America. David Levinsky did, along with the German American Jews of the previous era who were dragged down by his success.

Every book about Jews has posed the question of whether anti-Semitism was essential to Jewish survival during the Diaspora. At least for the part of the Diaspora that has coincided with the Jewish experience in America, one is tempted to say no. The determination of the first generations of American Jews to remain Jewish appears to be something that they brought with them from Europe and that had little to do with the persecution they encountered or did anything to encourage here. Unlike the Mormons, they did not have to build a tradition of persecution in the United States. Events in the world would have provided American Jews with sufficient reasons to hold onto their Jewishness even if the word "Jew" had never in America carried the slightest social stigma.

However, the "no" requires qualification. Since anti-Semitism did become part of the American landscape, it inevitably played a role in shaping American Jewish consciousness. The many American Jewish organizations formed in the twentieth century to combat anti-Semitism had the obvious aim of eliminating it. They also developed the double purpose of using it to maintain the boundaries of ethnic identity. In this respect, American Jews were no different from other groups who have played the outsider's role. American Jewish organizations have invested a great deal of labor in publicizing anti-Semitism. But, as is well known, other groups with their own memories of martyrdom have accused Jews of making far, far too much of what they have suffered. Combating anti-Semitism thus became the cause of further anti-Semitism.

As was usual in these cases, Jews memorialized their persecution as much to speak to the conscience of other Jews as to persuade or inform others. American anti-Semitism was perhaps not essential to the survival of Jewish consciousness, but arising as it did at a difficult time of uprooting, it gave American Jewish leaders time to reflect on the question of why anyone would want to maintain forever a separate Jewish identity in a liberal, open society. As a moral equivalent for the ghetto, it had short-term uses. In fact American anti-Semitism provoked a small social war in America in which Jews were able to turn their losses into victories. No doubt that is why throughout the entire half century, from 1900 to 1950, when anti-Semitism was the most pronounced in the United States, the Jewish love affair with America reached its greatest heights.

One cannot make a precise reckoning of the gains and losses from anti-Semitism. In the United States it was private rather than public, at least as those terms were understood legally in the first part of the twentieth century. It took the form of exclusion. First at Saratoga Springs, and then in the Catskills and along the Jersey shore, American Jews discovered that certain hotels and vacation retreats no longer would accommodate the "Sons of Abraham." By the end of the century, gentiles had invented additional ways to distinguish their social standing from that which economically prosperous Jews sought to buy. Country and city clubs refused to consider any more Jews for membership, even the children of Jews who were charter members of the clubs. In many socially prestigeous neighborhoods, Jews no longer were able to buy property. Established law firms did not hire them. College fraternities refused to pledge them. And, in a move that caused the most bitterness, major universities around the time of World War I started to set quotas on the number of Jewish applicants they accepted.[25] These patterns of exclusion lasted with varying degrees of rigor until well after World War II, and some remain quite pronounced in American life, albeit in de facto form.

Most of what American Jews lost as a result of these practices is obvious enough. Discrimination was an insult, particularly when it recalled centuries of persecution against people whose main sin was an inability to regard Christianity as anything but an odd deviation from Jewish monotheism. It was also a temptation to bale out of an identity that barred one from many universities, many professions, and many businesses. The reasons why many American Jews have so strongly attacked recently devised quota systems for university admissions are clear. Even if these newer quotas are designed to speed up rather than retard the entry of minorities into positions of economic wealth, they too easily recall an era when gentile elites regarded immigrant Jews as a polluting influence on high American culture and barred them from rewards equal to their talents. The psychological costs of demeaning stereotypes are hard to assess. Have American Jews been more prone to self-hatred than a Jehovah's witness or a Pentecostal? How can one ever be sure, especially since alleged Jewish self-hatred is in part an invention of Jewish sociologists to enforce Jewish identity.[26] Whatever the differences, Jews did manage to find compensating factors in discrimination.

Manhattan law firms that excluded Jews did themselves about as much good as Hitler did for himself when he barred Jewish scientists from service to the Third Reich. The Jewish law firm in contrast became an important focus of Jewish pride. Much has been made of the fact that many Jews had to make their fortunes in low status business pursuits that became an embarrassment to their children. One truly wonders how many Jewish businessmen who made their way as furriers, or landlords, or manufacturers of odd utensils felt any painful sting from knowing that they could not sit in the board room of Chase Manhattan. The prestige hierarchy of well-paying American occupations seriously concerns the perhaps one percent of population who know that such a thing exists. Jewish businesses were in fact a thing of unabashed boasting within the Jewish community; and if Jewish businessmen embarrassed their children, it is because the pride of the *nouveaux riches* always seems excessive to those who enjoy the luxury of not having to accumulate money for themselves.

Perhaps in the absence of gentile exclusionary policies, there would not have been Jewish resorts, Jewish law firms, Jewish neighborhoods, and Jewish country clubs. That seems doubtful however. The social and cultural discomforts that brought them into being, and the reasons why they were maintained, were not generated on only one side of the gentile-Jewish split. Gentiles may be more fun than Jewish stereotypes of them suggest, but the unease that upwardly mobile Jews felt in gentile social situations was just as pronounced as what gentiles felt in the less commonly experienced opposite situation. New York State passed a law as early as 1913 forbidding places of public accommodation to discriminate, but laws did not much change the social patterns that by then prevailed in the Catskill resorts. Jews preferred to vacation in the formerly gentile resorts they purchased in sweet revenge of the social slight or in the ones they built for themselves. They liked hotels with kosher tables as much for the people they kept away as for the people they attracted. American democratic ideals would have been better served if more Jews had gone to Harvard and Yale and Columbia in the period between the wars. This does not necessarily mean that in retrospect one would want to erase the lively intellectual environment that Jewish students created during that period at City College.

As with the other cases of religious discrimination in America, one can turn the issue of anti-Semitism in a number of ways. It made certain things impossible while providing the only way for other opportunities to emerge. What is important for our story is that it became comprehensible, endurable, and usable because Judaism provided a religious meaning for suffering. Many American Jews learned secular formulas to explain Jewish suffering. That is indisputably true. Marxists argued that Jews suffered as part of a proletariat whose collective mission was to destroy the injustices of capitalist civilization. Yet for most Eastern European Jewish immigrants in the first generation, whether they were in or out of the labor movement, anti-Semitism remained inextricably linked to the religious notion of chosenness. Like persecuted Christian groups in America who stressed martyrdom, discrimination provided Jews with a measure of group virtue. It also provided them with the useful idea that Jews had to work twice as hard as gentiles to get anything. As a result they worked twice as hard and frequently went twice as far.

In summing up this era of Jewish experience, one may say that traditional religion helped Eastern European Jews succeed in spite of the fact that it tried to make them stay something other than what most of them became. In the long run, a strict Orthodoxy fared no worse in the United States than it did in Europe. In both places the Orthodox Jew often left observance to others. His infrequent attendance in synagogue resembled the patterns of many Catholics and Protestants who firmly believed that good Christians should go to church but who rarely got around to it themselves. If secular forces worked quickly on the Eastern European Jews of America, Orthodoxy also set a limit on how far those forces could go. Rabbis who sadly watched so many of the old ways go to pieces could take consolation in noting that Orthodoxy in the early twentieth century accomplished one remarkable thing that endured. It broke the stranglehold that the Reform temples had on American Jewry and made certain that as East European Jews achieved the same educational and social standing in America as German Jews, they would not, whatever else they did, endorse the Pittsburgh Platform of 1885.

The anti-immigration measures passed in the 1920s pushed the story of American Jews into a new phase. In important ways, the measures were stabilizing and helpful to immigrant groups who were already here. In the case of American Jews, their population stopped increasing rapidly; and, as a percentage of the total population, it began to decline. Eastern European Jews, as they came to look more and more like other Americans, became less of a worry to German Jews. They in turn did not have to worry about threats to their own middle-class status caused by identification with disheveled new arrivals. Although America's Jewish community remained divided by nineteenth-century memories, those divisions eased and were not replaced by new ones. In the period from 1930 to 1950, when the majority of America's Jewish community turned into a native-born community, American Judaism as we now know it had time to emerge.[27] Neo-Orthodoxy established an institutional framework of unity as well as Yeshiva College (in 1928) to train its rabbis. Conservative Judaism and Reform Judaism redefined themselves under the influence of Mordecai Kaplan's Reconstructionism. Suddenly, after World War II, with Jews constituting only a small part of the American population, and an even tinier proportion of religiously active Americans, a rhetorical campaign commenced which sought to make Judaism, often subsumed under the "Judeo-Christian tradition," part of the American mainstream. Jews had no John Kennedy to dramatize the change, but they had something that was arguably better. They had considerable control over how the campaign was directed.

In another way, however, and quite apart from the disastrous effects of restrictive laws in efforts to save European Jewry, the new stage perpetuated in a different context what had always been the potential threat that America posed to Jewish identity. Jewish identity had survived nicely enough so long as a steady influx of new arrivals, who could not immediately eradicate their foreign roots and who kept other Jews mindful of roots that had not entirely disappeared, made the question of total Jewish assimilation largely academic. Now Jewish identity, cut off from immigration, had to survive the rhetorical embrace of the American mainstream. It had to find ways to deny the moral authority of that other popular metaphor of American acculturation, the melting pot.

Horace Kallen, a secularized Jew, was working on that problem long before it became fashionable to think of Jews as American insiders. Kallen did not invent the idea of American cultural pluralism. Thomas Paine probably deserves credit for making the first important strategical use of the idea in connection with his efforts to sever colonial loyalties to Britain. Americans of British ancestry, he said, were only one among many types of people in the colonies, and they had no special claims on setting cultural norms. As we saw in the last chapter, a rather unlikely set of conservative Catholic clerics had been cornered into championing a sort of cultural pluralism in the course of the nineteenth century. Kallen's version of cultural pluralism, formulated in response to the Americanization crusades of World War I, was important because that form of the idea finally caught the attention of twentieth-century American liberals. It persuaded some of them at least that tolerance did not mean a willingness to provide means for everyone to become the same. A tolerance of difference does not amount to much if there are no differences left to tolerate.

John Higham has indicated that Kallen's Harvard mentors saved him from acculturation. They awakened his interest in his Jewishness and started him on the path that led to his defense of particularism. William James raised pluralism to a metaphysical principle, although his influence was less decisive than that of Barrett Wendell. Wendell, whose Boston pedigree made him an unlikely source for philo-Semitism, was a good enough scholar to recognize the importance of the Old Testament prophets to America's Puritans. Apparently Kallen, through Wendell, came to understand that the story of the Jews was repeated in the story of New England. Chosenness, hard work, tribulation, and success were the central themes in both histories. Thus, according to Higham, Kallen learned that the Jewish past he was fleeing was central to the American identity he was pursuing. He decided that one could be "an unreconstructed Jew while belonging to the core of America."[28]

Higham has written very well about the weaknesses that attach to pluralist positions, including Kallen's, whether considered as analysis or as strategy. Higham suggests that as a philosophy or strategy of minority rights, pluralist assertions can appeal only to a group that had already made it economically. Kallen, a Jew, celebrated difference because at the time he wrote Jews were on their way out of poverty. Accepted and assimilated in crucial ways, they could afford the luxury of imagining that a permanent minority status, whose terms were largely of their choosing, might be advantageous to them. Their pluralist vision grew from a privileged flexibility. Jews could demand autonomy and separatism on the one hand and unimpeded influence in the larger society on the other. American blacks, a group that Kallen forgot to mention in his essays, were not yet in a position to cheer such an argument.

Without question, a pluralist position can become an ideal that ignores everything that can go wrong with it. Joshua Fishman wrote much later with respect to ethnicity in America that it could exist and yet not exist, be needed and yet be unimportant, be different and yet be the same, be integrated and yet be separate.[29] Although most American Jews before 1920 had not achieved such enviable chameleon capabilities, their rapid economic success and the attendant flexibility it provided did make them something of a special case among American outsiders. Pluralism became almost a romance. Thus, when Kallen's ideas were widely cited after World War II, often by Jewish academics, to celebrate the ways in which American group interests were mediated, those celebrations frequently overlooked crucial economic disparities in the actual situations of various groups.

Be that as it may, a hidden elitism was not the main problem with Kallen's argument, not as it affected Jewish consciousness. Kallen's writings may have reflected retrospective confidence; but as a prescribed strategy for group success, and a description of how the American system worked, whenever it did work, what Kallen said about pluralism was neither wrong nor inattentive to the realities of American life. Groups made claims on the mainstream by staying apart from it, and group pride became a vehicle for group acceptance. But for people seeking a permanent basis for group identity, the problem was that pluralism might be nothing more than a game that ended once a group had gained the social leverage it sought. If the assertion of minority consciousness was merely a strategy for gaining economic success in American life, then at some point it presumably became irrelevant and expendable. There is not much point in celebrating difference indefinitely merely for the exercise. Pluralism was usually less a formula for permanent apartness than a plea for letting the inevitable process of assimilation take a slower course. However exciting it was to find Jews in the center of the Puritan myth, that discovery simply implied the conflation of Jewish and Christian myth into a common American nationality. What else could melting-pot enthusiasts ask for? As Kallen himself recognized in his later work, he had not in his first writings about pluralism located a content for Jewish apartness or the apartness of any other group that would not over time disappear. For many American outsiders, that thought did not provoke a great deal of anxiety. For many Jews, it did.

The anxiety increased as Jewish leaders in the 1920s and beyond became more and more concerned about the viability of a religious base for Jewish identity. Although experience in the Western world over several centuries suggests that modern science is not fatal to religion, science does cause problems for anthropomorphic forms of religious belief. Traditional Judaism was rich in those forms; and one had to wonder whether American Jews, as they rapidly turned themselves into sophisticated urbanites, could maintain them in anything other than attenuated and ultimately meaningless ways.

Jewish consciousness in the United States has come to include more and more secular components that are clearly distinct from religion. The secular trend, already apparent in the first generation of Eastern European immigrants, was irreversible. Jews, who no longer could believe that God set them apart, had to find historical reasons to feel Jewish. Labor radicalism and *Yiddishkeit* declined in importance after the war, but Zionism was among the community commitments that emerged to replace them. In the beginning, Zionism in America got religious support from only a few non-Orthodox rabbis. Its prominent backers were nonreligious, thoroughly assimilated Jews, who were alarmed by the persistence of anti-Semitism largely as it affected others. Louis Brandeis and Felix Frankfurter were typical of the first American

Jewish intellectuals who were attracted to Zionism in the United States. While neither was deeply immersed in Jewish culture, Zionism represented a cause that linked Jews to a collective memory. Brandeis apparently regarded his support for a Jewish homeland in Palestine as akin to the support an Irish American gave to Irish home rule.[30] He never gave a thought to resettlement.

The many Jewish organizations formed in America outside the arena of religious life have doubtlessly in the twentieth century kept more Jews in touch with one another than attendance at Sabbath services. Moreover, the Holocaust created a very exclusive club and made the need for a consistent religious argument in defining Jewish identity somewhat beside the point. Even so, thoughtful Jews in the United States have not stopped worrying about the possibility that without some religious conception of Jewish life, the theoretical base of a Jewish identification is very shaky.

What after all are the alternative bases? Jewish suffering? Other people in the world have suffered enormously. Jewish nationality? The establishment of the state of Israel has made it clear that most American Jews have opted for the Diaspora, that they do not regard the United States as a land of *galut* (exile). Conceived simply as a national or ethnic group, Jews will, like other such groups who have settled permanently in the United States, find less and less to distinguish them from others around them. History? Americans forget history. Jewish chosenness? In anything other than a religious form, and perhaps even in a religious form, it looks nonegalitarian, undemocratic, boastful.[31] Chosenness comes close to asserting what anti-Semites charge: Jews really do think they are better. It becomes a competing version of the American myth; and as recent clashes between American blacks and American Jews suggest, it stirs deep resentment.

After World War II, American Jews who were concerned about Jewish survival had to consider certain facts. Anti-Semitism was sharply on the decline in the United States. At any rate, pollsters had more trouble finding people who were willing to say that they did not much like Jews. The rates of geographical dispersion and intermarriage were not increasing as dramatically as some Jews had feared, but they were increasing. Was it really enough to suggest, as some intellectuals did, that Jews might somehow continue to exist as permanent outsiders, alienated gadflys, without the Torah.[32] To be Jewish, if that is anything special, has to be more than to play the role of the intellectual in tension with the society around him. The love affair that ordinary American Jews have conducted with the United States suggests that there are limits to how much they will let their Jewishness set a distance between themselves and their nation. They will be Jewish, but only so long as their Jewishness defines their Americanness and is part of their pride in being American. Whatever Jewish intellectuals have sometimes said, Jewish experience in America has not been the experience of people usefully defined as social marginals.

In the context of the many post World War II discussions about the meaning of Jewishness and the survival of Jewish religion, Will Herberg's famous book of 1955, *Protestant, Catholic, Jew*, came as both good news and bad news. The good news for observant Jews was that American Jews, despite the many purported influences of secularism, defined their Judaism primarily as a religion. Moreover, that mode of identification was increasing rather than declining. Although a much lower percentage of Jews was affiliated with synagogues than Protestants or Catholics with churches, most American Jews identified with one of the major Jewish religious traditions in the United States. Eighty percent of them made sure that their children received some formal religious training. A second somewhat surprising fact, part of the good news to many, was that most American Jews who were religious had not in moving up the social ladder embraced Reform practices. The dominant form of American Judaism in the 1950s was Conservative Judaism, and by the 1970s its position had been only slightly weakened. Indeed, measured simply in terms of numbers of synagogues, Orthodoxy was faring better than any of the competition.[33]

The bad news in Herberg was that American Jews were increasing their religious affiliation not out of piety but because they regarded it as the socially acceptable thing to do. It was a habit picked up from gentiles, a way of conforming one's religious behavior fully to middle-class Protestant norms. One went to temple for business contacts, for the social hours, for the conservative outlook that decorous worship symbolized. Unlike the Spanish Marranos who had been Christian in public but faithfully Jewish at home, the American Jews were unfeelingly Jewish in both places because the difference between Christian and Jew no longer much mattered to anyone. The apparent triumph of Conservatism brought scant comfort to Jews who could not separate the religious significance of Judaism from the belief that the Torah was divine revelation. To the Orthodox, Conservative Judaism was a halfway house originally set up by German-American Jewish millionnaires in order to provide Eastern European Jews with some place to worship at a safe distance from their own Reform temples. Conservatives hired religiously strict rabbis to be good Jews for them. They then obeyed only so much of Torah as was convenient and historicized their personal belief to whatever degree was necessary to keep themselves from feeling ridiculous. Arnold Eisen has neatly summed up the situation of contemporary American Judaism: there are few pressures to abandon Judaism, even if apostasy has become more reasonable.[14]

Doubtlessly, so long as American Jews pour energy into debating questions of Jewish identity, they will not lack for one. Consensus might be the worst thing to befall Judaism. In many ways the situation of contemporary American Jews is not very different from that of earlier American Jews. For most American Jews, the choice was not between whether they should assimilate or whether they should remain Jews. The choice, which allowed for a wide range of debate, was what sort of Jew should they become as they became American. What Philip Roth has said about the present situation of American Jews applied equally well to the beginning: "I think the amazing thing which sort of brought the blessing and burden of having been brought up in America— was to have been given a psychology without a content, or with only the remains of a content, and then to invent off of that."[15] Jews came to the United States with a psychology that they could not shed, and found an unprecedented freedom, both from Jewish and from Christian authorities, to do with it what they liked. Many have doubted that what they did was, strictly speaking, Jewish. But their undoubted achievements still go by that name.

In opinion polls, people used to be asked if they thought that Jews were overrepresented in various areas of American life. A positive answer was taken as evidence of anti-Semitism; and in the context in which the question was posed, it was. Overrepresentation implied conspiracy. Nonetheless, the proper answer was that, yes indeed, Jews were overrepresented in some areas, sometimes unbelievably so. That was normal since various immigrant groups have made their marks in various fields. What seemed so striking about the Jewish case was that Jews had made a smashing success out of interpreting America to other Americans. They grasped in ways that will never be fully understood what a democratic public wanted, whether it was their clothes, their movies, or their Christmas tree ornaments.

Although this reflection suggests that Jews are securely part of the American mainstream, it also suggests that Jews were part of the mainstream long before ecumenical voices thought it nice to say so. Without a doubt, the idea that Judaism deserved equal status among American religions with Protestantism and Catholicism gained considerable popularity among writers after World War II. Whether the idea reflected much more than a wish to spruce up America's image in the era of the Cold War is less clear. It would be interesting to know whether fewer Americans in this "enlightened" period regard the United States as a Christian nation than was true a hundred years ago. The guess of this author is no. The likelihood of a Jew being elected president remains remote. Claims about the mainstream, as we have seen, are important because they reflect shifting perceptions. They do not tell us much unless we note who is trying to change perceptions and why.

In these matters, the parallels between Jews and the earlier religious groups we considered are almost exact. Mormons and Catholics have, without necessarily becoming more typically American in their values than they ever were, been granted mainstream status by a number of post World War II publicists. Many of their leaders have somewhat cautiously accepted it. They could hardly go on forever portraying themselves as persecuted outsiders when their economic position was going up, when discrimination against them was going down, and when their immigrant origins were becoming more distant. At the same time, they have been reluctant to let go completely of an outsider identification. Too much has been invested in it. Their sense of outsiderhood helped turn their religion into something more than religion. It became a separate culture, even an ethnic identity, for the Mormons. Rhetoric has softened the boundaries of that identity, but they remain part of the consciousness of a group. As long as the United States allows people to be American and to be something else, and as long as national and religious tensions have meaning anywhere in the world, American Jews are not likely to embrace insider rhetoric totally.

Whether that makes a difference is another question. In one way, perhaps it will. Jews comprise a group whose outsider status began long before their immigration to the United States. They had better reason than most other religious groups to know that fashions affecting the way a group is treated change. Perhaps that fact prepared them in the United States to see, although they often said otherwise, the relationship between their own problems and the problems of other groups. One of the oldest stereotypes about Jewish behavior is that Jews care only for other Jews. For many of them that is doubtlessly true; they have their reasons. However, the Jewish emphasis upon their particularity, the stress on their suffering which they insist is not like the suffering of anyone else, has not proved incompatible with general humanitarian concerns.

Where American Jews of the twentieth century have been most overrepresented in American life has been in the area of a politics that has tried to do something to alleviate social injustice. The Jewish God may take care of Jews first (although that has hardly been the most obvious lesson of history), but he does mean to take care of everyone. In the United States, Jews have been virtually the only religious group that has been overwhelmingly liberal in its politics. The radical social implications, which are arguably part of all outsider identities, in this case found political expression. Whereas many other religious groups were working for the first time in the United States within a minority framework and busily inventing and reinforcing their particularity, Jews had brought their customary minority status into a context that for the first time allowed them to glimpse what they had in common with others. Many would argue that the turmoil over Israel in the Middle East has changed that and turned Jewish particularism into another form of American conservatism. That may become so, but not before many things in the American Jewish past are forgotten.

PART TWO

The Progressive's Despair— Religions for Average Americans

CHAPTER FOUR

Christian Science and American Popular Religion

We are charged with lunacy in that we believe in Life instead of Death, Love instead of Hate, Truth instead of error, health instead of sickness; Light rather than darkness.   S. J. Hanna

I shall not forget the cost of investigating, for this age, the methods and power of error.   M. B. Eddy

By now, readers will have noted that these chapters do not fit into the category of what normally is classified as social history. The terms of reference, and the questions posed, owe more to the discourses of cultural and intellectual historians. However, the break between one sort of history and another sort of history is never complete. The arguments in this book have in fact been powerfully influenced by work in social history as well as in the various social sciences, especially sociology and anthropology. Most obviously, this study concerns itself with the lives of ordinary men and women. Although we have not tried to give every argument a statistical base, since number is not normally what is being placed in contention, we find ourselves again and again worrying about questions that have been of central concern to social scientists. These include social class, sexual role behavior, and relative social deprivation.

The influence is in part negative, a reflection of disatisfaction with ways in which some social scientists have described and separated deviant from typical behavior in American life. However, the articulation of that disatisfaction has required a constant return to social science literature for help. That has been especially so in this chapter because the temptation to apply the label "deviant" to Mary Baker Eddy and the early Christian Scientists is very great indeed. After all, Eddy's most clearly stated message was directed to people who felt themselves to be sick. Nonetheless, attempts to understand Christian Science as a movement founded by abnormal men and women who then appealed to other abnormal men and women encounter many of the same difficulties we noted in discussing the Mormons. If the first Christian Scientists were abnormal, then one is tempted to add that they were typically abnormal.

Writers in the late nineteenth century who were alarmed by the popularity of Eddy's doctrines frequently summed up their fears by using the word "occult," the same word that had been used earlier to attack Mormons and spiritualists. It was meant to draw into question the allegiance of those movements to sound democratic and Christian principles. Opponents of Christian Science wanted to link Eddy's church to an anti-Christian tradition that they said was trackable, despite the shrouded secrecy that had cloaked many of its activities, back to Mesmerism and the Illuminati Conspiracy, back to the Renaissance magic of Paracelsus and the devoted students of Hermes Trismegistus, back to the Gnostic and Neo-Platonic cults of the early Christian era.[1]

Yet in using the term "occult" to describe Christian Science, opponents of the movement saddled themselves with a problem. They had to account for the appeal of Eddy's "bizarre" and "diabolic" system in their supposedly enlightened and scientific age. A similar confusion had overtaken the opponents of Joseph Smith when they tried to explain how anyone as ridiculous as they believed him to be managed to get "sensible" Americans to listen to him. One possible answer was deceit. Eddy, it was claimed, wove her "fantastic and crude dogmas savoring of the occult and mystic East" with the "sacred tenets of the New Testament." By taking advantage of fears about real and imagined illness, she confused many good people of otherwise sound mind who were searching for reinterpretations of Christian principles to combat the materialism of their age.[2] To opponents, the very name Christian Science constituted false advertising since, in their minds, the movement was neither Christian nor scientific. And yet false advertising does not seem a sufficient explanation of Eddy's success. Neither does the observation that the late nineteenth century was marked by social dislocations.

Simply because the odds against any new religion getting off the ground are very high, even in the United States, the progress of Christian Science was remarkable. Certain things made the odds against it seem even longer than they were for other groups. Despite its obvious ties to Christian traditions, Christian Science presented itself as a break in history, as a church utterly distinct from all existing churches. Moreover, unlike some earlier American religious inventions that had succeeded, Mormonism, Shakerism, and Adventism, for example, Christian Science did not find its room to grow in sparsely populated areas of relatively recent settlement. Eddy launched Christian Science in Massachusetts as an urban church, and it remained one. She built the Mother Church in Boston. Those who regarded Boston as the oldest and most sane center of American Christianity could only shake their heads in disbelief. Boston too, it seemed, had produced a lunatic fringe of people whose personal unhappiness turned them into victims of disreputable religious novelty.

As we did in the case of Mormons, we mean to take exception to the suggestion that unusual social maladjustment is by itself an adequate explanation for understanding the prominence of Christian Science in American life. Yet, since nothing is simple, we also need to consider reasons why explanations based on deviant personalities are not either utterly beside the point. Eddy was a complicated person with a long history of nervous disorders and personal instability. She spent her lifetime searching for security and respect. She did not set out to found a controversial religious system and certainly not an occult one. However, like everyone else in this book, Eddy learned to work within an outsider's role that was partially thrust upon her and partially created by her. In trying to make that role work, she did things that gave her contemporaries reasons to link her with occultism and that gave later scholars reasons to raise questions about her psychological normality. No one should wonder that Eddy became a subject of psychobiography.[3]

Again the parallels to Joseph Smith are striking. Consciously or unconsciously, Eddy bore a heavy responsibility for creating her reputation as an oddball. She vehemently denied that her ideas owed anything to anyone or to any other ideas widespread in her culture. Her doctrines, she insisted, were "hopelessly original."[4] Understandably perhaps she resisted the frequent associations that were made between herself and Madame Blavatsky, who founded the Theosophical Society in the same year that *Science and Health* was first published. Eddy regarded the latter as an unsavory person whose Society formed part of Boston's "spiritual underground." Less understandably, unless one keeps in mind the usual way in which outsider identifications develop, she denied the influence of things that had been crucially important in shaping her life. In most scandalous fashion, she disclaimed a debt to Phineas Parkhurst Quimby, her "healer" and father figure who had set the direction for Eddy's entire career. She dismissed Quimby as a "mere" mesmerist in Portland, Maine, whom she had visited without benefit. How could he have taught her Christian Science, she asked, when he had never composed more than a dozen pages.[5]

Eddy's ideas were not as original as she claimed. That fact requires no elaboration. Yet with respect to the present discussion it scarcely mattered. What mattered was the claim that "the discoverer of Christian Science" was the vehicle that God had fitted "during many years, for the reception of a final revelation of the absolute Principle of scientific being, and of healing." Eddy encouraged would-be converts to believe that they were joining a movement without parallel in history.[6] Translated into the language of the social sciences, the invitation to become a Christian Scientist was, in more than a trivial way, an invitation to deviance.

Eddy did more than issue idle claims. She taught lessons; she organized a church; and she devised ritual ways to bring her followers together. Even a brief look at her practices makes it clear how the rumors about occultism got started. In the nineteenth century, as now, occult was commonly employed as a pejorative word without precise or steady meaning. It loosely suggested one or all of the following: magic, mysticism, superstition, and diabolicism. More precisely, it referred to what was hidden and concealed, to what was secret.[7] However, not every secret qualified as something occult. Those who searched for occult knowledge presumed to concern themselves with ultimate reality. According to occultist claims, the ordinary operations of the senses or of the intellect could not apprehend the highest forms of knowledge. Known to a few mystic brotherhoods in antiquity, the highest truths had been discovered, lost, and rediscovered in all later stages of human history.

Although standard occult texts had survived from past epochs, most "modern" occultists, which was the label affixed to Mary Eddy, did not content themselves with the wisdom of ancient writings. Having themselves advanced to the highest stages of consciousness and having glimpsed the nature of reality, they added their own texts to the stack of occult literature. In seeking followers, they formed societies that were bound together by secret rites. They initiated members gradually through various degrees that marked the stages of occult awareness. For the initiates, the payoff presumably was a greater mastery and power over fundamental life forces. As part of the program for maintaining strict secrecy, modern occult societies were usually authoritarian in leadership and elaborately hierarchical. Occult knowledge was most definitely not for everyone.

If one uses strict criteria for recognizing occult activities in nineteenth-century America, one will not find many. The only important pure manifestation of an occult society was Madame Blavatsky's Theosophical Society. Blavatsky proudly claimed the label "occult" as proper to her work since she was heir "of a greater knowledge concerning the mysteries of Nature and humanity than modern culture has yet evolved."[8] With Eddy the case was different. She repudiated occultism and insisted that none of its characteristics listed above applied to Christian Science. Yet that was not quite the truth. Her society was not elaborately occult, but it recalled some important features of occult systems.

In the first place, the early Christian Science fellowship was, by any reasonable construal of the term, a secret society. Eddy may have claimed that the classes of instruction which she ran were rational and practical demonstrations of her ideas, but the way that she divided her private instruction into stages of spiritual advancement looked very much like ritual initiation. She kept her students paying for more instruction by telling them that "she had important secrets relating to healing the sick which she had not theretofore imparted."[9] A humble seeker after truth had considerably more to do than read *Science and Health*, which to the ordinary eye is a very ordinary book. The "neophyte," with his "diseased physique," had to accept Eddy's belief that "the English language, or any other language with which we are familiar, is inadequate to fully convey a spiritual meaning with material terms."[10] Eddy carefully distinguished her neophytes, who could not yet clearly tell the difference between the material and the spiritual, from her "advanced Scientific students," who were ready to receive the higher truths of spiritual consciousness. Very few of the people who interested themselves in Christian Science made it into Eddy's inner circle of people who were sworn to the strictest secrecy.

Not everyone who got close to Eddy kept the secret. Apostates, whose testimony must be used cautiously, rushed to reveal the practices of Christian Science's inner circle. Arthur Cory, for example, who was once a Christian Scientist, broke with the discipline of the church and published a book purporting to contain the lessons of Christian Science class instruction. Cory indicated that he was fed up with a mentality that had turned these lessons into "one of the most closely guarded secrets of this age."[11] Eddy provided her followers with a way to answer the charge that they were occultists, but it did not much help. Secrecy was necessary, she said, because the words of her private lessons could not be understood apart from the oral instruction. In half-grasped fashion they might become instruments for doing evil. According to Eddy, there was a great danger in "promiscuously" teaching the metaphysics of "the power of the mind to do good" because the same power when not fully matured could cause great harm.[12] To opponents, such reasoning merely proved that Eddy was seeking non-Christian ways to manipulate cosmic powers. Not incidentally, Christian Science remains one of the least open of the American religions founded in the nineteenth century. In spite of the many Christian Science reading rooms that exist and the distribution of free information about its teachings, the Mother Church in Boston jealously guards its historical records. The belief in the potential of the neophyte to cause harm is still part of the faith.

When Eddy used the term "science," she was not taking as her model what most people understood by that term. She regarded most of the scientific advances of the nineteenth century as materialistic deceptions.[13] Eddy did not, to her own way of thinking, lack respect for empiricism and objectivity. She offered the many healings reported by Christian Science practitioners as "practical" demonstrations of Christian Science instruction that could be verified by visual observation. Nonetheless, the sort of empirical proof championed by Christian Science did not rest on repeatable experiments. The proof of Christian Science, its objectivity, lay in the endless collection of testimonies to small miracles, to unique events that supposedly confounded the laws of material science. In "experiencing" healing in one's own life, one dissolved the reality of the physical world and learned that the only important thing in the alleged material thing was its hidden spiritual significance.

Every important point in Eddy's teachings went toward undermining the ways in which human beings used their five material senses to order experience and to found common sense judgments. Our ordinary reading of a text, our ordinary reaction to something beautiful or ugly in nature, was an illusion. Somehow, one had to learn to read the inspired page, whether of a book or of a natural object, "through a higher than mortal sense."[14] This point of view was not necessarily un-Christian. A long line of Christian mystics had talked about a higher than mortal sense. Many years before Eddy was born, Jonathan Edwards had linked the Christian experience of conversion with the awakening of an inner spiritual light. Eddy, however, was not talking about ordinary Christian conversion. She was telling people that she could guide them toward a spritual awareness that no other church knew about. Whether God played any role in furthering Eddy's sort of spiritual enlightenment was left a bit unclear. Eddy did not reject the language of Christianity, and her "discovery" of metaphysical healing was rooted in her reading of the New Testament. On balance, however, in reviewing what she wrote about higher consciousness, one is struck by the connection that can be drawn between Eddy's teaching and that of a self-avowed twentieth-century occultist like P. D. Ouspensky. Both Eddy and Ouspensky believed in a knowledge which surpassed ordinary human knowledge, which was obscured by our five normal senses, and which was inaccessible to most people.

Critics might have passed lightly over Christian Science as a harmless and particularly vague sort of pantheistic mysticism, a commercialized Transcendentalism if you like, had it not been for something else which convinced them of a more ominous relation between it and systems of black and white magic. Eddy's claim to heal was not primarily what gained her the reputation for deviance. It was her belief in the power of the mind to cause harm, to act at a distance without physical mediation to cause pain, disease, and even death. Eddy called this power malicious animal magnetism, and it sounded to many citizens of Massachusetts suspiciously like the belief that had once led to the hanging of witches in Salem.

Since Eddy defined malicious animal magnetism as the use of mental power to destroy a person's well-being, it was in theory the opposite of Christian Science. It was part of the illusion, the false reality of normal consciousness, that Eddy's philosophy sought to dispel. Illusion or not, malicious animal magnetism was something that did a great deal of damage within the mental universe that Eddy and her followers occupied. It gave substance to her warning about Christian Science neophytes. Neophytes were dangerous because they acquired a power to do mischief before they had gained full spiritual enlightment. Nothing guaranteed that they would exercise their limited knowledge of metaphysical science only to heal. Apostates were especially apt to misuse what they had learned to revenge themselves against Eddy and those who remained loyal to her. The general public first learned about this aspect of Christian Science in the spring of 1878 when Lucretia L. S. Brown brought a suit against Daniel Spofford, a former Christian Scientist who had parted bitterly from Eddy, for practicing harmful mesmerism against her.[15] The startled court in Salem did better than its Puritan forebears and dismissed the charges. It was not persuaded by the warnings written into the early editions of *Science and Health* that "the peril of Salem witchcraft is not past."[16] The dismissal, however, did not end the controversy.

Well into the 1880s Eddy ignored the ridicule that greeted her public denunciations of malicious animal magnetism, and she spoke freely about MAM to the press. In 1882, when her third and last husband died, she told a reporter for the Boston *Globe* that he had been the victim of mental malpractice. The alleged activator of the fatal poison was again one of Eddy's former students. Eddy cautioned everyone who became close to her that, in so doing, they entered a targeted space where they would be in constant danger of hostile mental attacks. The invention of Christian Science, with its promise of dispelling illusion, had simultaneously created a counterforce that was just as strong. According to Eddy, "the mild forms of animal magnetism are disappearing, and its aggressive features are coming to the front. The looms of crime, hidden in the dark recesses of mortal thought, are every hour weaving webs more complicated and subtile."[17] Christian Science was supposed to be a monistic philosophy which recognized only one reality, but its everyday view of the world was Manichean. The forces of good were locked in combat with the forces of evil, and it was not entirely certain which side would prevail.

By the 1890s Eddy had decided or was persuaded by others that the fuss over malicious animal magnetism interfered too much with her goal of making her "hopelessly original" system of thought "respectable." She said less about the subject in public. Privately, little changed. Her concern with the mental attacks directed at her and her inner circle became something of an obsession. Frequently, journals got wind of her "secret" activities to ward off harm and published details about them as part of the muckraking literature of the early twentieth century. According to one unfriendly journalist, Eddy organized "watches" among her closest disciples to turn the effects of evil thoughts back upon particular enemies. She gathered students in a room and had them "treat in thought" someone she suspected of causing harm to herself. "Say to him," she instructed, "your sins have found you out. You are affected as you wish to affect me. Your evil thought reacts upon you. You are bilious, you are consumptive, you have liver trouble, you have been poisoned by arsenic."[18] If this report was true, then Eddy did not protect herself merely by dispelling the illusion of harmful mental attacks. She set the force of the evil back upon its perpetrator, thus using the resources of Christian Science to do something other than to heal.

Although one must suspect the accuracy of anything written by someone hostile to Eddy, her fear of malicious animal magnetism was confirmed in one sympathetic and affectionate account. Adam H. Dickey, Eddy's private secretary during the last three years of her life and for a time the chairman of the Board of Directors of the Mother Church, published a memoir of her last days to prove that his beloved friend and teacher was in the end "mentally murdered."[19] Christian Science officials, eager to be rid of their association with demonology after Eddy's death, suppressed Dickey's book, and it is not easy now to find a copy. However, the story that it tells is consistent with everything one knows about Eddy's final years.

According to Dickey, Eddy's failure to ward off the death administered by her enemies did not result from want of trying. Eddy turned her household into a mental fortress, dividing the night into four mental watches. Each watch was assigned to different mental workers, all residents of the house, who had specific instructions about how to counteract the "evil influence of mortal mind directed against our Leader and her establishment." The typewritten instructions designated in numerical order which phases of error they were supposed to combat. Some of the battles were waged against rather miscellaneous targets. Since the elderly Eddy had trouble getting around after a heavy snowfall, she directed her watches one winter to "make a law that there shall be no more snow this season." However, most of the effort went toward warding off severe mental attacks upon Eddy, and she participated in the watches along with everyone else. If Dickey was precise in his reporting, then much of the language she used strongly suggested the influence of occult and magical traditions. At one point she told her staff: "You don't any of you realize what is going on. This is a dark hour for the Cause and you do not seem to be awake to it. . . I am now working on a plane that would mean instantaneous death to any of you."[20] This sort of statement was not one that conventional Protestants in Boston were accustomed to hear from conventional Boston Protestant pulpits on Sunday morning.

We noted earlier that Eddy was not interested in making common cause with other independent religious teachers who claimed to see spiritual meanings behind material reality. She refused to acknowledge the significance of the fact that many people who were attracted to Christian Science were also attracted, as she had been, to spiritualism, Theosophy, and various mind cure movements. Moreover, she was irritated that at the World Parliament of Religions, assembled as part of the Chicago Exposition in 1893, several visiting Hindu teachers pointed to similarities between "the fundamental principles of modern Christian Science and those of that ancient system of philosophy known in India as Vendanta."[21] Yet she sometimes tried to have it both ways. When the occasion suited her, she allowed Christian Science to be asso-

ciated with the popularity of movements she had on other occasions attacked. Her journal in the 1890s offered for sale through
the Christian Science Publishing House such esoteric competitors
as J. H. Dewey's *Christian Theosophy*, Swedenborg's *Correspondences*, the *Bhagavad Gita*, and Warren Felt Evans's *Esoteric Christianity and Mental Therapeutics*.[22] If Eddy's enemies wanted to
demonstrate that the Christian Science movement was more
occult than its founder acknowledged, they could make a good
beginning by reading its advertising.

Such, then, is the evidence, or a sufficient sample of it, to justify
the hypothesis that a potential convert to Christian Science simply
could not approach the movement thinking of it as a perfectly normal enterprise. The occult connection was too pronounced. What
we must now consider is the other side of the coin. When Eddy's
contemporaries called Christian Science an occult aberration, they
were not, any more than critics of Joseph Smith, analyzing the
appeal of her movement. They were saying that they did not like
that aspect of their culture which explained its appeal. Eddy's philosophy, whether occult or not, did not come out of nowhere. Its
attraction, despite what might be said about the invitation to deviance, was not to people who were swelling the population of
American's mental asylums. From all the information we have,
Christian Science drew its membership mostly from people of
middle-class background. It became quite early in its history, and
remained, a wealthy church, probably the wealthiest of American
churches if measured by the per capita wealth of its membership
It exerted a special appeal to women. Presumably many of these
women had problems, but there is little to suggest that they were
crazy.

The outsider strategy that Eddy pursued was probably the only
strategy for a new entry on America's religious landscape. A great
deal of her energy therefore went into making distinctions. Even
so, historians must recognize the artificiality of some of those distinctions if they are to understand how Christian Science gained
sufficient plausibility to become useful to many people who were
suffering under "normal" pressures of American life. Christian
Science was one important nineteenth-century product of harmonial philosophy, which Sydney Ahlstrom has succinctly defined
as "those forms of piety and belief in which spiritual composure,
physical health, and even economic well-being are understood to

flow from a person's rapport with the cosmos."[23] Manifestations of it were everywhere present in the popular culture of nineteenth-century America. We know very little about this influential current of belief, but this fact has to do with the taste of scholars rather than its importance. Harmonial philosophy was the romanticism of the unlearned, that is, of virtually everyone. Its influence in the United States was spread through popular interest in Swedenborg, through Andrew Jackson Davis and LeRoy Sunderland, through mesmerism, spiritualism, and numerology, and through an almost infinite variety of healers who rejected the painful and useless heroic procedures that remained common medical practice throughout the nineteenth century. Eddy encountered the philosophy most concretely when she studied with Quimby, but she was exposed to it in other forms including spiritualism.

In all of its varieties, harmonial philosophy taught human perfectionism. Although human beings were not yet aware of the many ways in which they set their lives jarringly at odds with the fundamental order of the universe, they could learn to overcome their mistakes. Original sin was not a problem. The harmonialists taught that evil was an illusion, saw a spiritual meaning or correspondence behind every material reality, and insisted that science, properly understood, could as appropriately deal with the unseen world as with the seen. The unseen could be made visible. In almost every case, this philosophy of everlasting progress was tied to a greater or lesser extent with some philosophy of unorthodox healing. Harmonial philosophy was a philosophy whose practical consequences were emotional and physical health.

Eddy's version of harmonial philosophy was unusual only in the degree of its institutional elaboration. Most of the other nineteenth-century harmonialists, even within a single movement such as spiritualism, worked on their own, and only occasionally founded organizations that had more than an ephemeral existence. Eddy, in contrast, although it took her several years to determine exactly what sort of organization to give her movement, created a church, with a large building in Boston, governed by a hierarchical leadership that exercised authoritarian control over the dissemination of Christian Science teaching. Those who wished to modify doctrine or establish some sort of independent platform for expressing ideas were forced out of the church.

In spite of Eddy's disclaimers, the cluster of movements that collectively prepared the way for the emergence of Christian Science is not difficult to identify in nineteenth-century American culture. Most of them, in stressing as Eddy did the limits of what we can know through normal consciousness, drew consciously or unconsciously on occult associations. To be sure harmonial movements were typically eager to dilute and democratize occultism. Spiritualists and mesmerists, who were as sensitive as Eddy later was to the charge that they performed secret rites, insisted that anyone with eyes could confirm their claims. Spirits and hypnotic powers were simply another part of the visible world to be observed. They were not mysterious. Anyone could learn about them. Even so, seances generally took place in the dark. Mediums and mesmerists went into trances and became the source of phenomena that did not occur outside a gathered circle. One source of the appeal of harmonial philosophy was clearly that it hinted at something more than the religious knowledge taught within the traditional churches of Protestant Christianity. Those who charged Christian Science with occultism were not necessarily misrepresenting an important connection. What they had misrepresented was how deeply various bits of occult lore permeated America's popular religious culture.

Placed as it should be amid a myriad of other popular movements, Christian Science was as an intellectual system neither deviant nor especially innovative. Sydney Ahlstrom was absolutely right in concluding that despite unusual features—charismatic founders, elaborate rituals, an insistence on the 'secret' meanings of authoritative texts—harmonial philosophy fed a "vast and highly diffuse religious impulse" that cut across the normal lines of religious divisions. People interested themselves in it without necessarily changing their church affiliation. According to Ahlstrom, some of its motifs probably informed the religious life of most Americans.[24] That influence has continued to be marked in the twentieth century. The American press likes to announce occult revivals in which Americans react against the world view of "modern science." Yet the journalistic emphasis on ebb and flow seems much overdone. The truth is that we do not live in an uncomplicatedly secular age. The scientific revolution, wherever in time one wants to cut into it, has promoted in almost equal parts a respect for empiricism among experimental scientists and a more popular belief that experiment can push beyond the limits of ordinary sensory awareness.

One may call Christian Science and related phenomena a system of occult magic if one likes. Eddy gave her critics reasons to do so. But the label does not turn its beliefs into wierd anachronisms or hysterical forms of anti-scientism. Highly educated people, often people who work in technical fields, have been attracted to Christian Science and some of the nineteenth- and twentieth-century movements to which it bears a generic relation. These include Guy Ballard's I Am movement, the "in tune with the infinite" philosophy of Ralph Trine, the cosmic optimism of Emile Coué, the positive thinking of Norman Vincent Peale, and the yoga-based discipline of Transcendental Meditation. Harmonial philosophy, rather than being rendered archaic by scientific and technical progress, has, like science fiction, often gained credibility among those who have welcomed that progress. The people who believe in ESP, after all, do not think of themselves as criticizing science per se. In their minds, they are merely urging science to stretch beyond materialistic assumptions that proscribe certain types of research.[25]

The links that existed between Eddy's system of ideas and widely diffused popular beliefs did not necessarily "normalize" the particular forms she gave those beliefs or the people who joined her church. Intellectual plausibility is not the only issue. We need to consider what sort of people responded eagerly to Eddy's particular invitation, one which, as we have seen, tried hard to advertise its own deviance. A great many of the respondents were women, and we may usefully pursue our discussion with that fact primarily in mind.

The problems that middle-class women faced in nineteenth-century America have been discussed in many places. Crippling psychosomatic ailments that sent many of them to bed for months grew apparently from tensions that their culture imposed on them. As pampered creatures whose virtues were tenderly praised, but whose actual power was limited to certain realms within the household, many women were surely unhappy. Even though they had middle-class husbands who provided them with economic comfort and social status, they felt useless and expendable.

Most historians have quite reasonably associated the feelings of dissatisfaction that affected many middle-class women with their prominence in religious activities. Although barred from running the churches because of their sex, they constituted most of the membership of both large and small denominations. They taught the church schools, organized the social life of the church community, and overwhelmingly, with their children, filled the pews on Sunday morning. Religion offered not only an outlet for unfulfilled emotion, it was also one of the few nondomestic spheres of activity open to women where they could imagine they were doing something useful and creative. Religious life became one of the ways in which women searched for power or learned to do without it.

The fact that women were so prominent in Eddy's church was not in itself unusual. Piety was a conventional role for women, and it had its uses. Nonetheless, one scholar has suggested that movements associated with the occult and magic exert a particular appeal to people of marginal social status.[26] In that case, because of the widely advertised connection of Christian Science with the occult, women who were attracted to Eddy's teaching may have suffered from acute forms of felt deprivation that went well beyond the experience of most American women. We know that illness was frequently a complicating factor to the other emotional burdens they felt themselves to be carrying. On this point of relative unhappiness, evidence is not satisfactorily conclusive one way or the other. Yet even if Christian Science women suffered strong distress, how much should we read into that fact when making assessments of what was normal in American life? Surely there is reason to be cautious about equating unhappiness, even deep unhappiness, with cultural deviance. Most of the sociological literature on deviance deals with extreme cases of social marginality, with criminals in prison, prostitutes, gypsies, the insane, the desperately poor. Our subject is women who became Christian Scientists, and most of them did not live in a world abruptly cut off from the social networks of ordinary community life. They often had complaints that they did not even know how to describe, but behavior does not cease to be typical or normal merely because it has been spurred on by unhappiness. To maintain otherwise is to view human experience from a falsely rationalist perspective.

The bias in contemporary scholarship that links strong religious commitment to unbalanced or inadequate social adjustment is pronounced enough to risk overstatement in the other direction. The argument is usually that deprived people, who inaccurately perceive the nature of their deprivation or who are not in a position to work directly to eliminate the cause, seek a religious (read illusory) resolution of their problems. Others, with more understanding of the social causes of deprivation and with greater opportunities to exert a collective pressure against those causes, seek a secular (read political) solution.[27] Applied to the present analysis, one might say that the religious activity of Christian Science women in the nineteenth century, while it might have given them some sense of command, was really a way of rationalizing and finally accepting their culturally defined weaknesses. Religion, with an allegedly otherworldly outlook, provided women with no way to challenge the cultural roles laid down for them by existing social structures, and it squeezed their small bids for power into the molds of existing cultural norms. Even if Christian Science provided women with public roles that were normally closed to them, the end result of the activity was to reinforce stereotypes that guaranteed the perpetuation of a subordinate role for women.

With respect to this sort of analysis, several questions suggest themselves. Most important, is it really easy to tell what an accurate perception of one's plight would be? Eddy, as shall appear, understood her plight primarily in terms of poor health rather than in terms of humiliating social subordination. Thus, she said nothing that would satisfy a political feminist in our own time. On what grounds, however, can we say that she misperceived her plight other than our own set of political priorities? It is far from certain how we determine whether someone is working "directly" to relieve the cause of his or her plight. By any possible criteria of judgment, Mary Baker Eddy solved a number of personal problems by founding a church. Other women solved their problems by joining it. Can we assert with confidence that they would have more directly or more realistically solved their problems by throwing their energies behind a secular cause, say, for example, behind the suffragist movement? The notion that religious commitment is escapist, a *faute de mieux* strategy for the weak, and that political commitment flows from a hard-headed understanding of the causes of human unhappiness, is nonsense.

It assumes that all the various ills to which the human body and psyche are prey can be resolved on a single level of action.

In recalling the events of her own life, Eddy exaggerated certain aspects of the difficulties that she faced. That exaggeration is part of the general story we have been telling about the behavior of religious outsiders. The themes of pain, suffering, and opposition are as central to everything Eddy wrote as they were to everything Joseph Smith wrote. One of her critics was not far wrong when he said: "Mrs. Eddy had a perfect mania for trying to connect up every event of her life with some striking event in the life of Christ."[28] Victorian women, quite apart from any particular religious involvement they might have chosen, were bathed in a literature of martyrdom. The theoretical meaning of nurturing, as well as its practical consequences, was to sacrifice yourself in giving life and support to others. Yet, when a more than sufficient allowance is made for rhetorical invention, the fact remains that Eddy's life was not easy and that her story is best and most accurately told as a triumph over adversity.

Although she spent her early childhood in a relatively pleasant farm community, within a relatively uncomplicated family circle, she was afflicted from an early age with spinal and nervous ailments. She was unable to attend school regularly. In 1843 she married a family friend, George Washington Glover. His sudden death, just over a year later, plunged her into a long series of traumatic disasters. She gave birth to a son, but was physically and economically unable to take care of him. For the next nine years she was a sick woman with no economic security. She unintentionally compounded her difficulties in 1853 by marrying Dr. Daniel Patterson, an itinerant dentist. Dr. Patterson lacked what Victorian moralists called character, and Eddy gained neither health nor economic security through this unhappy union.

Her decision in 1862 to go to Portland, Maine, to seek help from Quimby was the first step in a gradual reversal of fortune; but the course of ascent was not steady. Quimby died in 1866 (again her dependence upon a man had failed her), and she shortly thereafter had the famous fall on the ice that injured her back. Eddy dates the birth of Christian Science from that incident, since "on the third day" after her injury, she healed herself and rose from her bed. Unfortunately for her, the significance of that celebrated healing was not immediately apparent to the world. She faced another hard decade of disappointing labor. She tried with little success to carry on Quimby's work and was briefly in a healing partnership with Richard Kennedy. He was the first of many young men with whom she worked closely and who later were bitterly estranged from her.

Although she only slowly developed her vision of a Christian Science organization, Eddy took two momentous steps in 1875: she published the first edition of *Science and Health* and she founded the Christian Science Association. A year later, having divorced Patterson several years before, she married Asa Eddy who dutifully helped her expand her organization over the next five years. By the end of the 1880s, Eddy was a wealthy and healthy person of almost seventy years. Her Christian Science Association was a national organization of twenty churches, ninety societies, and thirty-three teaching centers. In the 1890s, she built her publishing empire, which included not only the many revisions of *Science and Health* but also the *Christian Science Journal*, the *Christian Science Sentinel*, and the *Christian Science Monitor*. She also reorganized her association around the Mother Church in Boston, which was completed in 1895. Despite retirement, first to Concord, New Hampshire, and then to Brookline, Massachusetts, and her rare appearance in public, she was without question a famous and influential woman at the time of her death in 1910.

One could make a long catalogue of the things Eddy did not accomplish. Her church, although she thought that she was founding it in opposition to the existing materialism of American life, was pervaded in suffocating ways by an American middle-class outlook. Eddy not only never thought to make a statement protesting the plight of American woman in spite of her long and agonizing acquaintance with that plight, she said little that can be construed as serious or precise social criticism. In gaining a position unusual for a woman, Eddy defined everything that she did in terms of existing sexual stereotypes. Much like the many female spiritualist mediums of the nineteenth century, Eddy identified the virtues that had made her religious mission successful with the traits used by her culture to define femininity.[29] God had chosen her because she was passive and impressionable. She was sensitive to beauty and to moral values and had the innate motherly instinct to suffer in behalf of those who were weak and defenseless. The maternal imagery of the Christian Science Association was marked. Everyone who was close to Eddy, including the young men who substituted for the son she had not reared, called her "Mother."

These facts testify to the strength of certain social conventions that defined "respectability" in late nineteenth-century Massachusetts. Eddy's tolerance for ridicule was high, and she was not afraid of opposition. However, as was true of many other religious outsiders, Eddy explained opposition as the result of her rigorous adherence to the social ideals that were supposed to govern American culture. And, in fact, she "seemed" different not because she challenged the rules about the normal role of women, but because she interpreted those rules too literally. She took female virtue seriously enough to take it beyond the domestic household. Eddy's life, we should remember, had never given her reason to complain about the idealized life assigned to women. Her complaint was rather that she had never been allowed to live it. Only within her church did she finally find a place where she could gain the respect and authority that she thought women, as mothers, should command. She may have worked within stereotypes, but she solved her own life's problem by freeing herself of past dependencies upon men.

What then can we conclude with respect to issues of deviance and typicality? For Eddy's organization to have a chance of surviving against the competition, Eddy had to make sharp differentiations between herself and everyone else. Even when those differentiations were not nearly so important as her rhetoric sought to make them, they erected formidable psychological barriers for anyone flirting with the idea of becoming a Christian Scientist. Joining the Christian Science Association in the early years often required either a large share of courage or a large share of desperation, perhaps both. One did not affiliate with Eddy thinking of it as an ordinary thing to do. In numerical terms, it was in fact quite unusual. Becoming Christian Scientist was not a path taken by many people. At the end of the nineteenth century, Christian Scientists accounted for less than one percent of the American population.

However, to ask how many people joined the Christian Science church is not the only relevant question. It is equally important to ask how many people, given the proper circumstances of associations and opportunities, were susceptible to the movement's appeal and to movements with a similar appeal. When you pose that question, the movement becomes much more typical of nineteenth-century American life. It was easy for Eddy's contemporaries to make fun of malicious animal magnetism just as it is easy for pundits now to ridicule the idea of extrasensory perception. What is not so easy is explaining why soundings of public opinion invariably suggest that the majority of Americans, although they may not be sitting in back rooms trying to send mental messages to their neighbors, believe in the power of the mind to affect objects at a distance. To many Americans who felt no particular urge to join Eddy's church or begin formal instruction in her philosophy, the general ideas which she posed were perfectly acceptable. They interested themselves in them. Contrary to what many ministers feared, ordinary people managed to entertain the possibility of mental healing without abandoning loyalties to Christianity or to technological progress. Christian Science by and large encouraged optimistic expectations.

Since there is a difference between tolerant curiosity about a belief and fervent commitment to a movement, one must acknowledge the force of the proposition that many of the early Christian Scientists were in their religion reacting to unhappiness in their lives. The argument being pursued here merely insists on the normality of that response. Christian Science grew as a perfectly ordinary manifestation of tensions that were always present in American society. The notion that sectarianism as a factor in American religious life rises and falls in response to dramatic social upheaval does not seem to fit facts. The tensions that propelled some people toward Christian Science were uncomfortable but relatively routine. They pushed others toward Theosophy, or spiritualism, or New Thought, or perhaps more commonly, simply toward a reexamination of their religious life within a well-established denomination. Joining Eddy's church was not in itself a typical or frequent occurrence among Americans, but it was an altogether normal solution to the problem of the emotional dissatisfactions of everyday American life.

For some of the reasons suggested in the last paragraph, the history of Christian Science provides a useful perspective from which to discuss the religious inventiveness of the very recent American past. In the 1960s a number of religious groups, some of which had originated much earlier, gained public prominence. Some of them were domestic in origin. Others were imported, especially from Asia. A far from complete list would include the Church of Scientology, the Hare Krishna and Meher Baba movements, Subud, Transcendental Meditation, and the Unification church of the Reverend Sun Myung Moon.

Parallels with the early history of Christian Science are striking. For one thing, the American press has greeted these "new" movements with the same feelings of uneasiness as well as fascination that Eddy aroused almost a century earlier. The words "occult" and "fraudulent" are frequently used. So is the word "cult," since contemporary religious leaders, like Eddy, have stressed, not their similarities to other religious traditions, but their differences from them. Joining one of the new religions, according to critics, is a socially isolating event and therefore psychologically dangerous. The appeal of contemporary movements appears to be to young people rather than specifically to women, but the social segment most affected has been the middle class. As a result, a strong tendency has developed to analyze the movements as nonprogressive, ineffectual reactions to irrational social malaise.

Since the religious ferment that was widely publicized from the mid–1960s until the present so clearly follows from patterns of behavior that have formed a central aspect of American religious life in every decade, the question of why they provoke worry and uneasiness does pose itself. One answer is that they always have. Another is that these "new" religions abuse the license of free religious expression more than past groups did. Their critics cite evidence to suggest that young people entering these religions undergo coercive rites of initiation. Parents are abruptly cut off from their children. Cult leaders accumulate vast wealth that is not taxed. In one famous case, that of James Jones's Peoples Temple, an entire church enacted a suicide that may be implied in all cult withdrawal.

Making judgments about comparative abuse is a hazardous enterprise. A nineteenth-century Presbyterian minister, could he view the present religious scene in the United States, would very likely be reluctant to concede that the Reverend Moon is any more nefarious a character than Joseph Smith or Mary Eddy. In one form or another, the present charges against religious "cults," including that of brainwashing, were hurled against every new religious group organized in this country, and usually with some measure of justification. Religious enthusiasm has always been a dangerous thing. It sometimes inspires people to do noble things. With equal frequency, it does not. The religious prophet trying to lead people in a new direction is not likely to be without blemish.

The resistance to treating new religions as a legitimate and normal part of American life is part of an old story that we traced in the introduction to this book. To the resistance of Protestant churchmen who despair of ever finding their way to the unified reformed church, we must add the secularist's reluctance to admit the durability of religious behavior. The viability of a new religious group, particularly one that has attracted a college-educated generation, despite the mammoth implausibility of its claims, is bound to make secularists nervous. Rather than admit to the irredeemable inadequacy of "modern" forms of political and social life, secularists try to place new religious movements at the fringes of normal life. Yet, if the disappearance of a "normal, all-American" boy into the cult of the Reverend Moon was adequately explained by the word aberration, parents in America could rest more easily than they have any reason to do.

On the brighter side of things, which brings us back to one of the book's main themes, the eternal eruption of outsider religious groups in national experience represents more than the failure of American life. If they are signals of cultural and social stress, sometimes serious stress, they have not been a significant cause of it. In providing ways for people to adjust their discontents, they have been an important means of making America work. Arguably, they have permitted many Americans in each generation to bury their sorrows in religion and hand to their children the responsibility for doing something adequate to repair the inadequacies of American life. Whatever we think about that matter, we still must seek to understand why normal people faced with the normal problems of living do the things that they do. People escape from things that they cannot control to do things which they can control even if those things reflect intellectual shallowness and mediocrity.

Daniel Boorstin has been roundly criticized for calling the non-ideological fumblings of American society the mark of genius.

That criticism is proper, for the word "genius" is much too self-congratulatory and raises to a virtue the incapacity of Americans to criticize their own society with any perspicacity. Even so, if one wants to understand how the United States got as far as it did with relative political stability, Boorstin's views about America retain a certain force. Mary Baker Eddy did not grasp everything that there was to grasp about the shortcomings of American life. Neither did she reflect much on the social and psychological causes of her own distress. However, these are not reasons for a patronizing dismissal of her activity. Her Christian Science did not cure cancer or allow people with severed optic nerves to see again, but it cured many maladies that were a lot more common among American women and men.

If this assessment of Eddy and the impulse she typified seems too generous, wait a bit. We will in the next two chapters be looking at religious movements, which more than any of the others that are considered in these pages, would have reinforced the Marxist opinion that religion's only efficacy is as an opiate.

CHAPTER FIVE

Premillennial Christian Views of God's Justice and American Injustice

How unworthy and absurd to call that a Christian state in which the vast majority do not even confess the name of Christ, much less practice his commands.

The Prophetic Times (December 1864)

We have in the course of previous chapters touched on the issue of politics—specifically on the question of under what circumstances an outsider religious group might or might not become involved in taking political stands. In this chapter, which deals with premillennial traditions within American Protestant Christianity, we intend to make the political implications of religion the central concern. Somewhat paradoxically, premillennialism has in the twentieth century encouraged one of the following: an indifference to politics, outright hostility toward schemes of social and economic reform, or support for legislation advanced by the so-called "moral majority." The nature of the paradox will appear as we proceed, but the central problem lies in trying to explain why politically radical tendencies present in the nineteenth-century origins of various premillennial churches vanished in a later period. We intend to focus on three movements that have become important religious forces in American life: the Seventh-day Adventists, the Jehovah's witnesses, and the Pentecostals. Many of the points we will make apply also to that enormous segment of American Protestant life that we label Fundamentalism. However, since Fundamentalism is difficult to define and has a rather unusual status among outsider religious positions, encompassing as it does probably the largest number of American Protestants, we shall forgo specific reference to that movement until the next chapter.

Despite some specific doctrines that explain why theologically conservative premillennialists never warmed up to the Social Gospel notion that sin is partly caused by unhealthy social environments, their recent affinity for certain types of conservative politicians poses a few problems that need explaining. For one thing, and this point has received a great deal of attention from others besides Karl Marx, many strongly premillennial or millenarian religious groups attracted people whose relatively deprived economic circumstances might otherwise have turned them into natural antagonists of status quo social systems. Second, a social radicalism can be extracted from most prophetic traditions that expect Christ to return in physical form within a short time, destroy the political nations on the earth, and establish his spiritual kingdom. Radical here simply means holding a vision of a vastly different and more just society. How did Christian prophecies, which once centered on the moral decline of every human society, which had no trouble sharply distinguishing the government of God from any national government, and which imagined a common dismal fate awaiting the worldly superpowers, become entangled with patriotic rituals of frenzied flag waving and begin to proclaim the fundamental moral exceptionalism of the American nation? That is the question we are seeking to answer.

Politically progressive American Christians have good reason to regret the failure of premillennial perspectives to resist a marriage with conventional expressions of Cold War nationalism. Premillennialism had once formed an important alternative to the forms of American Protestantism that curled up comfortably with the postmillennial expectation that America could perfect itself without Christ's direct rule.[1] A lot of blame has fallen on poor Jonathan Edwards who, in making America the center of the redemptive drama, had already in the eighteenth century provincialized prophecy. Thereafter, and particularly after the American Revolution, many leading church figures accepted, in John Smylie's words, a view of their nation as the "primary agent of God's meaningful activity in history." According to Nathan Hatch, "the kingdom of God and the virtuous republic became for Americans one and the same empire."[2] A flood of religiously supported popularizations of "redeemer nation" themes emerged in the nineteenth century, themes that arguably became powerful engines of American imperialism and helped create a nationalistic spirit that eventually tolerated efforts to Americanize such unlikely places as Vietnam and Iran.[3] The premillennial tradition had its own problems, but one of them should not have been to suffer the influence of this sort of cultural blindness.

Despite the recent work of such scholars as Robert Mapes Anderson, Timothy Weber, and Ernest Sandeen, it is probably still necessary to insist that the premillennial strain is not a minor one in American religious thought.[4] In antebellum America, the belief in Christ's imminent second coming formed an important focus of Protestant controversy. In those years, and for the rest of the nineteenth century, Protestants in every section of the country, and in almost every denomination, reacted against efforts to define the Second Coming as a nonphysical and distant event. Groups founded on a specific premillennial eschatology became important denominations and enjoyed a steady growth. In the latest church censuses, the Assemblies of God, among the largest of the Pentecostal groups, counted more members than the American Baptist Churches in the U.S.A. The Church of God in Christ was pushing toward 4,000,000 adherents whereas neither the Episcopal church nor the United Presbyterian Church had reached 3,000,000. The Seventh-day Adventists and Jehovah's witnesses both showed larger followings than the Unitarian-Universalists.[5] In some specific regions, in the South and in Spanish-speaking sections of large cities, premillennial groups are a major numerical force. Nationally, denominations loyal to specific premillennial chronologies constitute a minority of organized American Protestants. However, as Timothy Weber has noted, nearly every major American revivalist since Dwight Moody has been a premillennialist.[6] The influence of premillennialism in some large denominations, perhaps especially the Southern Baptist Convention, has been powerful. Prophets of Armageddon crowd the television channels every Sunday morning in the United States and attract large sums of money. We are not talking about an exotic survival.[7]

The political implications of premillennial prophecy have changed. That is our argument. For the most part, the change owes little to evolution in the theological content of premillennialism. What seems to have happened is that premillennialists in different historical contexts have attached a different significance to similar doctrines. The terms of their social identifications have altered, and doctrines have affected their behavior in different ways. We know that in England in the seventeenth and eighteenth centuries millenarian thought was often linked to egalitarian movements that advocated radical social upheavals. The work of Christopher Hill, especially, on the Seekers, the Levellers, and the Ranters, has revealed the political significance of apocalyptic religious desires to turn the world upside down. More recently, J.F.C. Harrison, another British historian, has explored the possibility that well into the nineteenth century in England, political radicalism and religious millenarianism were not alternatives, as E.P. Thompson suggested in his magnificent book on the English working class, so much as different aspects of the same phenomenon. Harrison wrote: "Dig into the history of popular radicalism almost anywhere before 1850 and the chances are good that a millenarian reference will be unearthed."[8]

What Harrison concluded about early nineteenth-century England was also true in antebellum America. We can demonstrate this fact by looking at William Miller and the church that eventually grew out of the controversies he started, the Seventh-day Adventists. For much of his religious career, William Miller was an ordinary revivalist preacher whose influence was not generally viewed as disruptive. When his preaching became controversial in the early 1840s, it was not because his intense interest in Christ's Second Coming was unusal. His generation, perhaps more than any other generation in American history, sponsored communitarian experiments on the premise that humanity was teetering on a point of dramatic historical discontinuity. In this context of heightened expectation, Miller's teaching became divisive only after he set specific dates for Christ's Second Coming, the final one coming in 1844. That prediction among other things gave a special urgency to his denunciations of worldly impurity and started the exodus of his followers from the already organized churches.

What is interesting is how much the uncompromising stand that shaped some Millerite rhetoric in 1843 and 1844, as the world supposedly approached its end, resembled the comeouter postures adopted by the most uncompromising Christian abolitionists. The resemblance was more than casual. Miller believed in the justice of the abolitionist position. So did Joshua V. Himes, who probably did more than Miller himself to publicize Millerism. His Chardon Street Chapel in Boston served as a forum for Garrison's followers in the Massachusetts Anti-Slavery Society. Josiah Litch, Charles Fitch, Joseph Bates, and Geroge Strong were other leading Millerites who had contributed to the radical wing of Garrisonian abolitionism.[9] Many historians have found this connection puzzling and have remarked on it only briefly. For example, Angelina Grimké's distinguished biographer, Gerda Lerner, concluded that the Millerite fancies of that famous abolitionist marked but an unimportant lapse of "common sense practicality" brought on by her fears about pregnancy.[10] Rather than that, it just may be that Grimké's belief "in the downfall of every earthly throne, the overthrow of every political government, the annihilation of every Ecclesiastical Establishment" was a thoroughly ordinary conceit among antebellum American reformers.[11]

This latter possibility should not startle us, for Miller's apocalyptic sentiments were in less precise versions constantly reiterated in popular literature. Doubtlessly, the strongly held belief that Christ would return to earth on a fixed October night in 1844 reduced in the believer's mind the importance of any activity beyond getting ready for that event. Reformers became ex-reformers when they became single-minded Millerites. Nevertheess, the evidence from antebellum America is overwhelmingly on he side of proving a connection between a belief in Christ's mminent return and energetic efforts to perfect this world, or at least a part of it. The Shakers believed that the Second Coming of Christ had already been fulfilled in the person of Ann Lee. They foresaw the end of the world, declared sex evil, and stopped bearing children. That did not keep them from building communities that are usually labeled utopian. Joseph Smith's early followers keenly anticipated divine intervention in the world to establish Christ's reign on earth and to inaugurate the millennium. That expectation simply increased the astounding efforts they made to construct Zion. In assessing the impulses that Millerism encouraged, it is less relevant to recall the disappointing and lonely October night in 1844 when Miller's followers wept and wept until dawn, than to remember how quickly, after that shattering event, some people began to pick up the pieces and put together a worldly community. What Leon Festinger called "cognitive dissonance" surely operated on many of Miller's followers in the wake of an apparently failed prophecy; but as in many comparable cases, rather than giving up the prophecy, they merely adjusted one of the details.[12]

Hiram Edson, Ellen White, Joseph Bates, among others, decided that Miller had erred in marking 1844 as the year of Christ's physical return to earth. According to a vision received by Edson, on the fixed October date Christ had entered the heavenly sanctuary where, in preparation for his still imminent earthly reign, he began to judge the sins of the living and to plead the case of the righteous before God. That rendering of prophecy, along with the observance of the seventh day of the week as the proper sabbath and the adoption of special dietary and health regulations, became the distinctive features of a new church, organized in the 1850s, although not formally incorporated until 1863. The Seventh-day Adventists never again set a specific date for Christ's coming, but for the rest of the nineteenth century neither did they stop stressing its nearness.

In the thinking of the Adventists, one can recognize a familiar ambiguity that is almost always present in Christian prophetic movements. With respect to secular society, the prophet cries doom and destruction. Nothing matters but the coming of Christ's spiritual Kingdom. Yet, somewhere between the lines of his utterances the prophet leaves open a possibility that worldly activity by God's saints might alter the scenario for Doomsday. On the one hand, God's saints among the Millerites had nothing to do but wait for Christ. On the other hand, they were commanded to act as if the future were in their hands. In his study of Adventist behavior, Jonathan Butler put the ambiguity this way: "They wished to delay the end in order to preach that the end was soon."[13] Premillennial Adventism, however one wants to characterize the social despair that it preached, was in its origins neither otherworldly nor quietist. Indeed, the word "otherworldly" when applied to Christian groups is almost always misleading.

The connection of early Adventism to an American reform tradition, although problematic in many ways, should not therefore be discounted. The Adventist perspective firmly challenged what Reinhold Niebuhr at a later time called "the easy conscience" of modern man.[14] Adventists, unlike many secular and religious

Americans who promoted the notion that they were God's modern chosen people, either gave the United States no particular place in prophecy or saw in prophetic scripture a specific image of its fall into hopeless moral corruption. In all his careful searching through the Book of Daniel and Revelation, William Miller failed to find any references to America; it was not prefigured in any of the signs of the last days. Biblical texts, he thought, clearly foretold the date of 1898 when Napoleon moved to end the secular power of the Catholic church. Other parts of the world were well represented in Miller's unraveling of millennial dates; but Columbus's voyage, the Atlantic crossing of the Puritans, and the American Revolution had no scriptural figurations.

When Miller's successors finally did spot the United States in prophetic texts, they spotted something ill-suited to the task of swelling patriotic pride. J. N. Andrews was apparently the first Adventist to identify America with the beast with "two horns like a lamb" foreseen in the thirteenth chapter of Revelation. Ellen White, who was the major voice of Adventist teaching and prophecy in the late nineteenth century, and Uriah Smith, a leading editor and writer in the Adventist church, made the point an important tenet of Adventist faith.[15] The interpretation of the scriptural reference had two parts. The first was reassuring. The two horns, which represented the twin virtues of republicanism and Protestantism, and the lamb-like qualities of the American beast accounted for the "thus-far glorious record and noble achievements" of the young nation. The gloom began with the second part that foretold a "painful sequel" to America's glorious beginning, after the nation had forgotten its "principles of justice so pure and undefiled." Sometime around the middle of the nineteenth century, the lamb-like beast began to speak with its "dragon voice," an ominous trait also mentioned in Revelation.[16] In alliance with the Roman Catholic church, American politicians and most Protestants committed themselves to overthrowing the principle of free churches. As evidence of a conspiracy to bring about a perverse union of a corrupt religion and a corrupt state, Adventists in the late nineteenth century cited the legislative proposals to enforce a uniform national sabbath. Because these proposals sought to legislate a false Christianity, the United States faced the same awful judgments when Christ returned as all the other secular powers on earth.

Although Adventist prophecy supposedly pointed to inevitable events that Americans were powerless to change, the behavior of the early Adventist leaders suggested something else. Corruption demanded action, an imperative that in the early history of the Adventist church led Adventists to protest the cruelty of American slavery and to support generally the reconstruction policies of the Radical Republicans. By the end of the century it involved them in political maneuvers to fight against sabbath legislation and to promote temperance. In Battle Creek, Michigan, which became the first important Adventist community, Ellen White built a church organization that seemed determined to revolutionize the dietary habits of Americans along with their methods of medical and hospital care. Working with John Kellogg, who developed a palatable breakfast cereal and built a hospital that was in the vanguard of American medical practices, White demonstrated to her followers that one could prepare for the end without despising life or neglecting "practical" activities to improve its quality.[17] In fact, a good bit of what White said suggested that Americans might just turn the situation around and separate their fate from that of other nations. White pronounced God's wrath upon her society without consistently denying her American followers a special role in the coming millennium.

We do not wish to go overboard on this point. The Adventists were never political revolutionaries. Ellen White rarely wrote about public issues. On the occasions when she did, she said things that placed her more on the side of the haves than the have-nots. Her prescriptions for social improvement reflected the position of laissez-faire theorists. She stressed obedience to established governments; she opposed trade unions and strikes; and she blamed the poor for their "lack of diligence and economy," for their failure to "practice self-denial." Her writings were filled with exhortations to work hard, to eschew material comforts, and to depend upon self-help rather than charity. Although she encouraged missionary work among the "worthy poor" and attacked the rich for accumulating luxuries while many children cried for bread, she denied that God intended for everyone to have "an equal share in the temporal blessings." She concluded that "there are very few in our land of plenty who are really so poor as to need help," and those few needed not handouts but job skills. In any case, she did not believe that work among the outcasts of society was the chief "burden of our mission."[18]

Even so, the early Adventist movement contained more than one political possibility, and the question is why, as time passed, it moved in one direction rather than another. The eventual almost complete accommodation of Adventism to the "American way of life" required the obliteration of the opposite tendency that had marked its early history.[19] Eric Hobsbawm has puzzled over the problem of why some millenarian movements in southern Europe during the nineteenth century were absorbed by "modern" revolutionary movements (premillennial apocalyptic rhetoric became Marxist apocalyptic rhetoric), while others persevered in isolationist, apolitical stances that in effect sustained reactionary social and economic attitudes.[20] Before confronting that puzzle directly, we need to consider some other American examples of premillennial movements that wound up suppressing the condemnations of American life that originally were essential to their prophecy.

The Jehovah's witnesses were the most distinctive, and certainly the most militant, of the American churches organized in the nineteenth century that focused on an imminent Second Coming. This group of believers did not adopt its present name until the 1930s. In the beginning its adherents were simply referred to as Russellites to indicate their allegiance to the teachings of Charles Taze Russell. Unlike many other American religious innovators in the nineteenth century, Joseph Smith, Ellen White, Mary Baker Eddy, we do not have any adequate biography of Russell. That is too bad, for he is one of the most interesting. Naturally the career is controversial, and Russell spent an inordinate amount of time defending himself in court. A doggedness in pursuing litigation became an enduring tradition among the witnesses. Russell's institutional accomplishments were impressive. By the time of his death in 1916, he had founded the Zion's Watch Tower Society in Pennsylvania, set up missionary activities around the world, and, after buying Henry Beecher's old Plymouth Church, established an international headquarters and publishing empire in Brooklyn. That last achievement forms one of the most recognizable landmarks in the vicinity of the Brooklyn Bridge.[21]

Russell also produced an incredible amount of complex prophetic writing. His first millenarian musings were grounded in the teachings of the Adventist church; but in the 1870s, he and a colleague had moved to an independent position by teaching that Christ had returned to earth, invisibly, in 1874, and that his visible "presence" would commence shortly. Their rejection of the doctrine of the Trinity gave added distinction to their theology. Russell soon broke with his colleague and drew on personal financial resources to publicize his ideas. His millennial calendars became exceedingly difficult to follow, and we need not here try to sort out purported confusions, especially those relating to what Russell expected to happen in the year 1914. It is sufficient to note that a Russellite identity formed around a literal application of the notion that Christ was quickly filling out the biblical number of the 144,000 who would reign with him in heaven. Although this fixed number, presumably mostly taken up by the first generation of Russellites, was later supplemented to include an indeterminate number of "other sheep" who would survive Armageddon and enjoy a peaceful existence on earth, Russell taught his followers to regard themselves as a small remnant. Like the first generation of Adventists, Russell did not believe that God had special plans for America or for Americans. The vast majority of his countrymen were speeding, without hope of reversing direction, toward a miserable annihilation along with the rest of humankind.

J. H. Rutherford, Russell's autocratic successor, stressed this grim outlook, along with a separatist and isolationist identity, even more strongly. He took with undeviating seriousness the notion that witnesses should not think of themselves as being like anyone else (especially Seventh-day Adventists); and he promoted contentious postures for which the witnesses became well known, and frequently despised, during the 1920s and 1930s. The most distinctive practices that shaped the mentality of witnesses remain part of the tradition. Witnesses, although not technically pacifists because of their plans to fight at Armageddon, will not participate in the military either as combatants or in any form of alternate service. They do not vote or hold office. They instruct their children not to salute the American flag. They refuse to authorize blood transfusions for their members, even in life-threatening situations. They proselytize endlessly, no longer with the blaring loudspeakers they used in otherwise quiet neighborhoods during the 1920s and 1930s, but with sufficient uninvited persistence to spark hostile reactions. Witnesses have been persecuted; but in ways that rivaled the actions of the early Mormons, they placed themselves knowingly in the way of persecution and wound up making persecution essential to their religious identification.

The political outlook that has flowed from these postures has proved to be one that is not easily reducible to our usual categories. The journal literature of Jehovah's witnesses during the course of the twentieth century, particularly between the end of World War I and the early 1960s, consistently and stridently promoted anti-Semitism, anti-Catholicism, and anti-Communism, causes usually associated with extreme right-wing politics. At the same time, the witnesses have turned up, however unintentionally, in company at the other end of the political spectrum from rightist philosophies. Because of their opposition to World War I, they went to jail with Eugene Debs. In every subsequent war, they were proportionately by far the most overrepresented group jailed for opposition to the draft. Because of their opposition to Hitler's demands for patriotic salutes, they went to gas chambers with Germany's Jews. Because they refused to pledge allegiance to the American flag, the American Civil Liberties Union joined them in court to protest the abridgment of First Amendment Rights. Hardly passive when they were challenged, the Jehovah's witnesses bombarded the courts with constitutional questions that significantly changed and broadened judicial interpretation of civil liberties protections.[22] Not incidentally, witnesses in Africa have played a part both in anti-colonial movements and in efforts to end the exploitation of blacks.

To be sure none of these actions was undertaken with much expectation of making the world better. Witnesses have not regarded the elimination of laws they condemned as a step toward the general moral advance of the human race. Unjust laws were the expected obstacles that God allowed the Anti-Christ to establish during the last days in order to test the faith of God's remnant people. Resistance to those laws was a way of strengthening the commitment of the witnesses, not a strategy of social reform. In a fundamental way, any social change that witnesses would have perceived as improving the world contradicted their sense of religious identity. Even their proselytizing, an activity in which they have become expert, was meant to be something more than an attempt to convert the world. Since most of the world was bound to refuse conversion, dogged canvassing in unfriendly neighborhoods was in part a ritual that aimed at creating shared feelings of isolation among those called to perform a thankless task.

Many observers have puzzled over the stiffness and coldness that they see governing the relation of witnesses with one another. Their meetings are not filled with the joyous fellowship that one often finds, for example, in Pentecostal assemblies. Even in prison, witnesses sometimes appear to keep as much distance from one another as from other inmates. Nonetheless, the bonds created by shared trials are very strong among them.[23] What observers often miss is that witnesses regard what they do in meetings as a serious intellectual exercise. They are hammering out the meaning of difficult prophetic scriptures, something they learn to do with skill. Witnesses take enormous pleasure in their achievements. They master texts; they learn to be leaders; and they show infinite patience in teaching what they know to others. Witnesses provide as effective an example of interracial cooperation and mutual respect as one can find anywhere on the map of American Christianity.

In making sense of the political significance of all this, one needs to keep in mind a point roughly similar to the one made about Adventists. The premillennial stance of Jehovah's witnesses did not imply a conventional conservatism or a moral majority politics. A political spectrum that measures things from right to left is in fact useless in describing the worldly work of the group. The refusal of Jehovah's witnesses to participate in patriotic rituals has offended American politicians whether they describe themselves as liberal or conservative. During World War I, Shirley Jackson Case, one of the best known of the "modernist" theologians who then taught in the Divinity School at the University of Chicago, compared the subversive dangers of premillennial belief to those posed by the doctrines of the Industrial Workers of the World, America's most radical labor union. Both ideologies, he argued, sapped the national will to fight and make the world safe for democracy.[24] Since few people these days think to compare any of America's various premillennial churches with left-leaning labor organizations, Case's remarks suggest that we look more closely at differences in what premillennial rhetoric seemed to imply before and then after World War I. We still need to clarify why radical potential that was contained within premillennial outlooks never became strong and indeed grew weaker as the years passed.

Proceeding chronologically, we come to a third important group of American churches that put their faith in premillennial calendars—the Pentecostals. Pentecostalism grew out of the Holiness revivals of the late nineteenth century and out of the dispensational millennial theology that was imported from England and adopted by America's best-known revivalist ministers. Although at first linked to the broad current of theological fashions that created American Fundamentalism, the Pentecostal emphasis on speaking in tongues eventually in the early twentieth century differentiated the Pentecostal groups from Holiness churches, which gravitated back toward the middle-class respectability of Methodism, and from the somewhat less experience-oriented Biblical Fundamentalists. Alliances between Pentecostals and Fundamentalists have sometimes subsequently been repaired, but Fundamentalists do not appreciate a common mistake which acknowledges no difference between them and the "holy rollers."

One cannot study the Pentecostal churches without noticing class. Pentecostals built their first churches almost exclusively from socially disadvantaged men and women, both native-born and immigrant; and its alleged otherworldliness in the early days was expressed with noticeable Populist accents. They were most certainly lower on the social scale than the first Adventists and probably lower than the first Russellites (though not necessarily later generations of witnesses). Religious experience for the early Pentecostals in America was above all the experience of being equal. Frank Bartelman recalled the downpour of the "Latter Rain" during the famous Azusa Street revivals in Los Angeles in 1906 in this way: "Brother Seymour [who was black and one of the leaders in the early Pentecostal movement] was recognized as the nominal leader in charge. But we had no pope or hierarchy. We were 'brethren.' We had no human programme. The Lord Himself was leading. We had no priest class, nor priest craft. . . All were on a level. . . . We did not honor men for their advantage, in means or education, but rather for their God-given 'gifts'." He added: "Those were truly wonderful days. I have often said that I would rather live six months at that time than fifty years of ordinary life."[25]

The early Pentecostal accounts of dedicated followers who struggled to buy food and pay the rent never turned into anything remotely resembling systematic social analysis. All the same, Pentecostal ministers knew where their support came from and removed many of the social barriers that other Protestant churches, increasingly middle class, erected. Women took an active preaching role in the movement. None became more famous than Aimee Semple McPherson, but there were others. Blacks also were welcomed and given active roles. Even in the South, many of the early Pentecostal meetings were interracial. Despite their frequent negative comments about the trade union movement, since strikes and labor organizations were signs of Satan's activities, Pentecostals in the American Southwest reached many of the same people who made Oklahoma, briefly, the center of support for the Socialist party.[26]

Pentecostal premillennialism made early Pentecostals as resistant to uncritical patriotism as the Adventists and Jehovah's witnesses had been. When America entered World War I, many Pentecostals prepared themselves to sit on the sidelines. *The Pentecostal Holiness Advocate* warned: "There is nothing to be gained whichever side wins in this bloodly conflict."[27] Much of the tone was taken from Charles Parham, one of the best known of the early leaders, who referred to patriotism as the "embrace of the Molluck God," and said of the United States: "Ere long Justice with flaming sword will step from behind the pleading form of Mercy to punish a nation which has mingled the blood of thousands of human sacrifices upon the altar of her commercial and imperialistic expansion."[28] Parham foresaw America being torn apart by a great struggle between capital and labor, a "great struggle in which the government, the rich and the churches will be on one side and the masses on the other."[29] Pentecostals did not believe that the world's ills could be eliminated by political action; but their highly dramatic portrayals of social injustice, their attacks upon the rich, were charged all the same with political significance.

Clearly, the fears of Shirley Jackson Case at the time of American participation in World War I were not entirely misplaced. And yet a few years after the completion of the war, the emphasis had changed utterly. Rather than being reminded of the IWW's ideology, the *Christian Century* concluded that postwar premillennialist rhetoric was the answer to the social conservative's prayer: "When the capitalist discovers a brand of religion which has not the slightest interest in 'the social gospel,' but on the contrary intends to pass up all reforms to the Messiah who will return on the clouds of heaven, he has found just the thing he has been looking for."[30] The echoes of class struggle faded in Pentecostal literature, and in their place in the 1920s sounded the steady drumming of only three themes with political implications: anti-evolution, anti-Communism, and anti-Al Smith.

In strictest terms, the Pentecostal churches after World War I were not so much reactionary in their politics as apolitical, far more than the Fundamentalists we shall consider in the next chapter. One can read through the Pentecostal journals that appeared between the early 1930s and the late 1940s, years of a catastrophic depression and war, and get no sense that any events took place in the world other than the wonder working, soul-saving miracles of the Holy Ghost. There were implications in the silence, however. Robert Mapes Anderson, who has done the most important work on the early Pentecostal churches, had little trouble finding evidence to sustain his conclusion that their rhetorical pattern transformed from one of challenge to the social system to a "bulwark" of it.[31] What happened was quite simply the suppression of the egalitarian innovations in early Pentecostal practice. Interracial Pentecostal churches rapidly disappeared in the 1920s. Women continued to become Pentecostal ministers, but Pentecostal literature otherwise adopted a frame of conventional sexual stereotyping that subjected women to men. "Women," according to one Pentecostal source, "are not given undue prominence in the movement . . . and they are virtually silent with respect to doctrinal and governmental questions. . . women may speak in the church without violating their subjection to men."[32] One is tempted to say that obedience in all areas of life became an major concern. Unlike the Jehovah's witnesses, most Pentecostals never again after World War I challenged the government's right to conduct war or draft young men into the army. When Korea and Vietnam occurred, unlike the pattern set in World War I, few Pentecostals requested CO classification.

Liston Pope, in his classic study of millhands and preachers in Gastonia, North Carolina, in the late 1920s, has described a poignant moment in the history of Holiness churches and the

Churches of God.[33] In a drawn out strike against the textile mill operators, made famous because of the intervention of the Communist party, Southern workers engaged in one of the first of many futile efforts to unionize the South. Predictably, they received no support from the "respectable" churches. On the other hand, the ministers of the newer Pentecostal sects, who shared the low economic and social status of the workers, wavered. At the outset of the strike, despite their opposition to action that might divert attention from personal salvation and despite their traditional view that labor unions bore the mark of the beast, some of them supported it. Yet rather than growing in strength, the support quickly collapsed. The attacks on religion by the Communist party were in part responsible. The Pentecostal ministers drew back from political sympathy for the strikers and wound up remaining studiously indifferent to the economic grievances that a struggling union movement tried unsuccessfully to protest. Common class ties that had once drawn socialists and Pentecostals together in Oklahoma had a different result in Gastonia.

After 1920, the premillennial condemnations of patriotism in Pentecostal journals gave way to reproductions of the American flag. Whatever God's ultimate judgment upon the nation, Pentecostal readers were told not to forget "the genius of our system of government. . . We are still a favored nation under God."[34] Long before the Cold War, Aimee Semple McPherson, whose Los Angeles congregation included a large immigrant constituency, called upon "Uncle Sam to arrest the communist alien within our gates." Her identification of the Soviet Union with the Anti-Christ led her to encourage ecumenical feelings that were totally at odds with earlier Pentecostal beliefs. The deportation of radical reds became for her a cause to join Republicans and Democrats, Jews and gentiles, Catholics and Protestants. Temporarily forgetting Armageddon, she stretched out her arms to embrace everyone: "We are made of the same clay, worship the same God, and swear allegiance to the same country."[35]

Our assessments must be tentative. Certainly not all American Pentecostals support Moral Majority or reactionary political positions. Polls may indicate that the more one identifies with a theologically conservative or evangelical Christianity, the more one will express contentment with life in the United States and the less one will support government spending on social welfare, but opinions on such issues are not a reliable guide to voting behavior.[36] Pentecostals are more likely to be Democrats than Republicans. Nonetheless there is little evidence, except in some black churches, to contradict the general view that Pentecostal preaching, like that in the present-day Adventist churches and among the Jehovah's witnesses, encourages a right-of-center political posture. This has been notoriously true in Latin American countries where some of these churches have flourished. We are left once again with trying to understand why that has happened to a popular religious tradition that found its first support among people of low social standing and that taught those people to view the American political order as hopelessly, irreversibly unjust.

The simplest answer is to argue that conservative social principles always dominated teaching in the premillennial churches we have considered, and, from the beginning, effectively contained the tendencies that might have led in the other direction. For example, Pentecostals, recognizing the potential problems that their Antinomian emphasis on personal experience posed to discipline, carefully sought to rein in their wilder impulses with a counter emphasis on obedience. However rigid their distinction between God's people and the world, they did not put God's people above the law. Moreover, as groups that became exceedingly self-conscious about persecution, Adventists, Jehovah's witnesses, and Pentecostals inherited strong prejudices against state activity, particularly when it threatened to standardize religious or ethical practice. They were (and are) inconsistent in applying that prejudice, having made exception for any number of issues ranging from temperance to abortion; but their engrained habit is to view large collective entities suspiciously. That explains why their early rhetoric included attacks on corporations and other powerful private institutions controlled by the rich. It also explains what emerged as their more persistent assaults on trade unions and social welfare agencies of the national government.

Other important aspects of social conservatism were always equally evident. Pentecostal ministers, although acutely aware of their own struggles against economic hardship, taught that God provided for the faithful. They made this the central message of Pentecostal biographies and autobiographies.[37] If a Pentecostal was broke and needed money to pay the rent, the proper recourse was prayer. Everything in Pentecostal culture focused on miracle. The rituals of healing and speaking in tongues made that clear. For someone shaped by that culture, a turn toward the welfare system, a dependency upon government to provide what was necessary to this life, was a denial of faith. From such a perspective, the only real social problem, the only one that a Pentecostal vocabulary could define, was an unsaved soul.

Listing aspects of premillennial teaching that had conservative implications, as important as they are, does not entirely solve the problem. Premillennial ministers were not otherworldly quietists who were unmindful of the worldly consequences of what they did. They were actors and institution builders who had to provide their followers with something that counted for them in this world. Their energies had, in other historical contexts, been harnessed to movements that aimed to restructure society. Why then in America did these movements, which seemingly had made their own ideological way without any significant influence on them from some imagined hegemonic class, which indeed had never made ordinary respectability a goal, become captives of rhetoric that legitimated the standing order?

There remain an indefinite number of partial answers which are all useful. One argument is that premillennial eschatology simply grew less prominent in the collective mentality of the churches we have considered. The lamb-like beast of Revelation, which Adventists had linked to the United States, lost its dragon features and grew more to resemble the tame creature that followed Mary to school. Apocalpytic versions of premillennial prophecy are still vigorously asserted in all of these churches, but they are now incongruously juxtaposed to Cold War images of a righteous America battling a demon USSR. Religious people have come to hold conflicting notions, and the contradictions do not bother them. That is common and should not surprise us.[38]

Another argument explaining the drift toward conservatism links it to upward social mobility. Premillennials have made it into the middle class. Without question, premillennial churches have encouraged the sort of moral behavior that enhanced chances for, and in many cases resulted in, upward social mobility. Adventists boast an uncommonly high percentage of doctors and dentists in their population. Oral Roberts, who began as a Pentecostal, capped his spectacular bid for success in the modern world by becoming a Methodist, building a university and medical center, and thanking Billy Graham for opening his eyes to the merits of "mainstream" Christianity.[39]

To be sure, social mobility as an explanatory factor can get us only so far. Neither Jehovah's witnesses nor black Pentecostals have enjoyed any great degree of upward social mobility, but their churches have done little to foster active protest against social injustice. (Jehovah's witnesses after World War I probably declined in social status, from roughly lower middle-class to roughly working class, but that trend may have reversed itself in recent years.) Most black Pentecostal churches, whatever their role in building black pride, emphasized conservatism and obedience even during the period of the fiercest civil rights struggles, a period during which they enjoyed great growth. According to one sympathetic scholar of black Pentecostal churches in Boston, "the framework of meaning these churches have fashioned . . . provides no handles with which to grasp most (secular) political action. . .in religiously meaningful terms.[40] Nonetheless, with respect to explanations based on social mobility, one must recognize the force of the argument that thirty year mortgages tempt people to separate their timetable of everyday life from their religious eschatology.

In seeking to understand the full range of what has happened, we must remember one important thing that has stayed the same. Premillennial imagery is still used, as it was always used, to feed feelings of protest. What has changed is the way in which premillennial groups have come to define their protest. The symbols they have seized upon to give meaning to their protest have narrowed, and the political implications of those symbols have altered in accord with altered circumstances in the world. Obviously the constant attention given to the rise of godless communist powers has been a key element in changing the premillennial universe of meaning, logically throwing prophetic utterances into a high state of confusion.

The importance assigned to the Russian menace and the international rule of Anti-Christ represented by the League of Nations and its successor, the United Nations, is tied to something else. Jehovah's witnesses and Pentecostals especially have grown deeply uneasy about twentieth-century modernism and their place in the modern world. What George Marsden has written about

Fundamentalists applies to all twentieth-century religious groups that have retained premillennialism as an important theme: "Respectable 'evangelicals' in the 1870s, by the 1920s they had become a laughingstock, ideological strangers in their own land."[41] Adventists, witnesses, and Pentecostals in America had always thought of themselves as outsiders. But in the nineteenth century, that identification was softened by consciousness of something else. They were part of a popular Christian tradition that a religiously centered world took seriously. Their particular positions were sometimes ridiculed, but the controversy they took part in was respectable. Then, after World War I, although they still had a large audience, the intellectual prestige of the controversy lessened considerably. As a result, many premillennials began to spend a lot of time looking for people to hold responsible for the modernist drift that pushed America's most prestigeous centers of learning in the direction of secularism.

Twentieth-century political liberals, in their championing of programs of active state intervention, have always had trouble understanding why people without social and economic advantages remained indifferent to their proposals. They have not understood that they represent the cosmopolitan urban elites who, because of their arrogance, their indifference to religion, and the perceived immorality of their styles of life, have become the enemy against which Protestant premillennialism defined itself. Their "modern" reform was received as just another intrusion that worked more to the self-interests of the professionals who invented it than to the welfare of those toward whom it was directed. Thus, resentment against the expertise of liberal reformers, FDR's Brain Trusts being one of the first targets, became a predictable feature of premillennial rhetoric.[42]

The most visible change in the symbol system of premillennials has already been alluded to. Premillennial preachers in the nineteenth century and consistently up to the end of World War I portrayed patriotism as the religion of Anti-Christ. With the continuing and significant exception of Jehovah's witnesses, patriotic symbols after 1920 assumed a different meaning. Some of the people who continued to express strongly a sense of alienation from what they themselves regarded as the dominant and corrupt cultural forces in America nonetheless asserted their willingness to fight eagerly in the country's wars against communism. At the cost of turning a godless America into the promised land, superpatriotism became the premillennial Christian's way to protest the sophistication of liberal elite groups who no longer found it fashionable to accept the Bible or to wrap themselves in the flag. Those who wore American flags in their lapels recognized the Anti-Christ in those who did not. So disloyal had most Americans become that premillennialists could identify the "remnant" with those who cried when they heard the strains of "America the Beautiful." This oddity was, by the way, not quite a collapse into an acquiescent civil religion, for premillennialists remained forever suspicious of the political and moral drift of the United States.

At least two trends of the twentieth century were not foreseen by the young American moderns who began trying to change the face of their nation at the turn of the century. One was the decline in political participation, despite the institution of various measures aimed at democratizing the political process. The other was the ability of biblically literal-minded Protestants, including those who count the days to Armageddon, to hold their own against scientific and theologically liberal efforts to demythologize the world. These two trends are not causally related, but juxtaposing them does suggest a significant point. Apocalyptic religions have given many average, twentieth-century Americans an arena of significant action in the world. Ordinary people have found in their simple pieties a meaning of self that they have not been willing to abandon merely because liberal politicians have fallen over one another in promising to provide them with lives of greater fulfillment. Whatever their faults they have at least kept their distance from the liberals' faith in the moral progress of Americans.

The defensiveness that is part of the premillennial stance is often neither particularly lovely nor particularly effective. Declension, supposedly a sign that God is about to return to judge the world, can be reduced to a simple-minded message that change of any kind must be resisted. A strategy of opposition risks becoming merely that, a pointless negativism, a vision of our destruction no longer informed by any attractive notion of righteousness. The example of Jim Jones and his Peoples Temple, moreover, reminds us that it can be incredibly destructive. What happened at Guyana was madness, the end of a movement perhaps driven mad by some legitimate protest against the world's moral corruption and vast lostness, but nonetheless an example of how people whose imaginations dwell on the world-denying side of opposition can destroy, not the corrupt world, but themselves.

History offers its students few heroes, and premillennial Christians have to this point failed to become the exceptions. That is too bad, and social progressives are left wondering whether some other path might have been taken, one that might have merged with the theological conservatism of Reinhold Niebuhr who also criticized the Panglossian optimism of the Social Gospelers, but with radical politics in mind. All we caution is that regret should not substitute for historical analysis. It should not lead anyone who seeks to understand the United States to imagine that premillennial Christianity, in the forms we have been describing, was and is made up of demoralized, socially dysfunctional congregations led by demagogues and charlatans. That simply is wrong. If ordinary Americans have not behaved as we might have wanted them to, it may be because they lacked attractive alternatives that were also realistic. Once again we are not looking at the deviations of American religious life, but normal ways in which average Americans invested their lives with meaning. If we are, as E. P. Thompson once urged, to rescue the nameless majorities from the "enormous condescension of posterity," then we must recognize how many ways the average historian knows to be condescending, and in being condescending, how many ways he knows how to fool himself.

CHAPTER SIX

The Protestant Majority as a Lost Generation— A Look at Fundamentalism

In this era of the Insider it may shock us for a moment to remember that the greatest Outsider of all time is Jesus Christ . . . If we follow Him we shall be outsiders too.

Vance Harner, *Moody's Bible Institute Monthly*
(December 1963)

One would scarcely know how to discuss contemporary American Christianity without using the word "Fundamentalism." Unhappily, the familiarity of the term has not clarified what phenomena are properly and fairly encompassed by the label. For example, is Fundamentalism synonymous with present-day evangelicalism, a proselytizing Christianity that places primary emphasis on the experience of being born-again in Christ? Can it be related to Neo-Orthodoxy, another twentieth-century movement that has rejected theological liberalism? Is Pentecostalism, which we examined in the last chapter, a variety of Fundamentalism or do Pentecostalism's roots in the Antinomian wing of the Wesleyan movement distinguish its experience-oriented behavior from more sober, more Calvinist, more Biblically-oriented Fundamentalism? Is twentieth-century Fundamentalism exclusively a Protestant movement or does it bear a sociologically meaningful relationship to movements one can locate within contemporary American Catholicism and American Judaism? What is the relation of Fundamentalism to the Moral Majority or to nonreligious expressions of discontent with cultural modernism and science? Is Fundamentalism best located in the independent ministries of those who have withdrawn from the fellowship of major denominations, or is it a tendency that one can find in all the large American Protestant churches? None of these questions has an absolutely clear answer based on historical or contemporary employments of the term.

No matter how one defines Fundamentalism, one risks joining together in Christian fellowship a lot of people who would prefer to remain apart. Let us try out, for example, the utterly reasonable characterization of Fundamentalism as a militant brand of Protestant conservatism, distinct from Neo-Orthodoxy, that opposes Higher Criticism, Social Gospel liberalism, and Darwinian science, and that endorses literal readings of Biblical texts, premillennialism, and family-oriented moral values. Probably the majority of American Protestants in the twentieth century have endorsed in more or less strict forms most of these patterns of belief. But one searches in vain for an organization that has come close to bringing that majority together. Many theologically conservative Christians who accept the label "evangelical" resist an association with "Fundamentalism" because they associate that word with an aggressive and judgmental separatism. Only a minority of Protestants whose theological position can be described as Fundamentalist belong to bodies affiliated with the American Council of Christian Churches that Carl McIntire founded in 1940 or the more conciliatory National Association of Evangelicals founded two years later.

Other splits illustrate the extent of the problem. Neither the Churches of Christ, nor the Church of the Nazarene, nor the Missouri Synod Lutherans, all militantly anti-liberal in their theology, are very close in their historical origins to each other or to the specifically Fundamentalist movement that was launched by the World's Christian Fundamentals Association in 1919.[1] The Southern Baptist Convention, a predominantly white and certainly Fundamentalist-oriented organization, has not over the years shared much fellowship with the National Baptist Convention, which also leans toward Fundamentalism but which is almost totally black. Although Pentecostalism was a product of many of the same cultural impulses that formed a more narrowly defined Fundamentalist consciousness, its ritualistic focus on subjective experience often made for an uneasy association with the literal-mindedness of many Fundamentalist ministers. The latter defined subjectivity as the disease of the twentieth century and insisted that their old-time religion, the jeers of their critics notwithstanding, made its primary appeal to the head.[2]

With respect to many issues, these differences are important. However if one is to appreciate the degree to which popular American Protestantism has remained immune to various sophisticated theological positions that have circulated in most of America's prestigeous divinity schools for over a century, and even at Princeton for a half-century, one has to live with a fairly loose definition of Fundamentalism and be somewhat indulgent about the lines that common usages of the word blur. At the same time, one is well advised to discuss Fundamentalism with the books of Ernest Sandeen and George Marsden in hand, for these two scholars have furnished the best guides to what one may sensibly include as part of the movement.[3] Since the present discussion tries to stay within the spirit of their findings, we should briefly summarize their conclusions that are important to a definition of the movement.

The simple but important point that both Sandeen and Marsden underline is that twentieth-century Fundamentalism was principally a religious movement, one with historical roots in intellectually respectable Protestant beliefs of the nineteenth century. Sandeen traces direct and continuous connections. Contemporary Fundamentalism, he argues, grew out of a merger of Dispensational Premillennialism and Princeton Theology, two theologically innovative movements of the nineteenth century, which for somewhat different reasons eschewed any sort of Biblical hermeneutics that had been influenced either by Inner Light doctrines or by the Higher Criticism. Both insisted that the Bible was inerrant in its every reference, statistic, and quotation.

As a corrective to Sandeen, Marsden has described a less continuous historical passage from the nineteenth to the twentieth century. Although contemporary Fundamentalists uniformly reject the view that the world is becoming more moral, Marsden does not believe that premillennialism was nearly as important in shaping the consciousness of modern Fundamentalism as Sandeen does. According to Marsden, Fundamentalism grew from a more general opposition to modernist theology. That opposition was often tied to beliefs in scriptural inerrancy and Dispensational Premillennialism, but it also reached beyond the specific movements stressed by Sandeen. For Marsden, twentieth-century Fundamentalism, born in the period of World War I, was essentially something new on the map of American Christianity. Its tone was far more defensive than that of earlier theological conservatives. No longer able to carry off their ruffled feelings to such orthodox and respectable places as Yale, Princeton, or Andover, twentieth-century theological conservatives had to take refuge in Bob Jones University and academically marginal Bible institutes.

A choice between Sandeen and Marsden is not necessary. Both stress the importance of religious issues in shaping the Fundamentalist mentality, and the two theological influences which Sandeen emphasized were in fact more important than any others. As Marsden recognizes, if one restricts one's definition of twentieth-century Fundamentalism to the mentality of those ministers who in the 1920s broke away from the major Calvinist denominations, Sandeen's analysis works extremely well. The advantage of Marsden's narrative, although it underestimates the degree to which Princeton Theology and Dispensational Premillennialism in the nineteenth century were also uneasy reactions to modernism, is that it allows one more easily to spot the Fundamentalist influence not merely among the militant twentieth-century "exclusivists" who formed independent churches, but also among many people who remained affiliated with large Protestant denominations.

These pages will waver a bit between discussing Fundamentalism at times with reference to its sectarian extremes and at other times with reference to its nonseparatist manifestations that usually carry in current disputes the less contentious labels "evangelical" or "conservative." The justification for this joint consideration is that sectarian and denominational Fundamentalisms are part of the same historical story. In the era around World War I, Fundamentalism arose as a self-conscious force within already existing Protestant denominations, originally and especially the Baptist and Presbyterian. And even in the cases where it broke with those denominations, it spoke with a voice that many of those who stayed in their old churches continued to appreciate. Jerry Falwell may not be part of the Southern Baptist fold, but a good number of those who are sympathetic to his message are. The phrase "theological conservatives," when here applied to twentieth-century Protestants, is a synonym for Fundamentalism. The reader will understand that it is not meant to include the

Neo-Orthodoxy of Reinhold Niebuhr, which Fundamentalists regard as hopelessly modernist.

The political implications of Fundamentalism are largely continuous with the story we told in the last chapter. Twentieth-century Fundamentalists gravitated toward a social outlook that distinguished them from many nineteenth-century ministers who closely resembled them in theological terms. In the nineteenth century, theologically conservative Protestants, the strict Calvinists among the Presbyterians, the Baptists, and the Congregationalists, were less likely than liberal or Arminian evangelicals to ally themselves with legislative proposals to promote moral reform. They were also less likely to become ensnared in messianic visions of America as a redeemer nation. It was the theological party leaning toward Unitarianism which in Massachusetts and Connecticut fought to preserve the church establishment. The separatist-minded Calvinist Baptists provided the support for Jefferson's Deistically inspired wish to maintain strict boundaries between church and state.

Compared to what has happened in the twentieth century, the earlier sectional patterns look all wrong. Southern ministers offered the stiffest resistance to what we might call the nineteenth-century Moral Majority. Southern hostility to the moral stance of the abolitionists, who claimed Northern evangelical support, was in good measure responsible for that. In Dixie, abolitionism turned ministers who interested themselves in any kind of politics into "clerical agitators" who prostituted "the high and holy office of the Gospel ministry."[4] Abolitionism does not tell the whole story, however. When the largest Protestant denominations broke apart in the decade preceding the Civil War, the offended Southerners expressed themselves in a manner consistent with an earlier opposition to New England evangelicals. The latter had not been certain whether independent churches could promote enough Christian virtue to preserve the nation, and had therefore regarded legislation a proper means to achieve moral aims. If Southern ministers predictably acted with hostility toward legislative abolitionism, they also, despite their strong disapproval of drunkenness and sabbath desecration, backed away from temperance and Sabbatarian legislation. They were not the ones who wanted to have Christ's name written into the Constitution. In the antebellum South, the religious struggle to enhance moral behavior did not become a political crusade.

Throughout the nineteenth century one can locate strong resistance among Southern evangelicals to moral legislation. One militant on the subject was David Lipscomb. Originally part of the Disciples movement founded by Alexander Campbell, he sharply distinguished his stance from Campbell's when the latter was swept away by grandiose visions of Anglo-Saxon destiny.[5] In a split that foreshadowed the eventual formal separation of the liberal, mostly Northern Disciples of Christ, from the conservative, mostly Southern Churches of Christ, Lipscomb maintained that Christians ought not to "use the civil power to enforce morality, righteousness, or religion." When his Northern brethren began to promote the Social Gospel and America's manifest destiny in the world ("the Government of the United States is the richest gift of Protestantism to the world"), Lipscomb and his Southern followers argued that Christians should pay their taxes and obey the laws but otherwise have nothing to do with worldly governments.[6] The most interesting political result of Southern antipathy to liberally inspired moral legislation was the unlikely alliance of conservative Protestants, who were deeply hostile to Catholicism, and Roman Catholic voters. Such was one miracle of the Democratic party which even now has not quite been undone.

We forget all of this because, after 1900, the Southern evangelical opposition to moral legislation broke down, particularly in the matter of temperance. The temptation to take public action to mark America as a Christian nation was too strong, especially since Yankees seemed to be backing away from the cause. We also forget that theological conservatism in the nineteenth century, even when it was not insisting on a rigid form of church-state separation, did not invariably support political conservatism as has seemed so remarkably the case with much of twentieth-century Fundamentalism. The *New York Times*, in trying to explain what its editors thought was a sudden rush of evangelical Christians to endorse conservative politicians in the late 1970s, quoted Harold O. J. Brown's view that "evangelicals suddenly found themselves standing almost alone on the front line of socio-political conflict, defending what had once automatically been assumed to be general American values."[7] That won't quite do as explanation. The perception of aloneness among evangelical Protestants, whether Northern or Southern, goes back well into the past. The late nineteenth-century independent ministers who most directly influenced the later Fundamentalist ministers, Dwight Moody, Arthur T. Pierson, and James Brookes, for example, rarely expressed strong confidence that the country and its government were safely Christian. According to them, it was a "lonely time to believers," and the children of God were like "a few scattered sheep in the wilderness."[8]

Nineteenth-century theological conservatives believed no less strongly than their twentieth-century counterparts that American values were in jeopardy. They also believed in the paramount importance of soul-saving. But they responded to social questions with a mild sort of social progressivism that has continued to be influential in British evangelical circles.[9] The effect of their premillennial theology on their social outlook was similar to what we saw in our discussion of Adventists, Jehovah's witnesses, and Pentecostals. They deplored excessive patriotism. In the North, conservative evangelicals criticized slavery. After the Civil War they spoke out against unjust treatment of American Indians. After the war with Spain, they protested imperialism. Their Bible ministries often reached the poor, and their criticisms of great wealth led to occasional support of the trade union movement. Even Billy Sunday, who is sometimes cited as the prototype of twentieth-century Fundamentalist evangelicals who tied their personal fortunes to their support of American capitalism, preached a sort of social populism that vanished only in Sunday's post-World War I career.[10]

We hesitate to linger too long over a phenomenon we have already tried to analyze, but the changed political meaning of conservative Protestant theology does invite a discussion slightly different from the one of the last chapter. The change is most dramatically evident at the extremes of the twentieth-century Fundamentalist movement. One writer's phrase, "Apostles of Discord," to characterize such men as Carl McIntire, Gerald Winrod, and Billy James Hargis, is not unfair to the subjects.[11] These men stridently denounced every trend that could remotely be construed as theologically or politically liberal. They equated their religious behavior with American patriotism. During the 1930s the ugliness of their attacks arguably slipped into fascism. In his savage journal, *The Defender*, Winrod denied an association with Fascism because he had identified Mussolini with the Anti-Christ when American liberals were still admiring Italian trains that ran on time. Nonetheless, until the Japanese raid on Pearl Harbor, Winrod wrote appreciatively of Hitler's attacks on world Jewry and Russian Bolshevism. Franklin Roosevelt's perceived animosity toward the German leader was only one of Winrod's excuses to attack the New Deal and the welfare state. From the early 1930s until the present, most of the separatist wing of Fundamentalism has explicitly and outspokenly supported the ultra right in American politics.[12]

No movement should be judged by its extremes. The alleged connection between contemporary Protestant Fundamentalism, broadly considered, and political conservatism is by no means made of steel. Theologically conservative Christians, even if they report conservative social views, do often vote for politically liberal candidates. But this much seems beyond doubt. A theological position that was once resistant to the moral blandishments of political activists is currently one constituency, though not the largest, of today's politically oriented "Moral Majority." Fundamentalist leaders and laypeople, whether separated from or joined to large Protestant denominations, have contributed money and labor to defeat legislation providing public support of abortions and sex counseling, equal rights for women and homosexuals, and day-care centers for working mothers. They have rarely been in the forefront of the movement for racial equality; they have consistently been hostile to trade unionism; and they have adopted virtually the whole range of conservative rhetoric about welfare cheats, coddled criminals, and the threat of global communism. Nowhere is the shift in the theologically conservative position more obvious than in the change from a stand which in the nineteenth century often came very close to pacifism to one that endorses whatever needs America's military planners express.

Fundamentalists can claim with a measure of truth that their political activities have been responses to Social Gospel activism. That is, they have not tried to enact moral legislation so much as to defeat moral legislation proposed by others. Anyone who has traveled very much in present-day Southern Baptist culture knows that Southern Baptists are not a particularly politically minded people and that the Southern Baptist minister who says more than a phrase or two about politics in his sermons is rare. The reputation for conservatism that the black National Baptist Convention gained was based not on its active opposition to civil rights legislation, but on its indifference. In 1963, just after the assassination of John Kennedy, the publication of the Moody Bible Institute polled its readers to name the top news stories of the year. The results serve as an important reminder that Fundamentalists do not assign a priority to politics in anywhere near the degree that their critics imagine. In first place was the prayer and Bible reading controversy in the schools followed, in order, by changes in the Catholic church, the racial issue, Billy Graham's Southern California crusade, and the charismatic revival.[13]

In speaking, then, of present-day Fundamentalism as politically conservative, we are not necessarily referring to explicit efforts of theologically conservative Christian leaders to rally support for conservative politicians or lobbying groups. When Fundamentalist rallies have collectively demanded laws to end abortion, individual Fundamentalists have regarded their support, not as improper church encouragement of moral legislation, but as a defensive reaction against the measures of liberals who are held responsible for turning the morality of abortion into a political question. The plea is genuine as far as it goes. But it cannot go far simply because the always difficult task of separating moral issues, which Protestant churches believe they must address, from political issues has in the twentieth century become absolutely impossible. Social planners in government have tried even harder than Fundamentalist spokesmen to pretend otherwise, but the alleged separation of politics and morality has not even served a useful fiction. In ignoring that, Fundamentalists have, along with everyone else, driven themselves into corners of self-deception and outright hypocrisy.

J. Franklyn Norris provides an example. He is one of the extreme cases, but he poses the problem we are trying to characterize. During his long career, which stretched from the early twentieth century until his death in 1952, Norris consistently denied that he took political stands. When he, for example, denounced church leaders who said that the government ought to take over the automobile plants in Detroit, Norris argued that his criticism did not mean that the government ought not to take over the plants. He merely meant that ministers had no business addressing the issue.[14] The disclaimer was at best naive. Norris's many prior caustic remarks about government regulation rendered his criticisms unmistakably political. Among other things, Norris was minister to the largest church in Detroit, and he regularly accepted favors from the car manufacturers. He did not miss many opportunities to heap public praise on Henry Ford and the Chrysler Corporation. In contrast, he said that Walter Reuther was "an excellent example of millions of others of foreign lineage who have grown up in America without understanding the capitalistic system."[15] Although Norris frequently attacked individual men who possessed power and wealth, not one line in all of his massive public and private writing gainsays the singular appropriateness of his having been the religious tutor of John Birch. When the Fort Worth Chamber of Commerce appointed Norris an ambassador of good will on one of his world tours, it knew what it was doing.

This does not mean that the political involvement of Fundamentalists was cheerfully chosen. Their view of the twentieth century, when stripped of its hysterical assertions of conspiracy, provides a not unreasonable account of what actually happened. American government began to grow in unprecedented ways shortly after 1900. From that day to the present, a great deal of legislation was passed, which though often defended in the language of a value-neutral social science, bristled with moral implications. It did not take religious Fundamentalists long to conclude that they were being caught in a trap. They were losing control of their lives, and the lives of their children, to a new class of experts who denied the force of moral authority as a guide to pragmatic social planning but who in fact were engineering a revolution in the moral behavior of the country. With a few more turns of the screw, Christopher Lasch and Jerry Falwell might jump into one another's arms.[16] Ronald Reagan, although a divorced man, has been successful with evangelical audiences not only because of his stands on morality, but also because of a personal presence that is completely untouched by the signs that indelibly mark the professional expert in contemporary America.

This sort of analysis perhaps helps to make clear why the Scopes-Darwin trial in 1925 was such an important event in shaping contemporary Fundamentalist consciousness. At least until recently, it was the last occasion when a man with a long history of involvement in populist-progressive politics spoke, without any sense of contradiction, in behalf of Biblical literalism. The bruising that William Jennings Bryan received from scientific experts as a result of the role that he played in Dayton, Tennessee, goes a long way toward explaining the silences that followed.

Since the enormous literature about the Scopes trial contains some misleading stereotypes about Fundamentalism, we need to preface our discussion with a reminder. Fundamentalism was not in its origins or in its development confined to the South and to rural people who were "untouched by the thrilling cosmopolitan appeals which daily challenge their urban neighbors."[17] In the 1920s Fundamentalism enjoyed its greatest numerical strength, both in leadership and following, in the Middle Atlantic and East North-Central states.[18] The Protestants who grew most alarmed about evolutionary theory were not Southern ministers, who after all rarely encountered a real Darwinist, but relatively sophisticated Northerners. William Bell Riley was pastor of a Baptist church in Minneapolis; John Roach Straton preached to a Baptist congregation in New York City, and J. Gresham Machen was a professor at the Princeton Theological Seminary. The conflict at Dayton did enhance, both among Fundamentalists and their opponents, the impression of a vast cultural split between two sorts of Americans. But that split followed geographical lines or even urban-rural lines only in the imagination of H. L. Mencken.

Ostensibly, the Scopes trial was about the constitutional protections afforded by the First Amendment. In an acknowledged violation of a Tennessee statute that forbade the teaching of evolutionary theory in public schools, John Scopes claimed to be exercising his rights of free speech. The state of Tennessee disagreed and took him to court. The young and aggressive leaders of the newly formed American Civil Liberties Union agreed with Scopes, having encouraged his act of defiance in the first place, and provided a legal team headed by Clarence Darrow to defend him. Since the constitutional issue was never resolved by an appellate court and never argued in the trial court, most observers regarded the Scopes trial as a confrontation between the claims of modern scientific theories and the claims of Fundamentalist religion. That was certainly what provided the drama in Darrow's famous cross-examination of Bryan concerning purported inconsistencies in the Book of Genesis.

In legal terms, the prosecution won its case at Dayton. The jury found Scopes guilty. Tennessee's appellate court ordered a retrial, but it never took place. As a result, the Tennessee statute remained in force, as did similar statutes in a number of other states. The battle, however, was not merely over legalisms. The ridicule heaped upon the Fundamentalist position sent clear signals to theological conservatives that they operated in a different intellectual universe from the one their fathers had known in the nineteenth century. They were left to nurture an enormous grievance that they had been willfully misunderstood by Darrow who had freely used the word "bigot" in the courtroom. The Fundamentalists did not wish to be understood as anti-scientific, and they eventually merged with a party of Creationists who zealously collected scientific testimony to combat Darwin. In their minds, the scientific evidence for Darwinian theory was far more flawed with contradictions than anything one could uncover in Genesis. The attitude they wanted to combat was not atheism but one that regarded religion as irrelevant. To them, Darrow seemed to be arguing that only things done in the name of science mattered.

Bryan's role in the affair was sad. His whole career had spanned a period of intellectual changes that were forever undermining his credibility. His opponents refused to acknowledge that he had anything to do with the modern world. Bryan willingly bore the charge of anachronism because, by his view of things, he was fighting for common people. He sought to raise them above the indignities that they suffered and to protect their right to preserve ways of life that they believed were threatened. His life's mission was as clear at Dayton as it had been in the earlier crusades for the Populist party and free silver. Darrow claimed that the proponents of Tennessee's anti-evolution law wished to block the truth-fulfilling mission of unprejudiced scientific endeavors. Bryan in effect questioned whether modern science was a neutral activity. If science meant Darwinian "theory," theory being a word that Fundamentalists used to distinguish Darwinism from a science of indisputable facts, then science threatened to destroy not only providential Christian religion but also a society that could distinguish moral from immoral behavior. Darwin tumbled the rock of ages that was supposed never to change and led people out into the starless night of a world without design.

Bryan had his point. Anyone who thinks that he monopolized the forces of idiocy that exploded in Dayton should read the contradictory scientific testimony that the defense tried unsuccessfully to introduce as evidence. If the exercise is not sufficiently sobering, a look at the admiring preface written by Henry Fairchild Osborn for Madison Grant's *The Passing of a Great Race* might be. Osborn was perhaps America's most distinguished paleontologist in the 1920s. He predictably attacked Bryan. Yet he also lent his reputation to the most famous racist tract of the early twentieth century. The opinion surveys that Bryan liked to cite, those which demonstrated a correlation between a college education and religious skepticism and which showed a sharp decline of religious belief among biologists, were unsystematic. But who would doubt the general trends that they pointed to? The widespread acceptance of Darwinian evolutionary theory changed the way that people reacted to a whole range of seemingly unrelated issues.

The question of whether science is or is not neutral is probably a badly phrased question that can generate only polemics. What is indisputably true, and Bryan knew it, is that the benefits of science, like the benefits of anything else, cost something. People have the right to resist the slogans of professional scientists and to ask whether the costs are worth paying. In recent years, liberal theologians have felt twinges of regret that in the year when Bryan fumbled his effort to find viable Biblical support for his opposition to Darwin, and for a long time thereafter, they cheerfully fell over one another in insisting that scientific advances must necessarily serve human interests.[19]

The problem with Bryan's last Populist crusade was that it required him to close his mind and close it tightly. Unfortunately for him, he confronted a true dilemma and he lacked the intellectual resources to escape from it. As a result, his defense of religion turned into a denying and a defying anti-intellectualism that Fundamentalism's main architects, skilled debaters who welcomed public confrontations with their critics, had wanted to avoid. Bryan solved the problem for himself by dying, not even one week after the Scopes trial. Other Fundamentalists were left to live with that problem as well as the problem of a political involvement that was both Populist and reactionary. The controversy over Scopes seduced Fundamentalists into pinning their hopes on science, hopes that vainly tried to make creationism as respectable a scientific theory as Darwinism. It also rallied them around support for an exercise of state power that sought to defend the rights of common folk by keeping them ignorant. Possibly this was history's revenge on them for the anti-Catholicism that had helped bring the troublesome public school system into being in the first place.

The attitudes taken at the Scopes trial are part of the bits of evidence to suggest that in the period around World War I, theologically conservative Protestants began to step self-consciously into outsider roles. They turned themselves into America's other Lost Generation. The break between nineteenth-and twentieth-century rhetoric was not complete. Nineteenth-century ministers often spoke in the way that Timothy Smith has found typical of twentieth-century Fundamentalists—that is, as a "beleaguered minority fighting with their backs to the wall."[20] But the position never became obligatory. Dwight Moody, who was the most famous and successful of the late nineteenth-century Protestant evangelicals who believed in Biblical inerrancy, said almost nothing indicative of status anxiety. Moody encountered criticism in his work and ruefully noted that his theologically sound Christianity had become a minority position in America. For all that, he never much exploited outsider rhetoric because he did not find it particularly necessary or useful.[21]

Other theologically conservative Protestants in the nineteenth century more frequently alluded to persecution and ridicule, but the nineteenth century does not furnish any close parallels to what one can find among separatist-minded Fundamentalists in the twentieth century. We come back to J. Franklyn Norris as a forceful example of what happened at the extremes. Norris's willful efforts to appear outrageous (in this case there seems little question about the consciousness of the intent) was remarkable if only because he was a successful preacher from the beginning of his career. Born in Dadeville, Alabama, he moved in 1888 to Texas and took degrees at Baylor, in Waco, Texas, and at the Southern Baptist Seminary in Louisville, Kentucky. From 1905 to 1908 he was the pastor at the McKinney Baptist Church in Dallas and then for the rest of his life the pastor of the First Baptist Church in Forth Worth. Theological modernism was scarcely a grand problem among Texas Baptists, but Norris did not let that stand in the way of his crusade against it. He belligerently picked quarrels with some of the leading figures in the Texas Baptist General Convention, in particular, Samuel P. Brooks, J. M. Dawson, and George W. Truett. In 1919, Norris had not only become a major figure in the World's Christian Fundamentals Association, but his Fort Worth church had the largest membership of any Protestant congregation in the United States.[22]

As the success mounted, so did his talents for stirring turmoil and opposition. We mention only the highlights. In 1912 he was very nearly imprisoned on charges of having set fire to his own church building. His critics said, perhaps correctly, that he had written most of the letters attacking him that he read from his pulpit. A bitter schism early in his ministry cost his church 1000 members. In 1924 he was excluded from the Baptist General Convention of Texas. In 1926, a man appeared in his church parlor who was outraged by Norris's pulpit attack on the mayor of Fort Worth. Norris shot and killed him. Acquitted by a jury in Austin of homicide, Norris returned to a cheering audience of 8000 followers in Fort Worth. During the 1930s, when Norris's brand of religious conservatism was supposedly on the decline, he continued to build his empire. In 1935, without relinquishing his position in Fort Worth, he took over the Temple Baptist Church in Detroit and made it into the second largest church in America. In the last decade of his life, he was able to seek favors from Texas politicians in Washington (Lyndon Johnson and Tom Connally), have an audience with the Pope (the Anti-Christ being partially forgiven because of his strong anti-communism), and visit the first president of Israel (the state of Israel being warmly endorsed as a sign of the approaching millennium). And yet he continued until he drew his last breath to break bitterly with those who should have been his closest supporters.[23]

Many of Norris's battles against "all the ecclesiastical powers from the regions below" seemed aimless and confused, but many related to strategies that should by now be familiar. As often as Norris emphasized his lonely martyrdom, he bragged about his power and influence. It is difficult to say whether over the years he exaggerated more his importance or his unimportance.[24] Shortly after his exclusion from the Baptist General Convention in 1924, Norris wrote to a friend saying: "There are a few that think I am dying to get in, that I need to get in. . . My work has prospered more by my being 'out,' more people have turned in sympathy toward my work than if I were in."[25] This sort of appeal clearly worked among the independent Baptists to whom Norris preached, and among Carl McIntire's followers who were told constantly that they "no longer counted" in American life. More significantly, the appeal struck a responsive chord among conservative, evangelical Protestants who remained affiliated with large and long-established denominations.

The outsider consciousness that developed among average American Protestants was a defensive reaction to intellectual insecurity. In America's best-known centers of learning, they were losing a battle of prestige. That fact, however, did not turn Fundamentalism into a disappearing aspect of American Protestantism. It did not lose its force after the Scopes trial. The alleged influence of theological modernism in the twentieth century has been vastly overrated, and the strength of the basic theological positions associated with Fundamentalism has not oscillated nearly so wildly as some accounts of twentieth-century religion have suggested. If Fundamentalists have suffered from hurt feelings in twentieth-century America, they have also had available to them a large cushion of public support on which to rest their bruised egos. Whatever aspects of minority consciousness they assumed and whatever divisions they maintained among themselves, their point of view represented the majority of American Protestants who held strong religious commitments. We need to understand why that fact is vigorously suppressed in some quarters and simply forgotten in others.

The Fundamentalist movement organized itself out of a determination to draw some lines between true Christianity and theological modernism.[26] Especially during the 1920s Fundamentalists began campaigns to force national church bodies to adopt confessions of faith. The aim was to separate orthodox ministers from rank heretics. For the most part, it was a knowledge of their strength, not feelings of powerlessness, that prompted the "exclusivists" in their course of action. They judged correctly that modernist views advocated by such men as Harry Emerson Fosdick, Shirley Jackson Case, or Shailer Mathews, despite the publicity accorded to them, had touched only a minority of American Protestants. The battle they had to fight was not with modernists, who lacked the numerical strength to force the major denominations toward their own confessional views, but with other theological conservatives who were not necessarily convinced that a purge of liberals was either desirable or necessary. The exclusivists pushed the issue because the generally well-educated and articulate modernists were overrepresented in leadership roles in national Protestant organizations, most particularly in the Federal Council of Churches which had been formed in 1908. The most bitter struggles over exclusion in the 1920s were fought among Northern Presbyterians and Northern Baptists who produced some of America's best known modernist ministers.[27]

In most of these struggles, save for isolated victories such as Fosdick's resignation from his Presbyterian pulpit, the exclusivists lost. But we must remember what was being contested. By the end of the 1920s, modernists had narrowly but decisively won their right to exist in several major Protestant denominations, and their voice in those denominations remained influential. Important as that was, modernists did not thereby sharply increase their influence beyond what it was. William Bell Riley, one of the leaders of the early Fundamentalist movement, remained in the Northern Baptist Convention until the last year of his life; and his views remained as representative of the ordinary layperson as those of modernists. Fundamentalist views retained a hold on one wing of the Lutheran Church. And in some important American denominations, modernism was not a strong enough force even to become an important issue in the 1920s.

Despite the continuing appeal of their theological perspective the most disgruntled exclusivists decided to embark on an independent course. By way of justifying their action, they declared that they could not remain in denominations "controlled" by modernists or liberals. The thirties witnessed the creation of such separatist Fundamentalist groups as the General Association of Regular Baptists, J. Gresham Machen's Orthodox Presbyterian Church of America, and Carl McIntire's Bible Presbyterian Church. These men schooled their followers as well as less militant Protestant conservatives to think of themselves as "outside the gate." In effect they abandoned the role of the insider to the liberals who were more than willing to seize it.[28] By any reckoning of numbers, Fosdick should have reacted to his treatment from conservatives by casting himself as the outsider. However, he specifically rejected the martyr's role and never conceded victory to his opponents. "In this bitter controversy," he said, "I was all the time supported by powerful backing from those by whom one would most choose to be backed."[29] He happily became the pastor of New York City's Riverside Church, drawing on the same inexhaustible Rockefeller wealth that was responsible for the modernist faculty at the University of Chicago Divinity School.

The roles became complicated. Although the ones assumed by theological conservatives and liberals in this period bore a relation to their respective intellectual prestige, they nonetheless distorted what was happening to American Protestantism. According to many accounts, Fundamentalism settled at the fringes of American religion in the thirties, briefly reappeared in the popular religion of the intellectually feckless fifties, and then inexplicably became a major force in the 1970s under the more respectable label of evangelicalism. Even a minimal respect for historical continuity suggests a cautious reaction to the notion that theologically conservatives have only recently begun to recover the following they supposedly lost during the battles of the 1920s. No one seems to doubt the current levels of strength. A Gallup survey conducted in 1982 reported that 35 percent of all adult Americans, not just church members or Protestants, claimed to have been born again in Christ; 45 percent had encouraged someone else to accept Jesus Christ; and 37 percent subscribed to the view that "the Bible is the actual word of God and is to be taken literally, word for word." Seventeen percent of the Gallup respondents, a figure that would project to about 27 million adults, subscribed to all three views; and that figure climbed to 55 percent among those who also said that religion was very important to their lives.[30]

In general the Gallup figures were consistent with other estimates that have numbered present evangelical and/or Fundamentalist strength at between 27,000,000 and 40,000,000.[31] The differences in the figures stem mainly from different definitions. If one defines Fundamentalism by the view that causes the most dismay among liberals, the acceptance of Bible literalism, then modernism has a long way to go before it can claim a decisive victory. Although the 1982 figure was down from the 65 percent of adult Americans who had in 1962 identified themselves as Biblical literalists, 47 percent of all Protestants fell into that category, and 75 percent of those who described themselves as having a "very high spiritual commitment." In a poll conducted in 1961, 74 percent of American clergymen professed to hold Fundamentalist or conservative views, while a scant 12 percent claimed liberal views and an only slightly less scant 14 percent owned the label Neo-Orthodox. Such a balance in the pulpits may explain why 44 percent of participants in a 1982 poll accepted the statement that "God created man pretty much in his present form at one time within the last 10,000 years"; whereas only 9 percent accepted the view that "man has developed over millions of years from less advanced forms of life. God had no part in this process."[32]

The *New York Times* in 1982 had no trouble finding Protestant clergy who were shocked at the persistence of anti-Darwinist views, a shock no doubt resulting from a willful forgetfulness about the long-standing resistance of many Americans to evolutionary theory.[33] That resistance, contrary to the usual interpretation, probably grew even stronger after the Scopes trial. After all, the controversy of the 1920s helped popularize the view that one had to choose between Darwin and religion. Secularist theorists grievously misjudged how most American Protestants had settled the choice.

The failure of Fundamentalist leaders to hold their forces together after the 1920s helped create the perception that American Protestantism was modernizing itself faster than it actually was. Theological issues should have united Fundamentalists, but it turned out that they had other sorts of identification to keep separate. The World's Christian Fundamentals Association was an empty fellowship by the end of the 1920s. Conservative Protestants thereafter were never able to devise a national organization that reflected their total numbers. Fundamentalists lived apart, as much in contention with one another as with theological liberals. They maintained their strength in local congregations, in an uncountable number of independent churches, rapidly expanding Bible institutes, and in the ministries of radio and television preachers. But, for many reasons, it was easy to overlook the collective force of these things. Only after World War II, when Billy Graham came along and gathered enormous audiences in football stadiums and large indoor auditoriums, did theological moderns begin to suspect that the outcome of the 1920s was not quite what they had thought.[34]

Twentieth-century Fundamentalism, therefore, provides us with the most puzzling case we have yet seen of how to assess

what is typical religious experience in America. By most objective
criteria, the Fundamentalist viewpoint, defined as conservative
Protestant theology, should have defined a party of religious insiders. Modernization has taken a toll in many important parts of
American culture, but it has not destroyed the notion in other
equally important parts that the Bible means what it says. Fundamentalists, for the most part, suffered from none of the disabilities
that initially prompted an outsider consciousness among other
religious groups. They were mostly white; they were mostly middle class; they were mostly native-born; and they were all, let us
not forget, Protestant. Their faith was a traditional one. Yet
somehow in accounts of American culture, they became the Mormons of the twentieth century. Religious historians admitted that
they were around if you bothered to look; but since they were
certain that secularization or theological modernism was the trend
of the twentieth century, they could not really say why. To reas-
sure themselves, they took the most separatist-minded Fundamentalists at their word and assumed that after the mid–1920s Fundamentalism was a disappearing impulse.

In this particular saga of American religious life, the cultivation
of a consciousness of beleagueredness may have been a needless
mistake. One's judgment about this depends in part on what one
imagines the more militant Fundamentalists were after. Calling
themselves a powerless minority and splitting their forces certainly diluted the influence that they might otherwise have had on
the nation's churches, and theological influence was one thing
they unquestionably wanted. Had the Fundamentalists avoided
ruinous contention among themselves, had they maintained the
World's Christian Fundamentals Association whose viability they
themselves destroyed, they had the numbers to make their way in
the twentieth century as perfectly respectable people who set the
tone for most Protestant churches. Attacking Darwin no doubt
made one a laughing stock in many Ivy League dining halls, but
there were perhaps ways of turning the tables without making so
much out of that fact.

The realization that respectability was a role that theologically
conservative Christians might have chosen to play in the twentieth century has recently begun to influence one sizable group of
them. Karl F. H. Henry's journal *Christianity Today* has for many
years urged Bible-believing Protestants not to define themselves

by a belligerent negativeness.[35] One group of Protestant conservatives, as we have noted, much prefers the label "evangelical" to that of Fundamentalist because they wish to free themselves from the defensive posture that they think has for too long governed the reactions of conservative Protestants. The first step toward respectability was easy. They merely had to state the previously unthinkable thought that liberalism had not won after all. According to one of the "new evangelicals," "it now seems indisputable that evangelicalism is beginning to assume a dominance on the American religious scene that it has not had previously in this century."[36] According to another, "it is conceivable that evangelicalism soon may become if it is not already the dominant religious orientation in Protestant America."[37] The facts had always been on the side of evangelical dominance, but both authors recognized the importance of what we have discussed elsewhere. The perception of facts was the thing that mattered. Calling attention to evangelical numerical dominance was more than a casual reporting of statistics. It was an effort to alter long established attitudes and the behavior that went along with them.

To some of the young evangelicals of the 1960s and 1970s, the aspect of Fundamentalist behavior that most needed altering was political behavior. A consciousness of their respectability, it was hoped, would liberate theologically conservative Protestants from their uncritical suspicion of every aspect of modern culture including the social programs of political liberals. The populist rhetoric that had been turned in self-defeating ways on political liberalism might thereby find more appropriate targets in the circles of America's power elites.

The young evangelicals can take heart in several recent developments. Carl McIntire was ousted from his own organization because of his attacks on efforts to promote racial equality. In 1983 the black National Baptist Convention retired their longtime president, the Reverend Joseph Jackson, who had quarreled with Martin Luther King, defended the Vietnam War, and endorsed welfare cuts; his replacement, the Reverend T. J. Jamison joined his executive board in endorsing a nuclear freeze and pledged to make the denomination more socially active. Billy Graham has spoken against the nuclear arms race. The leaders of the Fundamentalist Fuller Seminary in Pasadena, one of America's largest theological seminaries, have rejected the Moral Majority stands of Jerry Falwell. Jimmy Carter, John Anderson, Mark Hatfield, and Jesse Jackson have made clear that a conservative Christian background, tied to a strong concern about morality, does not necessarily yield right-wing politics. The polling statistics which suggest that strict Protestant evangelicals are more likely to be right-of-center in their political views than other Protestants seem to reflect the group's general contentment with their lives rather than a rigid ideological conservatism. In the 1980 election, they voted in the majority for Carter rather than for Reagan and for Democrats rather than Republicans.[38] The black element in the evangelical movement accounted for some of this, but apparently not all of it.

In view of the past, one must remain a bit skeptical about whether the Fundamentalist and evangelical mood will become more politically liberal if Fundamentalists and evangelicals accept the mood of respectability being tailored for them in some quarters. Martin Marty, no doubt recalling what H. Richard Niebuhr said about the worldly accommodation signified by a shift from a sectarian to a church mentality, has suggested that if a theologically conservative evangelicalism really did turn out to be *the* Protestant mainstream, it would "increasingly take on the burdens of typicality and of cultural predominance."[39] One of the young evangelicals, David Moberg, warned:[40]

> As its future becomes more promising in terms of numerical strength and ecclesiastical recognition, evangelicalism stands even more exposed to the danger of becoming conformed to sinful worldly aspects of the social system. Already prone to capitulating to the civil religion, to giving an uncritical blessing to political and industrial power structures, to sanctifying the social and cultural system, and to blessing materialism, which is the contemporary form the worship of mammon against which Jesus so clearly spoke, evangelicals, if impressed by their own new status, will become even more susceptible to the temptation to bow their knees before the economic and political Baals of modern society.

Moberg may have been pondering what another evangelical, Senator Mark Hatfield, told a group at a Congressional prayer breakfast. He said that "the wealthy and powerful" should not forget that those who followed Christ "will more often find themselves not only with comfortable majorities, but with miserable minorities."[41] Both Moberg and Hatfield knew, according to all available evidence, that the habit of sitting with the wealthy and powerful caused exactly that form of forgetfulness. The most recent chartings of how respectability has affected the political behavior of Fundamentalists and evangelicals may not reflect a permanent trend, but they have surely cheered Reagan's followers.

In any case, theologically conservative Protestants, even those who prefer the name "evangelical" to Fundamentalist, are not likely to shed completely the minority self-image that Fundamentalists have applied to themselves since the 1920s. What after all prompted the perception in the first place? It was not, as we have seen, a response to declining social importance and economic status so much as response to diminished intellectual prestige. In many obvious ways, the Fundamentalist response to the quarrels of the 1920s was a repetition of what New Side Presbyterians had done during the Great Awakening of the eighteenth century. The latter split from churches which they could not purge of unGodly rationalism and were quickly charged with arrogant contentiousness. The crucial difference was that their opponents could not make the charge of intellectual backwardness stick.[42] In contrast, the Fundamentalist mentality stands no better with the scientific community than it did at the time of the Scopes trial. Until all the world goes to Harvard, the outsider pose will remain useful to American Protestants who insist on saying what modern biology insists they cannot possibly say.

CHAPTER SEVEN

Black Culture and Black Churches—The Quest for an Autonomous Identity

Is Norman Podhoretz more assimilated than Count Basie?
Albert Murray (1970)

The fact is, we are thoroughly Americans, and by reason of the fact that we have been here longer than the majority of the new American race, we have developed more fully than they, the characteristics by which it is known?
African Methodist Episcopal Church (1868)

Debates among black intellectuals in the 1960s forced everyone who took a serious interest in American experience to make some long overdue reappraisals. Back at the turn of the century W. E. B. DuBois had suggested a simple enough historical truth when he asked: "Would America have been America without her Negro people?"[1] Understanding the development of the United States required careful attention to the presence of black people. However, until the explosive racial developments that were part of the Vietnam decade, most American historians went about their work as if they were trying to prove how aptly Ralph Ellison had titled his famous postwar novel. The leading textbooks used in American schools, which reflected the primary concerns of historical research, ignored the insight suggested by DuBois. America's story began with the landing at Plymouth Rock in 1620. Usually, although some pages later, the arrival of black Americans a year earlier was mentioned. But no writer thought to lavish on these "first families" the sort of generous attention that was routinely allotted the Puritan settlers of New England. DuBois had been right, but it took something more than his voice to change the categories of perception.

Since the end of the 1960s Americans have not lacked for alternate texts to give their schoolchildren. The lines and lines of writing that are now carefully meted out to acknowledge black contributions to American life have largely erased the problem of invisibility. What remains are problems of interpretation. Writers of the revised texts have not had an easy time deciding what to say. Since blacks were thrust into American experience by force and were not able for several hundred years to leave their own records concerning what it meant to them, historians have been groping for formulas to confer historical importance. A sticky controversy has developed around the question of whether American blacks ever had a culture other than what white Americans had given to them. If they did not, it was hard to see how black Americans could precede white Americans in historical narrative. Blacks would figure in the story not because they had been primary in setting the conditions of American experience but because of limited ways in which they had been able to modify those conditions.

The question of culture has been an especially difficult one to treat because it is a political as well as a scholarly question. Nathan Glazer found himself branded a racist when he floated the hypothesis that American blacks lacked the kind of ethnic identity that formed part of the heritage of, for example, Irish Americans and Jewish Americans.[2] This despite the fact that a black sociologist and historian, E. Franklin Frazier, made a comparable point in his analysis of the most crucial component of black cultural life—the independent black churches.[3] Lawrence Levine and Eugene Genovese, among others, wrote books to prove Glazer wrong, and Glazer himself saw fit to modify his comments.[4] A great deal was at stake. If American blacks had no culture other than a parasitic one, they were uniquely crippled among the various identifiable groups that comprised American society. They were outsiders who lacked a positive content for the racial identity that stigmatized them. They were therefore unable to use outsider strategies advantageously as had other groups in America's past. Since the past had provided them with no basis for autonomy, they could only go on in the future trying to wrest an identity out of what their oppressors chose to give them.

The seriousness of the political issues enormously complicated the scholarly enterprise of historical revision. If white historians wrote books to remind blacks of a proud and independent cultural past that they had forgotten or were misguidedly ashamed to acknowledge, were white scholars in their belated zeal for DuBois not merely putting the problem of cultural paternalism in a new form? Melville Herskovits, a white ethnologist at Columbia University, came forward to teach American blacks about Africa.[5] The black scholars who in the 1960s demanded the field of Black Studies to themselves knew what they were doing. Scholarly objectivity was very well and good. But equally important was the question of who was going to get credit for inventing a past usable for blacks in their conflicts with white America.

Passions now are calmer than they were in the 1960s, although not so calm as to allow a perfectly clear perspective on where our revision has taken us. The outcome of what is being risked politically in contemporary rhetorical inventions remains very much up in the air. However, although we remain uncertain about the implications of what we have learned, we do know more, especially about the special circumstances of the black experience in the United States, than we used to know. With respect to culture, and this fact has emerged from our efforts to learn about black churches, paternalism was in fact a complicating factor in black efforts at self-definition. On the other hand, American blacks, within such limits as their circumstances imposed on them, have worked to establish an autonomous cultural identity for themselves for as long as we have historical records. If those attempts to this point have not worked as well for blacks as similar efforts have for some other groups, it is not because the efforts lacked inventiveness or were somehow "non-authentic." (Authenticity, as we have seen, is only one component of ethnic consciousness in America.) It is because blacks were a large, scattered, and, until recently, rural people.[6] The things that united them were difficult to articulate, and what was articulated was difficult to share.

The problem of paternalism was rooted in the dependent conditions of slave life, and in various ways. In cultural terms, what was crucially important in determining the effects of American slavery on the freedmen was that white Protestant evangelicals, especially Baptists and Methodists, were able with stunning success to convert the slaves to Christianity and to supervise the formation of their religious life. We will never know precisely how many slaves became Christian in the period between 1800 and the onset of the Civil War. The best estimates suggest that 12 to 15 percent of the slaves were church members by the middle of the nineteenth century.[7] That figure compares favorably with the church membership figures for white Protestants, and Protestant Christianity was no doubt the nominal religion of many slaves who were not church members as it was for many unchurched white Americans. American Protestant missionaries never again achieved such an impressive wholesale conversion.

To be sure, black slaves, as the slavemaster had originally feared, turned Protestant Christianity into something quite different from what was preached and practiced in white churches. Even though the law tried to keep it carefully under white scrutiny, slave religion developed a point of view that located sin not in the venial misdeeds common in the slavequarters but in the beliefs of those who held them in bondage.[8] Reversing the mythology of the Puritans, black spirituals, which were the most original creation of American music in the antebellum period, taught the slaves to regard the United States not as Zion but as Egypt. The white men who led America were not enlightened statesmen but Pharoah. Gabriel Prosser, Denmark Vesey, and Nat Turner expressed overtly the rebellion that was a covert part of black Christianity. Their defeat left many American slaves with no way to talk about the promised land except as heaven and no better Moses than Abraham Lincoln. Slave religion, however, was not otherworldly. It was a way of making difficult lives workable and bearable. It was resistance of the only kind that a realistic look at "this" world allowed.

Without underestimating the transformed meanings in black Christian worship, we must still assign weight to the prior point. American blacks were "given" major components of their religion; and that fact, however wrongheadly, created a mentality of indebtedness which became one of the heaviest burdens imposed on black America by white paternalism. We are not forgetting about the important influence of African survivals in shaping black Christianity. Most scholars are convinced that the slave spirituals, the "ring shout," the ecstatic behavior of black religious meetings, and the rhythmic style of the black minister came as much from Africa as from evangelical America. They also suspect that if we had ways to penetrate the secret and illegal religious meetings that were apparently widespread among American slaves, we would uncover many other folk practices with African roots. Nonetheless, if African religion had survived in more systematic ways— that is, in ways fully comparable to what Jewish and Catholic immigrants retained of their cultural baggage—Protestant proselytizers would have had a far tougher time among American blacks than they did. The impressive evidence of African survivals that Herskovits found among black slaves in the Caribbean served to weaken the case he wanted to make about black slaves who absorbed Christianity in the American South.[9] The ending of the African slave trade to the United States was a victory of sorts for humanitarianism, but it also stopped the major source of African immigration. Black slaves were left without an easily renewed access to their homeland, and black mythmakers in the days that followed slavery faced a tough job.

A good bit of the problem that white Christianity caused American black slaves and their successors is encapsulated in the image of Uncle Tom. Harriet Beecher Stowe's famous character quickly became a favorite American example of Christ-like sacrifice. Uncle Tom lived the Christian law of love. He exemplified dignified manhood in submission, powerful self-assertion in humble loyalty. Through his suffering for righteousness' sake, he gave himself up to a martyrdom that, in Stowe's fiction, was meant to purchase the redemption of the American nation. As an image that provided a meaning for black suffering, Uncle Tom inevitably had a significant influence on the religion taught in black churches. What else can explain why Booker T. Washington's Atlanta Exposition Speech appealed to black America a generation after the circumstances which had justified Uncle Tom's posture had disappeared? Only someone who had been taught to aspire to the spiritual composure of Uncle Tom could find dignity in Washington's promise to white Southerners: "We shall stand by you with a devotion that no foreigner can approach, ready to lay down our lives, if need be, in defense of yours."[10]

Admirable he was. Yet Uncle Tom was a heavy moral burden for black Americans to carry. Stowe's book was not written for the slave, and Uncle Tom died pointlessly to redeem the soul of white America. Stowe, like most other abolitionists, predicated the end of slavery on changing the conscience of white America. Small wonder then that some black leaders from the beginning warned that the Uncle Tom myth contained a trap. In the 1960s denouncing it became a touchstone of black militance even after Martin Luther King, Jr., demonstrated ways to link submissiveness to effective protest. King's opponents ignored the victories of passive resistance because they thought that they should have been won long before. They used the past to argue the foolishness of urging black Americans to wait for liberation until white Americans grew ashamed of themselves. The experience of other groups suggested that patience was not a necessity. It was a virtue that only black Protestantism, among all the varieties of American religion, seemed to take seriously. That was, many said, because black Protestants had become what white Protestants wanted them to become.[11] The counter assertion that blacks had gained their autonomy by becoming better Christians than white Americans could not quite blunt the force of that judgment.

The black militants of the 1960s were not seeking to recount the history of black Protestantism in the United States in a dispassionate way, and their criticism moves us well ahead of our story. We mention them at this point because in the decade of the sixties circumstances permitted a large number of black leaders, representing a wide range of tactical positions, to gain perspective on certain dilemmas that their historical experience in America had created. American blacks had unknowingly faced a series of Hobson's choices: when they rejected one option as clearly unacceptable, they found that their refusal left them with nothing. No matter what they did, they could not entirely escape an agenda that others had set for them. The lives of American slaves reveal how some of these dilemmas were set. But similar difficulties confronted free blacks who lived in the North during the antebellum period.

Examples are handy. Successful efforts to form independent black churches in Northern cities provided striking evidence of what a militant black consciousness could accomplish. Well before the abolitionist movement provided a platform for black voices of protest, black Protestants had created numerous separate congregations, including the St. Thomas African Episcopal Church in Philadelphia, the Abyssinian Baptist Church in New

York City, and two Methodist organizations, the African Methodist Episcopal Church and the African Methodist Episcopal Church Zion. When Richard Allen and Absalon Jones despaired of equal treatment in white congregations, they expressed their disgust by separation.[12] The black churches which they then formed prospered because they provided black Americans with opportunities for leadership and achievement. They served as symbols that free blacks were determined to run their own affairs. We are talking about a small minority of the black population in antebellum America, 90 percent of whom were still enslaved in the South in 1860; but free blacks in the antebellum North and their descendants were for a long time to come greatly overrepresented among the leaders who emerged in the black community.

The independent church movement was not the only way for black pride in the antebellum North to assert itself, for a number of outspoken black religious leaders chose to protest from within existing white Protestant denominations. Of the eight black ministers who helped found the American and Foreign Anti-Slavery Society in 1840, five were Presbyterians and a sixth, Alexander Crummel, was an Episcopalian.[13] However, independence was clearly an important and indeed an essential step in any black strategy for gaining full civil rights. The problem was that circumstances beyond anyone's control put difficulties in the way of what the movement could accomplish. One ironic thing that dramatically undercut achievements of the independent black churches was emancipation. The need to accommodate a large population of unskilled and largely illiterate people placed an unbearable strain on their resources and their reputation both in the North and the South. That complication was unavoidable. But so was another one although it touched an issue where black religious leaders had an apparent choice.

In 1816 a number of white Americans who opposed slavery founded the American Colonization Society. It was the first important organization to sponsor ideas that would later be associated with ideologies of black nationalism. Marcus Garvey could scarcely have improved on some of the arguments. Colonizers told free blacks that slavery was wrong and that their importation into the United States constituted a grievous wrong. They urged blacks to accept proudly the responsibilities of their racial identity and warned them that the white American majority would never treat them as equals. Logic led to a single conclusion: blacks ought to rediscover their homeland, return to Africa, and there build a civilization worthy of that important continent. White colonizers pled their case energetically before black religious leaders because they understood correctly that the response of the latter would be decisive. It was, although it proved to be the opposite of what the colonizers had hoped for. Until the 1850s, black churchmen without exception reacted as David Walker who wrote: "Why should they send us into a far country to die? See the thousands of foreigners emigrating to America every year: and if there be ground sufficient for them to cultivate, and bread for them to eat; why would they wish to send the *first tillers* of the land away?"[14]

The response was the appropriate one. How could first families have reacted in any other way? The leaders of the African Methodist Episcopal church were not engaging in an act of self-hatred when they declared that black Americans had dwelt in North America for three centuries and retained nothing of Africa.[15] They were stating a fact about their lives. Under the circumstances, for free blacks to have forsworn the determination to have the full rights of American citizens would have been tantamount to admitting that they were not as good as immigrants who were just off the boat. Only thinly veiled in the arguments of white sponsors of black colonization was the notion that blacks were too lazy, too primitive, and too mentally slow to survive as free agents within the American system. Richard Allen concluded that the main aim of the colonizers was to remove from the view of the slaves the "potentially insurrectionary example of free men of colour enjoying liberty."[16] A fairer judgment would have been that the white colonizers wanted to solve a racial problem which they had created by putting blacks for a second time to the greatest possible inconvenience.

Appropriate or not, rejecting colonization meant passing up the chance to pursue another important opportunity that those immigrant groups who were just arriving in the United States exploited as a matter of course. The dilemma was this: to combat the racist stereotypes that prompted white-sponsored colonization schemes, black leaders had to accept racist stereotypes of another sort— those which demeaned the cultural attainments of black Africans. In rejecting Africa, or at least those parts of Africa from where most of them had come, as a possible source of cultural identity, free blacks in the North left themselves with only the cultural heritage of the Puritans to exploit. Arguably, once black religious leaders endorsed white middle-class standards as the measure of worth, they were dooming the great mass of black Americans, once freedom came, to a sense of failure. Rejecting one option as unviable had left them with nothing.

If blacks were to succeed as an outsider group, they clearly needed strong forms of cultural identification to maintain group pride. What black Americans had on the eve of emancipation was an identification based in large part upon color. How could that become a source of pride if the majority of the black people in the world were viewed as cursed and primitive? The dilemma was painful. On the one hand, efforts on the part of black leaders in the North to connect themselves in a positive way with Africa would have required a large amount of implausible mythmaking. On the other hand, if they did not invent the myths someone else would. In trying to make the best of a bad situation, many black Americans ended by accepting a myth that involved a fatal inversion of the chosen people concept. They believed that God had allowed them to be carried off into slavery so that they could learn white Christian culture and return, as Phyllis Wheatley said, to disperse "the thick cloud of ignorance" from their "benighted country."[17] Most of the black Protestant missionaries who did return to Africa to work beginning in the middle of the nineteenth century approached black Africa with the same cultural chauvinism that was used to justify European imperialism. Visions of a dark and savage continent became the uncertain basis for American black pride.[18]

The situation had to be the way it was, for the material to quickly build a myth out of African material was rendered useless by the belief in African backwardness. Nonetheless, the disastrous aftermath of slavery suggested that somewhere along the line black leaders had to start recovering a cultural past that could separate black people from the negative images of black culture that white groups perpetuated. This was the importance of the various black nationalist and "Back-to-Africa" movements that were launched in the nineteenth century. Implausible they might have been. Yet Joseph Smith had worked with implausible material, and American Jews were later to invent a homeland for themselves out of a past far more distant that the one that separated black Americans from Africa. As early as 1852, Martin Delaney, who was bitterly disillusioned by passage of the Fugitive Slave Law, suggested that black Americans needed to seize the initiative from whites in promoting colonization schemes. His book, *The Condition, Elevation, Emigration, and Destiny of the Colored People of the United States*, introduced a new element into discussions of how blacks ought to regard their past and future in North America. Eventually, that element gained credibility, but it was bound to take a long time.

The initial failures of Afro-American mythmaking have been widely noted. For one thing, the nineteenth-century Back-to-Africa movements did not shake themselves free of condescending attitudes toward African culture. Edward Blyden was unusual in his admiration of Islam. He viewed it as a religion better suited for free blacks than Christianity. The latter, he said, had taught blacks living in New York to entreat God to extend his "lily white hands" and grant a blessing to their all black congregations.[19] Blyden remained a Christian, however, and his knowledge of Africa was confined to the Islamic regions. Henry McNeal Turner, a bishop in the African Methodist Episcopal Church, who organized the most important of the Back-to-Africa movements of the nineteenth century, justified his movement using much of the language that Phyllis Wheatley had used.[20] Secondly, none of the nineteenth-century colonization plans sparked much emigration to Africa. Some American blacks did participate in the colonization of Liberia, but by and large they confirmed the deepness of their American roots by becoming the least likely of American people to expatriate themselves or repatriate themselves.

What was surprising in all of this was not the limitations of the early colonization proposals. After all, blacks seeking to find a way back to Africa were developing a concept virtually from scratch. The more notable fact was that white enthusiasm for colonization schemes disappeared almost as soon as blacks began to sponsor them. Whites regarded colonization in one way when they controlled the discourse. They looked at the same programs very differently when black leaders sought to define the issues. Delaney, Blyden, Turner and the other religious leaders of the black nationalist minority were attempting something difficult but not something pointless.

By far, most of the black churches formed after emancipation either showed no interest in black nationalist schemes or attacked them. That is one reason, though by no means the most important one, why many present-day scholars judge them harshly.[21] Given how little we know about what was preached in black churches, judgments of any kind are surely hasty. Such evidence as we have, which often comes in the form of polemic, can justify a range of generalization. Some writers have argued that the churches fostered black pride. Others have said that they encouraged blacks to imitate whites. Some have pointed to their functional role in building a black community. Others have insisted that they erected authoritarian structures that encouraged blacks to accept passively whatever happened to them. One assertion seems as based on realities as the other. And perhaps it will always be that way no matter what further evidence is accumulated. What strikes one writer as an assertion of black pride will appear to another as capitulation to racial stereotypes created by whites. The ambiguities are that shifty, and a lot of meaning hinged not on what was said but on who was saying it and to whom.

We can nonetheless venture a few generalizations both about what black Protestantism managed to accomplish in the last half of the nineteenth century as well as about what factors limited the accomplishments. Of most importance, emancipation made it possible for the freedmen to organize their own churches away from direct white surveillance, and they immediately seized the opportunity.[22] In following the example that had been set by the majority of blacks in the North, Southern blacks determined one aspect of the Jim Crow patterns of segregation for themselves. They associated the theoretically integrated churches of the antebellum period, which had forced mostly black congregations to listen to white preachers and to submit to discriminatory patterns of seating, with servitude. By 1906 the Colored Methodist Episcopal church in the South counted 172,996 members, and the largely Southern National Baptist Convention had grown to a membership of 2,201,549. In the meantime, in the North, the antebellum patterns persisted. At the end of the century, the population of the African Methodist Episcopal Church was 494,777 and that of the African Methodist Episcopal Church Zion, 184,542. Only about 474,880 of the blacks living in America were affiliated with mostly white churches.[23]

A second important point followed naturally. Black ministers used their position to preach black pride. An editorial circulated in 1886 by the African Methodist Episcopal Church was typical. It said: "We must learn to love ourselves."[24] The "Black is Beautiful" theme that was so prominent in the 1960s was part of the heritage of the black churches. Blacks in the nineteenth century used their congregations to organize community affairs, to assert themselves, and to work cooperatively. They also continued, as they had in the days of slavery, to turn black Protestantism into something different from what white evangelicals had given them. They could not change the fact that the major texts and symbols of their religion came from white culture. But, as we have learned from many studies of popular culture, people without education read or misread selectively from the texts they are handed. Their arrangements and emphases amount to an act of cultural creation.[25]

The other and less positive side of the coin of course remains important. The largely illiterate population that made up most black congregations after emancipation had precious little experience with independence. Lacking the self-confidence to appreciate fully what they had in their music and their services marked by joyous emotionalism, they were tempted to regard what they had created as a debasement of white culture. For this reason behavior associated with the independent black churches in the last part of the nineteenth century does not let us quite forget Edward Blyden's accusation that they were governed by a slave mentality. Blyden wrote: "To be as like the white man as possible—to copy his outward appearance, his peculiarities, his manners, the arrangement of his toilet, that is the aim of the Christian Negro—that is his aspiration."[26]

Physical separation provided blacks with some of the freedom they had lacked under slavery, but conditions in the post Civil War South, especially after the end of Reconstruction, allowed whites to continue to monitor in covert and overt ways what went on in black churches. At the most benign level, whites knew how to make blacks feel grateful to them. That, as we suggested earlier, was one of the legacies of the paternalistic ethic engrained in American slavery. Whites gave blacks money to build their churches and quite commonly contributed to the minister's salary. They further provided ways for ministers to distribute patronage among their followers. Not surprisingly, under such circumstances the voice of the white community was more often heard in black churches than vice versa.[27] At less benign levels, the white community in the South did not hesitate to threaten physical violence against black ministers who protested racial injustice. Black ministers often accommodated the white community. That was surely a fact of black religious life. They did so because of the prestige it brought them and because they had no choice.

In assessing the achievements of the black churches after emancipation, we must not forget conditions that isolated black people from one another and accustomed them to look for help from nearby whites rather than to distant blacks. Black churches touched more black people than any other institution. They became for most American blacks the primary form of identification. They could not, however, forge a common consciousness for all black people. Although a great deal has been written about the richness of community life in the slave quarters, we may, as Peter Kolchin has observed, in correcting notions about the cultureless slave have moved too far in the direction of romance.[28] The hard fact is that most slaves were forced to submit to a form of ghettoization without the saving virtue of autonomy. Slaves learned, by way of protest, to avoid responsibilities, but most of them were given none to manage. Recent studies have made it hard to decide which was worse: a West Indian slavery that was physically brutal but that left the blacks who survived with a determination to take care of themselves, or the more gentle American system that caused the deaths of far fewer Africans but that exposed comparatively few blacks to areas of collective responsibility. Black churches inherited a situation they could do little to overcome without a lot of work. Unfortunately but unavoidably, a lot of what they did reinforced the problem.

A number of people have argued that the American principle of voluntary churches, whatever good it did for other groups, was a disaster in the case of black Protestantism. It fragmented the one thing that might have provided desperately needed unity. In the nineteenth century, most American blacks had no historical memory of anything other than slavery and no knowledge of a country larger than a Southern county. They had their churches, and too many of them.[29] Despite the grouping of most black Protestants into four or five major denominations, black church organizations were more splintered than their white counterparts; their individual churches more independent from one another; their sects and cults more short-lived. The pattern persisted. By the 1930s, in Cincinnati, where blacks comprised 10.6 percent of the total population, black churches accounted for 32 percent of all churches. In Detroit and Philadelphia, where the black population was 7.7 percent and 11.3 percent respectively, black churches constituted 24 percent of the total number of churches.[30] Part of the reason lay in the competition among ministers. The black church provided roles of leadership, but it provided too few of them. Thus, as one writer has suggested, the politics of black neighborhoods remained parochial and was turned inward on themselves.[31] The only way to create more ministers, hence more leaders, was to create more churches. Perhaps too many of those churches were autocratically ruled by charismatic leaders who spent more time attacking other black ministers around the block than in talking about common features of black experience.

Fragmentation was also a consequence of class distinctions in the black community. The things that became most characteristic of black worship in the nineteenth century were also things that became offensive to black Protestants as they moved up the social scale.[32] Although other religious groups faced the same sort of problem, the task of maintaining pride in traditional or folk forms of religious expression appears to have been especially complicated in the case of American blacks. Blacks struggled to control the discourse about themselves, and they did not begin in an advantageous position.[33] The pattern of having a token black appear on a largely white panel to discuss "The Future of the American Negro," a pattern so distressingly common in the twentieth century, was established very early. In the nineteenth century the "token" black was usually a minister. In discussions effectively controlled by more educated whites, a lonely black participant had a difficult time turning stereotypes about "emotionalism" in black religion into a source of pride. Within the stereotype, emotionalism represented the childish mental condition of slaves who were unprepared for freedom. Since black leaders in the nineteenth century were trying to free themselves from images that slaveholders had used to justify their system, they thought it important to disassociate black churches from images of indecorous worship. Snobbery or cowardice was not the reason why men like Alexander Payne, Delaney, Blyden, and Crummel criticized the emotionalism of black religion.[34] In this matter, they were dealing with another form of the dilemma that black church-men faced in responding to colonization proposals.

The two most famous black leaders to emerge in the United States toward the end of the nineteenth century, Booker T. Washington and W.E.B. DuBois, found no completely satisfactory way to turn stereotyped views about black folkways into an acceptable base on which to build group pride. Washington tried to sidestep the problem by apparently accepting the view that blacks had no past to recapture, only a past to overcome. Slavery, he said, had left blacks without skills, without a collective sense of responsibility, without means to make positive and independent contributions to American life. Everyone who has studied the complicated figure of Washington has realized that there was more to his game than passive acquiescence in "second-class citizenship," the policy that is usually linked to his name. The only things that interested Washington were black pride and black power, with or without consent from whites. However, since he was convinced that most American blacks had many things to learn about how to help themselves, he counseled blacks that they would have to wait for the things they wanted, perhaps a long time.

Washington's quest for black autonomy led him to urge blacks to keep their distance from white America. That advice was consistent with the experience of other outsider groups. It was also consistent with the experience of black churches whose ministers Washington often privately criticized but from whom he drew a large measure of his support. Unfortunately, the independence that Washington advocated was designed within a system of legal segregation and discrimination imposed by whites. It was therefore hard to turn it into a policy that promoted either pride or power. Because Washington was unable either to locate a black culture worthy of the name or to suggest quick ways to create one (other than placing blacks at the center of a conventional version of the American dream), he inevitably, however unwillingly, suggested that blacks were inferior to other groups who, although hampered by a lack of skills and by educational disadvantages, had shown that group pride grew not merely from separation but also from direct confrontations with discrimination. Washington saw the world with uncommon clarity, but his clear vision left him with a program that gave too much pleasure to whites who were setting the legal terms of black existence.

DuBois recognized the flaws in the strategies that Washington proposed. He argued that the kind of independence Washington wanted was just a name for giving up. What DuBois's career exemplifies is the fact that knowledge alone cannot always cut through a dilemma. No one at the turn of the century understood the reasons for the impasse in American racial relations better than DuBois. No one wrote with such insight and feeling about the black experience as he did. Indeed, given how little had been articulated about that experience, his early books, especially *The Souls of Black Folk* and *The Negro Church*, amounted to virtual revelations. Even so, many of his famous formulations were phrased as questions for which DuBois had trouble finding answers. "How does it feel to be a problem?," DuBois wrote in the first paragraph of *The Souls of Black Folk*. Undoubtedly, DuBois had pinpointed something important about black psychology. But what was one to do about it?

DuBois searched for a strategy to reconcile two tendencies that he believed pulled blacks in opposite directions—their blackness and their sense of being American. In his early career, DuBois did what leaders of other minority groups did. He expressed no embarrassment about his group identity and asserted his claims to full rights as an American citizen. With that militant posture he ran smack into the paternalism of the almost totally white-run National Association for the Advancement of Colored People. The NAACP was an important milestone in black history, but it gave blacks no immediate control over discourse concerning the black problem.[35] DuBois's later career reflected more searching and less certainty. Although he never stopped insisting on full rights for black Americans, he lost interest in "integration" as a solution to discrimination. Coming to doubt whether blacks would ever find the most important parts of their identity in their American past, he worked his way through Marxism and various programs of Pan-Africanism. Potentially the greatest of twentieth-century mythmakers, DuBois was also a Harvard-trained intellectual who had difficulty approving of the mass movements that most appealed to blacks. He knew too well what white Americans thought and could never entirely separate himself from their stereotypes and the value judgments which those stereotypes carried. He never brought his blackness and his Americanness satisfactorily together nor did he succeed in keeping them far enough apart so that they did not compete for attention.

Discrimination was not by itself the critical difference that separated black experience from the experience of immigrants who entered the United States in the last part of the nineteenth century. It was what discrimination coupled with a long period of dependence had done to self-image. DuBois counted on a cadre of talented blacks to overcome the damage to black self-image; but it was far from certain, however impatient DuBois seemed to be, that his "talented tenth" would get blacks any further or any faster than what Washington proposed. DuBois had a wonderful gift for describing black people, but no particular gift for working with them in ways that united them. In their tendency to spark sectarianism, the record of black intellectuals has been no better than that of white intellectuals.

When American blacks did start using their freedom to uproot themselves in large numbers, the direction of their movement was not to Africa but to the city. The importance of this step, which marks one of the most important demographic transitions in twentieth-century America, lay not in the fact that American blacks started breathing the free air of the North. In fact, what free air there was tended to vanish once Southern blacks started crossing the Mason-Dixon line in large numbers during and after World War I. In the long run, the massing together of blacks in Atlanta, Birmingham, and New Orleans was just as important as their movement into New York City and Chicago. Urbanization, which is still a relatively new experience for American blacks, was important because it created for them a totally new scale for collective action.

The possibilities first became evident in Harlem. By the end of World War I this area of New York City had become the major reference point for black writers and artists, even for those who did not live there. The intellectual "renaissance" that stirred Harlem gave credence to the "New Negro" movement that Alain Locke and others announced in the middle of the 1920s. James Weldon Johnson had been waiting a long time for something like Harlem to happen. He had had a successful career as a "colored man" in white America that dated back to the administration of

Theodore Roosevelt, but he had turned away from that. Harlem promised to be the "home" that black Americans had never had. Johnson described Harlem as a place relatively free of racial tension, a place with a low crime rate, a place where blacks could discover their creativity. In Harlem, American slavery would finally end.[36]

As it turned out, Johnson's hopes were premature. And in part they rested on the wrong thing. The black intellectuals of Harlem who created such a stir in the decade that followed World War I found themselves confronting the same problem that DuBois had confronted. Their ideas about what black culture should be did not deeply stir the masses of black Americans who were moving to the city. The one Harlem figure who did know how to generate a popular movement among blacks was not a person whom most of the intellectuals respected. This was Marcus Garvey. Garvey saw in Harlem something other than a place to build black theatres and black nightclubs that drew a largely white clientele. Harlem was the chance to gather blacks in the streets for mass demonstrations and parades, something never before possible on such a scale, and bring them together by creating a new racial myth.

The Jamaican-born Garvey has not lacked for critics. Even those who have admired what he attempted to do have regretted his flamboyance, his desire for personal aggrandizement, his carelessness in financial management. He gave his enemies all the ammunition they needed to bring him down. The most damning charge against Garvey is that he failed. He wanted blacks to take pride in their color, to create institutions that would give them financial independence, and to begin a mass return to their homeland. Instead, this man who stirred an unprecedented degree of optimism among ordinary black Americans was deported from the United States and became yet another symbol of black incompetence. What Marcus Garvey had begun brought little comfort to black Americans when economic conditions devastated Harlem in the 1930s.

Garvey is probably best understood as one of America's religious prophets who did not quite make it. The religious dimensions of his movement have been well marked.[37] Garvey's joint endeavors with the Episcopal priest, George Alexander McGuire, were not always smooth. But the African Orthodox church, which McGuire headed, was a crucial experiment that gained substantial elements of support from the black Protestant ministry. Garvey believed, as had some earlier black nationalist leaders, that a good part of the problem with black consciousness lay in religious symbols. Black Christians in America worshiped a white God. He might be a God who planned to free them, but He was not particular to them in the way that the Jewish God was to Jews or the Mormon God was to Mormons. Garvey insisted on a black God whose concern for the black man was prior to His concern for all other racial or national groups. If that seemed an extreme claim, it was meant to. Other religious movements in America had made a success out of claims that were attacked as extreme. Garvey failed to establish a permanent movement or a successful church, but the most important reasons had little to do with the extravagance of his racial doctrines. That extravagance was the one thing that large numbers of black Americans did not forget.

Garvey was not the only important would-be religious prophet who emerged in the new urban context that affected the lives of black Americans. Father Divine and Daddy Grace were two others who built significant personal followings, although they were not able to solve the problem of succession.[38] More successful in the last respect was Elijah Muhammad (born Elijah Poole) who founded the Nation of Islam, known later as the Black Muslims. Muhammad's turn to the Islamic world looked back to the work of Timothy Drew, an American black who in 1913 took the name Noble Drew Ali and founded the Moorish American Science Temple in Newark, New Jersey. However, Elijah Muhammad apparently learned about Islam from a figure about whom we know practically nothing, Wallace Fard. He convinced Muhammad that Afro-Americans were all Muslim by heritage and had to return to Islam to get in touch with their past and self-identity. Fard's views were unorthodox by world Islamic standards which stressed human brotherhood. Nonetheless, Muhammad's Nation of Islam incorporated a racially based doctrine that was intended to help blacks, the "original" race, overcome their subordinate position to "satanic" white oppressors.

The Muslims grew and became the most important new religious movement to emerge in America in the twentieth century.[39] Joseph Washington, among others, has severely criticized the Muslims. He wrote that they exemplified "the final catastrophe of a religion without authentic roots, and action without social conscience."[40] That is too harsh a view. If black religion truly lacked authentic roots, then the Muslims, rather than a catastrophe, pointed to one way out of an impossible situation. The Muslims arrived at a moment when the earlier myths invented to sustain black pride had been repeated long enough to start gathering plausibility. The cultural factors that had permitted some Americans in the 1830s to believe that Joseph Smith had translated golden tablets were no stronger than the cultural factors that permitted some black Americans in the 1930s to believe that Yakub, a black scientist in rebellion against Allah, had created a cunning and deceitful white race who used power to wage war and to enslave the once superior black race. You did not have to live in a black urban neighborhood to see evidence that sustained notions of white demonology, but it was impossible not to if you did.

We do not mean to evoke the name of Joseph Smith too often, but parallels between his religious inventions and various black nationalist movements are striking. The Black Muslims in the 1950s and 1960s attempted to do precisely what the Mormons had done. They reinvented the myth of creation. They used ritual and tight discipline to bind themselves into a community. They aspired to territorial separation, not in Africa, but in land ceded to them within the United States. What they accomplished brought on them the same criticism that was used against Joseph Smith and Brigham Young. Muslim leaders were denounced as religious impostors who aimed to glorify themselves and destroy Christianity. They were charged with sponsoring an economic isolationism that provoked needless animosities with their neighbors. The once-existing Muslim paramilitary organization, the Fruit of Islam, caused the same fears that the Mormon Band of Danites once aroused. Critics of the Muslims said that they were disloyal, that they plotted against the United States government, that they controlled every aspect of the behavior of their members. The same denunciations were applied just as convincingly to nineteenth-century Mormons who in fact bloc-voted, used every conceivable means to undermine the authority of the territorial government established over them, and finally went underground to evade criminal indictments. No direct influence exists. Even so, the Mormons, who in the nineteenth century were commonly associated with the "barbarian" practices of the slaveholder, can serve as an example to justify one form of contemporary black militance.

The Muslims may or may not have the long-range success of the Mormons. Splits have appeared in the movement. The most charismatic of the Muslim leaders, Malcolm X, traveled to Mecca in 1964 and returned to the United States ready to reject the racial doctrines of Elijah Muhammad. His break with Muhammad was prelude to his assassination. When Muhammad himself died in 1975, his son, Warith Deen Muhammad, took the Black Muslim movement in the direction of Malcolm X and Islamic orthodoxy. Renaming his organization the American Muslim Mission, Warith Muhammad urged his followers to quit blaming their problems on a demon white race and become good and responsible citizens of the United States. Tension remains between this part of the Black Muslims and members of the growing immigrant Muslim community in the United States; but Warith Muhammad has been recognized as a brother in Islam by leaders of the immigrant Muslim community, and he is respected in Islamic centers abroad.

Louis Farrakhan, in contrast to Elijah's Muhammad's son, has kept alive the Nation of Islam following the teachings of the founder. To him, Islam in America has to be interpreted in a way to take account of the oppression of American blacks. What Warith Muhammad taught might work for middle-class blacks, but "orthodoxy" was meaningless in building pride in black ghettos. In the long run, both formulas may prove important, especially since the total number of American adherents to Islam may soon equal the total number of American adherents to Judaism.

A sympathetic reading of Muslim experiments is not meant to suggest that Islam can hope to provide a cultural identity for all, or even very many, black Americans living in the United States.[41] American blacks are too large, too complex, too diverse a racial group to be given a single cultural identity. Most black Protestants are unlikely to walk out of their Protestant churches, except in the direction of the religious indifference that affects many other Americans. Nonetheless, Muslim strategies are perfectly appropriate given the way other groups have worked within the American context. They have the potential to galvanize the energies of a significant number of black people. Interestingly, the one Mormon sin that was not added to the list of complaints against the Muslims was the charge of deviance from middle-class morality.

The Muslims, whether now following Farrakhan or Warith Deen Mohammad, dress neatly in business suits; they forbid the use of drugs, alcohol, and tobacco; and they are committed to principles of sexual monogamy that are unusual only because they are taken seriously. Their religious inventions, whatever their influence on the international Islamic community, are thoroughly American.

The importance and influence of contemporary black nationalist movements can perhaps be best demonstrated by noting the degree of controversy they stirred in the black Protestant churches. Sometime at the end of the 1950s, partly as a result of the intensified feelings generated by the civil rights movements, traditional black churches came to life and entered a period of creativity unmatched by anything since the early days of Reconstruction. In some ways, the burst of creativity simply accelerated the tendency toward disunity that had previously weakened the efforts of the black churches to teach racial pride. Certainly the range of postures taken by black churches in recent decades has been wide. At one end of the scale were the black Pentecostal churches which in the main paid little attention to the social problems of the American black community. Along the spectrum, one significant step away from political indifference, was the powerful figure of the Reverend Joseph Jackson who controlled the National Baptist Convention from 1953 until 1983. He expelled Martin Luther King, Jr., from his organization in 1961 and spent the rest of that decade taking stands that linked him closely to the political right.

King in the meantime built a powerful movement that pushed black Protestantism into the forefront of social protest. It was, however, an independent movement and King's relations with many other militant preachers, Adam Clayton Powell, Jr., and James Cleage, for example, were never close. Militance promoted sectarian divisions. Caught somewhere in the middle of religious controversies were many black professionals who belonged to largely white denominations. As a number of studies have demonstrated, these people were the most likely of any group of blacks to be political activists.[42] Ministers whom they supported issued the powerful "Statement by the National Committee of Negro Churchmen" in 1966. Far from trying to escape their uncomfortable racial identity, as they had been accused of doing, many members of the black bourgeoisie had carried their identity proudly into uncomfortable circumstances and insisted on a voice. Their political disagreements with black religious leaders who wanted nothing to do with the white churches were not great, but angry rhetoric often made united action difficult.

Nonetheless, although black Christians remained fragmented in the period after 1960, a number of signs indicated that fragmentation mattered a good bit less than it had. Black voices, whatever they were saying, had grown less deferential to white opinion. Scholars argue about the degree to which paternalistically bred habits still hamper black efforts to rise economically, but they agree that black churches are breaking free of older patterns of dependence.[43] At the end of the 1960s a group of militant black Christians dramatically demanded $500 million from American churches and synagogues as restitution for past wrongs.[44] Had the demand been made in perfect seriousness, it might have indicated that blacks still looked to whites to solve their problems. Instead, the demand was meant to reveal the phoniness of purported white beneficence. What whites owed by way of significant help lay immeasurably beyond what they were willing to give. And even if they did give anything reasonably near what they had taken, black people were not prepared to say thank you. The burden of gratitude is not entirely a thing of the past, but during the 1960s anger gained a legitimacy in black Protestantism that it had not had for a long time.

At least two other important things changed the meaning of diversity within the black churches. First, an increasing number of black ministers tailored their sermons to emphasize the distinctiveness of black religion, whatever form it took. James Cleage, the pastor of the Church of the Black Madonna in Detroit, represented an extreme of this insistence. So did the theological writing of James Cone.[45] The extremes were less important than the general awareness they reflected. Black ministers of a variety of persuasions worked to spell out an idea that had not been articulated as part of the original program to form independent black churches: black Christianity and white Christianity were not the same thing. Leon Watts pointed to an unquestioned, even if neglected, historical face when he wrote: "Black religion. . . is a separate religious force in American life, different in all aspects from the tenets of the American Religious Establishment, primarily because its basis and base of operation relates exclusively to an oppressed community."[46]

The second thing of importance was that in the decade of the 1960s blacks won a major part of their battle to control discourses about themselves. American blacks still write the smaller part of what is said about their historical experience, even their religious experience. In this sense they remain public property to a greater degree than American Mormons, Jews, or Catholics. Yet others who write about them tread lightly. So long as the assumption of cultureless blacks prevailed, there was no reason to think that the mere fact of being black gave one special insight into that condition. Once perceptions were altered sufficiently to permit an appreciation for various autonomous aspects of black culture, growing up black carried a presumption of a certain kind of expertise.

These things taken together meant that fragmentation among black religious leaders was no longer any more or less important than it was among American Jewish leaders. Carter Woodson once noted that Jews were proud of the traditions that non-Jews demeaned, even when they no longer adhered to them, whereas blacks seemed to be embarrassed by their religious folkways even when they still enjoyed them.[47] We have commented on reasons why Woodson's judgment has the ring of truth for much of the post-emancipation period. The psychology that underlies Jewish consciousness and black consciousness is now more similar. Blacks are better able to exploit stereotypes in ways that promote group pride. The cause of white supremacy and the view of black culture that it maintained have gone on the defensive. Blacks may quarrel about who they are without damaging their collective interests because they have gained confidence that who they are has mattered a great deal to American experience.

The powerful example of Jewish self-esteem has in fact long served as a model for black leaders in America. Booker Washington, who himself was dubbed the Negro Moses, wrote about the Jews:

> There is, perhaps, no race that has suffered so much, not so much in America as in some of the countries of Europe. But these people have clung together. They have had a certain amount of unity, pride, and love of race; and as the years go on, they will be more

and more influential in this country,—a country where they were
once despised, and looked upon with scorn and derision. It is
largely because the Jewish race has had faith in itself. Unless the
Negro learns more and more to imitate the Jew in these matters,
to have faith in himself, he cannot expect to have any degree of
success.[48]

Several things explain why similar statements were made so frequently in the black community. When American blacks started
moving to cities in the Northeast, they were well-placed to
observe the truth of Washington's observation. Since many black
spirituals and sermons took their examples of suffering and
redemption from the Old Testament, blacks naturally compared
their destiny with that of another people who had been forced out
of their homeland. The psychological bond was strengthened
because after the turn of the century American Jews were the only
significant section of the white community to support blacks in
efforts to overcome racial discrimination. W.E.B. DuBois, among
others, gratefully acknowledged the Jewish contribution.

Perhaps oddly, one sign of how much blacks have taken from
the Jewish example is bad feeling between them. The concord
that once existed between black and Jewish intellectuals has
grown severely strained in recent years. As we have had ample
reason to see, tension and strain are the normal pattern of relations
among outsider groups. They define themselves as much against
one another as against groups who supposedly hold power. The
same demographic move that brought blacks and Jews together in
an urban context and gave blacks a chance to observe what Jewish
group consciousness had accomplished often placed blacks in
positions of economic subservience to Jews. Because Jews were
storeowners and landlords in Harlem, they replaced Southern
patricians in the eyes of blacks as the white power structure. They
also replaced Southern whites as the people to whom they were
supposed to be grateful. After some black leaders decided that the
time had come to renounce their debts to white America, the fact
that the debt to Jews was relatively great only made matters
worse. When competition also developed between the well-being
of the state of Israel and various Pan-African programs, the stage
was set for a verbal battle in which Jewish leaders charged blacks
with fomenting anti-Semitism, and blacks charged Jews with
vastly exaggerating the degree to which they had suffered in

America. The campaign that the Reverend Jesse Jackson conducted for the presidency in 1984 made clear that blacks can no longer particularly count on Jews to help make their political fortune.

Ethnic and religious groups as they gain the power to make demands commonly find themselves clinging to different priorities that are not easily compromised. Much of the tension that has been generated between blacks and Jews has revolved around issues of education. American Jews, following their history of devotion to study, worked hard in the United States to establish the priority of rewarding academic talent. They used the public and private schools to gain professional skills and were only secondarily concerned with whether schools protected Jewish culture. Other means existed to protect Jewish culture. Blacks, on the other hand, although they enthusiastically entered school houses after emancipation, quickly learned that quality education did not necessarily move them upward and was not widely available to them in any case. Much like the Irish Catholics in the middle of the nineteenth century, many black leaders began to regard questions of academic excellence as secondary to questions of whether school curricula provided blacks with a favorable self-image. Given this historical background, the recent angry disputes that have tied many universities and school districts in knots are best viewed not as aberrations but as battles that the American system guaranteed.

Through all of the tension, black leaders accused of anti-Semitism did not stop using the example of Jews as one to emulate. The anger that Harold Cruse directed at American Jews in his remarkable book, *The Crisis of the Negro Intellectual*, stemmed from his belief that the blacks' so-called Jewish allies tried to make blacks pursue strategies that Jews themselves eschewed when their own group interests were at stake. His fiercest resentment was directed at the paternalism of Jewish communist leaders in America who, according to Cruse, urged blacks to be universalists while they remained particularist in any matter that concerned Jews.[49] Beneath his anger was Cruse's tacit acknowledgment that the particularism he had learned from Jews was precisely what American blacks needed. The public addresses of Malcolm X, who was also widely accused of anti-Semitism, illustrated the same point. Malcolm X criticized the selfishness that he associated with Zionism. Yet, in explaining his opposition to the strategies of Martin Luther King, Jr., he told a *Playboy* interviewer: "The Jew never went sitting-in and crawling-in and sliding-in and freedom-riding, like he teaches and helps Negroes to do. The Jews stood up and stood together, and they used their ultimate power, the economic weapon... The Jews pooled their money and bought the hotels that barred them."[50] Malcolm X accepted the stereotype of the pushy Jew because he admired it. A backhanded compliment no doubt, but more of a compliment than one found in more classic cases of anti-Semitism.

If black strategies of self-advancement, especially as worked out in black churches, are now comparable to those of many other groups, they are nonetheless the products of a different historical experience. The strategies have faced harder tasks of invention and recovery. They have had to pretend that the large population of American blacks shared a common culture when virtually no institutions of common culture, save very congregational churches, had existed to maintain and spread one. The past that black mythmakers had to discover was unknown not because there had not been one but because the oral culture of blacks made it difficult to transmit from one generation to the next. African immigration to America had begun early and ended early. These things may mean that in the long run that blacks will care less about an indentification based on a separate nationality than some other groups who arrived in America later. DuBois was not so much interested in preserving a specifically African culture as he was in using a program of black culture for as long as it was necessary to enable black Americans to claim their rights. Full assimilation was not a prospect that worried him.

But whatever else happens to the idea of black culture, the distinctiveness assigned to black churches seems to be indelibly established as a part of American consciousness. In that area black mythmakers have always had plenty of historical material to work with. All they had to do was to await the time when American blacks could communicate with one another about the richness of a life that had contributed a rhythm to American music and a cadence to American speech that became recognizable around the world.

The identification rooted in being first families may also yet turn out to be an important badge of cultural distinctiveness. Black

Christians have long been taught that they carried through their religion the best version of the American dream. If there is any sincere feeling left in American public rhetoric, and that is debatable, black ministers deserve much of the credit. They arguably are the only people around who could read aloud Lincoln's Second Inaugural Address and make anyone in the United States believe it. The black Protestant church, shaped as it was by both slavery and emancipation, held out the possibility that the American commitment to equality might fail, but it did not insist that it would. The power of the black church derived from, and derives from, the hope that it might succeed. It is an utterly pragmatic proposition that still places a large burden for making it become true on the black churches. At least for the moment, American blacks are carrying the burden primarily for themselves.

Civil and Uncivil Religions—
Describing Religious Pluralism

What then is the point? In the Introduction we traced the history of a Protestant desire. Throughout the nineteenth century most Protestant evangelicals who could be located within the Calvinist, Methodist, or Lutheran traditions warmly endorsed America's experiment in religious disestablishment. At the same time, they expected Americans to move toward a common faith which they thought would resemble their own sectarian outlooks. They were prepared to tolerate diversity, but they did not regard diversity as in itself a good thing. Too many sharply distinctive faiths in fact nullified not only their belief in the unity of the Reformed church but their idea of a virtuous republic as well. To them, maintaining a sensible piety among the American people was a public concern.

Jefferson had spoken of a "wall of separation" between church and state, but Jefferson was not much of an evangelical. His metaphor badly characterized the attitude of ministers who took the lead in describing America's religious system. They viewed the United States as a Protestant Christian nation. Many of them wanted the Constitution to say so explicitly, and they lobbied for legislation that laid down broad guidelines for religious and moral behavior. The freedom to worship in odd ways did not, they believed, require governments to encourage people to exercise that freedom. Unfolding events in the nineteenth century did little to sustain the hopes of Protestants who were waiting for a fundamental religious unity to emerge. However, the situation was sufficiently complicated to lend plausibility to any number of interpretations. What one chose to describe remained very much under the influence of what one wished to prescribe.

By the middle of the twentieth century, the nineteenth-century Protestant desire clearly needed recasting. The permanence of diversity, diversity that included non-Protestant religious traditions, could no longer be doubted. Nonetheless, those who wanted to continue to emphasize some form of essential religious unity found ways to do so, none more persuasively than the American sociologist Robert Bellah.[1] Bellah described the emergence of a civil religion in the United States which, while it did not replace or compete with individual churches, formed an arch of consensus over them. Civil religion, according to Bellah, had a life and institutional base of its own. Bellah argued that its major tenets were not even originally Protestant. But even if they were, the American mission which they sanctified had long ago expanded to include Catholics and Jews. Bellah found a good bit of the evidence for what he wanted to argue in the inaugural address of John Kennedy. America's first Catholic president molded his phrases to fit a tradition of public religious rhetoric that went all the way back to John Winthrop.

Without question, Bellah was onto something important, and he was not the only distinguished scholar who in the post-World War II era managed to locate an American faith that transcended the crazy quilt pattern of denominational divisions.[2] Americans are nationalistic like other people, and their nationalism was and is frequently expressed in religious terms. The paradox has not been lost on European observers. A nation that supposedly is neutral about religion has made religion an obligatory part of public ceremonies. Americans cannot even begin a football game without calling on a clergyman, and it scarcely matters of what faith, to invoke the divine blessing that they assume is peculiarly theirs. Yet if the rites of civil religion suggest that Americans share religious myths, mere reference to them does not settle the issue of how much of themselves Americans invest in nonacrimonious religious observance and how much of themselves they invest in using religious lines to separate themselves from one another. Civil religion exists, but it too, like more ordinary religions, may have split Americans into separate camps as often as it has brought them together.

Common myths do not have to be read in the same way. That is one important caveat. Studies of popular culture have begun to take account of how people misread or creatively misinterpret

texts that are assumed to have a clear and single meaning.[3] Public
ceremonies are no different from texts. Most Americans celebrate
the commercially promoted holidays of Christmas and Thanks-
giving, but what their private recreations on those days mean to
them is anyone's guess. The same can be said about Inauguration
Days, Fourth of July celebrations, and Memorial Days. Americans
may or may not pay much attention to what presidents say when
they take office; but since the ritual utterances are in the main
bland (Jefferson, Lincoln, and Kennedy are exceptions), Americans are not forced into a single pattern of understanding meaning. Americans may remember on the Fourth of July that they are
glad to be American, but whether that memory in most cases
relates to feelings solemn or specific enough to qualify as religion
is subject to doubt. Memorial Day celebrations in small towns
give as much evidence of patterns of geographical tribalism as of
a common faith. Insofar as the rites of a public religion evoke
strong emotional response, they do most certainly reinforce
American patriotism. However, as we have seen, patriotic flag
waving permits a language that proclaims difference. A civil religion therefore turns into an arena of contested meanings where
Americans make assertions about what makes them different from
other Americans. The Civil War stands as an ample reminder of
just how bad things can get. A functional unity of the majority
may in normal times be the product of civic piety, but we ought
not on that account forget the differences, or the ways in which
what is called civil religion can reinforce the least attractive common denominators of the American people.

The last point, although acknowledged, is deemphasized in the
prescriptive outlook that clearly underlies much of what has been
written on the subject of civil religion. At its best, according to
Bellah, American civil religion recognized that the nation stood
under transcendent judgment. If regular denominational religions
have had trouble keeping that point of view in mind, we should
not be surprised that past American politicians have in their public
piety fallen shorter of Bellah's idealism than Bellah wished to concede. When the "sixties" were over, some proponents of civil
religion followed Bellah in writing sadly about the "empty and
broken shell" of American civil religion.[4] There was reason for
sadness, but what they thought had failed was not failing for the
first time in American life. Gratitude is due to anyone who tries

to hold America to high expectations, but only historical forget-fulness can permit us to believe that the American past furnishes consistent encouragement to those expectations. What the origi-nal tribal inhabitants of North America learned about America's sense of national destiny was as relevant to understanding the uses of civil religion as Lincoln's Second Inaugural Address.

The success that the American people have had with their insti-tutions was not necessarily in the design, for the system has often worked in ways that would have confounded the designers. Mad-ison, in the celebrated tenth paper that he wrote to argue the Fed-eralist position, came as close as anyone ever has to explaining the "genius" of American politics. Societies, according to Madison, are collections of groups or factions that seek to satisfy selfish, frequently economic, interests. In pure democracies or in small republics, factions posed grave dangers to individual liberty. Any one of them had a fair chance to become a majority and thus gain the unchecked power to impose its particular interests on every-one else. In a large republic, such as the United States was intended to be, the danger of factionalism was significantly reduced. Elected assemblies imposed a check on popular majori-ties. More important, large republics, spread over an extensive geographical area, multiplied the number of factions to the point that no one of them could become the majority. As a result, fac-tions had to compromise and to be content with only part of what they wanted. They sometimes even had to concern themselves with the public good. Madison never imagined that the selfish desires responsible for the formation of factions would disappear or cease to be a primary motive in political behavior. He merely predicted, with reasonable accuracy, that the projected American system could control the dangerous consequences of factionalism.

The analysis that Madison applied to political behavior was just as prescient with respect to the American system of church vol-untarism. American religious sects are a species of faction, and the religious history of the United States gives us little reason to think that tolerance would remain an entirely safe principle if any one of them gained an overwhelming majority. Will Herberg was being uncharacteristically Pollyanna-ish when he concluded that the "American tends to feel rather strongly that total religious uni-formity. . . would be something undesirable and wrong."[5] Perhaps recently, a pluralism of religions and churches has become "axiomatic" to most Americans. However, the full extension of religious tolerance, if indeed full tolerance describes the present state of religious affairs in the United States, was more the product of conditions of pluralism which no one sect had the power to overcome as of an abstract belief in the value of pluralism. Contemporary studies that point to a strong correlation between religious affiliation and prejudice should remind us that religious tolerance was not the free gift of a dominant religious group, the Constitution notwithstanding, but the product of uneasy arrangements made between groups that did not much like one another.[6] If Americans are now more religiously tolerant than they were in the nineteenth century, it is not because they are collectively more high-minded but because they care less about religion. A civil religion that guarantees an absolutely unqualified religious liberty to everyone has about the same standing in American life as Madison's realm of the public good. One has no trouble finding it proclaimed and respected, but it owes its existence to the frustration of sectarian interests rather than to the disappearance of selfish ambitions and dark suspicions about the value of someone else's religion.

In raising questions about the degree of religious consensus in the United States, we most certainly run the risk of exaggerating divergence. Any number of observers have remarked with respect to political behavior that the ideological differences among Americans have been relatively insignificant. Otherwise the American party system could not have operated as it has. An analogous observation about American religion suggests that although one can count hundreds of religious groups in the United States, the vast majority of religious Americans have gravitated toward a small number of "mainline" denominations. Edwin Gaustad, for example, argued on the basis of religious statistics gathered in 1965, that is, in a period marked by a seemingly large amount of religious splintering, that only ten major Christian denominational families existed in the United States.[7] Despite journalistic attention given to new religions that attracted young students, the ten major denominational families together comprised 57.9 percent of the total national population and 90 percent of church membership.

Gaustad sensibly suggested, therefore, that America's system of religious pluralism has stopped well short of religious anarchy. He confirmed what nineteenth-century religious statisticians had observed: in whatever time period, most Americans who affiliated with churches confined their enthusiasms within the structures of no more than ten main groups. In fact, judged by these measures, the degree of unity is increasing. That is, the ten largest denominations at the end of the nineteenth century, as counted by H. K. Carroll, comprised a smaller proportion of total church adherents than they do now (75 percent as opposed to 90 percent). But Gaustad made nothing of the trend. His main thought was to demonstrate that the names of the "mainline" denominations change, but the number of them stays roughly the same.

Although religious census statistics are not wrong (at least no more wrong than statistics about religion always are), one still feels a bit like blind men before the elephant. Most of what one describes depends upon what one happens to touch, and it is not at all clear how best to sum up the whole. As noted, Gaustad might have used census statistics to suggest more unity than he did. In 1965 only two denominational families counted more than 10 percent of the national population—Roman Catholics with 23.8 percent and Baptists with 12.2 percent. (The proportional predominance of both groups has increased since 1965.) Together these two major denominational families claimed 36 percent of the national population and 56 percent of the church population. Measured against such statistical preponderance, one wonders what else could qualify as major. Perhaps Methodism, which housed 7 percent of the national population. Beyond that, none of the other denominational families labeled as "major" by Gaustad accounted for more than 5 percent of the national population, and only one, the Lutherans, exceeded 4 percent. The bottom seven of the "major" denominational families divided a scant 14.5 percent of the national population, and only 22.5 percent of the church population. Statistically, Presbyterians (2.3 percent of the national population) and Episcopalians (1.8 percent) were closer, much closer, to Christian Scientists and Pentecostals than to Catholics and Baptists. It is hard to see the choice of the number "ten" to count "major" families as anything more than a wish to have a list long enough to seem tolerant but not so long as to appear indiscriminate.

Gaustad is an astute observer of American religious life, and he did not rest his conclusions on statistics alone. He noted correctly that members of most of the smaller denominations on his list of ten were proportionately overrepresented in the most influential institutions that comprise American society. Moreover, although theoretically split by family lines, some were on the verge of forming a Christian Union that would put them numerically in the same league with Baptists. Still, one is left with questions about splits in the major "denominational families." Baptists are the largest Protestant family precisely because their name covers any number of conventions and congregations which encourage a consciousness of separation. Catholics, who despite large numbers have only recently made it onto lists of "mainline" churches, have managed to advance in America despite the well-known ethnic parochialism that in reality divides the church. Any grouping of denominational "families" is bound to underestimate the degree to which religious Americans have made their primary allegiance to numerically small groups.

The same caution holds true even if one ignores families and counts separate denominations. The latest census, published in 1984, showed four Christian denominations with over five million members; nine more with over two million; and twenty-two total with over one million. Although diversity already becomes more apparent if we separate Baptists, Methodists, Presbyterians, and others into their various national organizations, we ought to go further. We ought to be looking at individual churches which have always been among America's strongest local institutions. The label "denomination" conceals any number of class, ethnic, and racial differences, not to mention distinctive theological perspectives and styles. The fact that individual Americans frequently change denominations, despite strong denominational loyalties, is a sign of that. In moving from one place to another, and faced with the need to sink instant roots into something particular and familiar, people sometimes find a denominational name of little help in deciding where to turn.

America's system of religious pluralism is not anarchy. We have no quarrel with that statement. We have, however, wished to reiterate several things that are not always apparent in efforts to draw lines between "mainline" and "non-mainline" churches in the United States, lines which place even many of those born on American soil in the latter category. The gulfs that religious Americans have invented to distinguish their various religious groups have not always, or even usually, had much to do with theology. Ecumenicists have been perfectly correct in saying that America does not need so many faiths as it has to house the range of its theological opinion. Any sophisticated theological perspective could instantly dissolve the importance of most beliefs that divide American Protestant groups. But religious modernists, who have yearned for a tolerance that flows from consensus, have tried to let an abstract possibility serve as reality. They have misread the facts that sectarian division is contrived, that religious groups exaggerate the differences that separate them, as evidence of incipient unity. What they have forgotten to ponder is why the divisions do not easily go away.

Andrew Greeley has persuasively noted that American churches have succeeded not merely because they have provided their adherents with a framework of religious meaning sufficient to explain the world they live in.[8] If that were the only thing, secularism would long ago have worked more corrosively on American religious loyalties than it has. American churches have also provided a shelter for people who otherwise had no clear niche in a bewilderingly unstructured society. Americans needed an unusual differentiation of religious persuasions because they had an unusual need for a wise variety of social identities. The separation of church and state in America has not done as much for the virtue of either church or state as its proponents usually claim. It did not much help Americans to find God or public virtue. What it did do was enable them to find themselves.

This returns us to the problem of understanding the paradoxical relation between outsider religious groups and so-called "mainline" churches. What we have tried to suggest is that "mainline" has too often been misleadingly used to label what is "normal" in American religious life and "outsider" to characterize what is aberrational or not-yet-American. In fact the American religious system may be said to be "working" only when it is creating cracks within denominations, when it is producing novelty, even when it is fueling antagonisms. These things are not things which, properly understood, are going on at the edges or fringes of American life. They are what give energy to church life and substance to the claim that Americans are the most religious people on the face of the earth. This often unexamined cliche by the way only means that a lot of Americans go to church. It does not mean, at least not without more proof than is offered here, that Americans are an especially spiritually minded people.

All of the examples we have presented were meant to change the meaning of our common vocabularies by revealing their ambiguity. As the argument ends, we may concede that the Mormon church in 1840 is not usefully characterized as "mainline." Nonetheless, nothing was more central to American culture at the time than the Mormon "controversy." Americans discovered who they were by locating themselves with respect to it. Furthermore, nothing was more "normal" or "typical" of American life than the process of carving out a separate self-identification, a goal toward which all the early Mormon enterprise was directed. The same effort was being made by much larger groups, the Catholics for example, as well as by churches that already thought of themselves as being on the "inside." Unitarian belligerency in the face of Transcendentalism was the response of a group that was trying to balance feelings of cultural superiority with fears of social extinction. There is no way to deal with questions of inside and outside without sharply qualifying the objectivity which those labels seem to claim. What was in conventional terms outside the American religious mainstream turned American religious history into an interesting story. Pluralism may not have meant anarchy. But it did mean pluralism.

Many of the religious groups we have written about in these pages attracted people with strongly felt social insecurities. But what should we make of that? To call their activities marginal blinds us to the great number of Americans who have had to find ways to confront social insecurities. To call certain religious positions escapist or unrealistic because they failed to encourage political activity that promised relief to downtrodden groups conceals how little many people have gotten from politics even in what is theoretically as democratic a country as exists in the world. As the reader was warned in the beginning, the point of view of this analysis is not particularly optimistic.

On the other hand, if the time has long come when Americans must stop writing about their unique success, they may take certain satisfactions in reviewing the historical record. The United States absorbed a vast number of people who had no opportunities elsewhere. It did not do that without violence, oppression, and exploitation, but one can imagine a far worse scenario. On balance, the proliferation of religious identifications helped contain the worst tendencies in American life. That was not because the various religions taught brotherly love, although most of them did. Nor was it because religions sought to avoid antagonism. Quite the contrary. Nor was it because diversity did not really entail distinctiveness. What the proliferation did was to provide ways for many people to invest their life with a significance that eased their sense of frustration. For many, no doubt, that meant coming to terms with and accepting social and political powerlessness. For others, it led directly to gaining conventional forms of power in a world that was no longer primarily religious. America was potentially as great a religious battleground as had existed in the course of Western Civilization. That it did not become one of the worst is probably enough of a success so far as history goes. Consensus as a myth became believable, and the long-range effects of very real conflict were blunted. Whether that success, the result of a providential mistake, will continue in the future is another matter.

Notes

PREFACE

1. R. Laurence Moore, "Insiders and Outsiders in American Historical Narrative and American History," *American Historical Review* 87 (April 1982): 390–412; Moore, "The Occult Connection? Mormonism, Christian Science, and Spiritualism," in Howard Kerr and Charles L. Crow eds., *The Occult in America. New Historical Perspectives* (Urbana, 1983), 135–61.

2. Robert Bellah, "Civil Religion in America," *Daedalus* 96 (Winter 1967): 1–21.

3. Moore, "Insiders and Outsiders."

4. For an especially cogent discussion, see Jonathan D. Culler, *On Deconstruction. Theory and Criticism after Structuralism* (Ithaca, 1982).

INTRODUCTION

1. A provocative corrective to older views is Philip F. Gura, *A Glimpse of Sion's Glory. Puritan Radicalism in New England, 1620–1660* (Middletown, Conn., 1984).

2. Thomas Branagan, *A Concise View of the Principal Religious Denominations in the United States of America* (Philadelphia, 1811). The only nineteenth-century account of American religions, which can at all match Branagan's in its sympathetic inclusiveness, is I(srael) Daniel Rupp, comp., *He Pasa Ekklesia: An Original History of the Religious Denominations at Present Existing in the United States* (Philadelphia, 1844). Rupp strove for neutrality by letting a member of each of the forty-three groups included write the individual account. The book is more interesting and more useful than Branagan's but lacks any overall point of view. Rupp published a number of revised editions of the work.

3. Robert Baird, *Religion in America, or, an Account of the Origin, Relation to the State, and Present Condition of the Evangelical Churches in the United States* (New York, 1856, first published, 1844), Books 6 & 7.

4. Ibid., 443, 456, 463, 497.

5. Ibid., 566, 571.

6. Ibid., 579.

7. Quoted in Martin E. Marty, *A Nation of Behavers* (Chicago, 1976), 174.

8. Philip Schaff, *America. A Sketch of Its Political, Social, and Religious Character* (Cambridge, Mass., 1961, first published, 1854), 198–204.

9. Ibid., 10–11.

10. Ibid., 98–99.

11. Ibid., 80.

12. Ibid., 191.

13. Daniel Dorchester, *Christianity in the United States from the First Settlement Down to the Present Time* (New York, 1888), 23.

14. Ibid., 24.

15. Ibid., 25.

16. Ibid., 48.

17. Ibid., 63.

18. Ibid., 65–66.

19. Ibid., 190–91.

20. Ibid., 763–64.

21. Ibid., 618.

22. Ibid., 641, 780.

23. H. K. Carroll, *The Religious Forces of the United States Enumerated, Classified, and Described on the Basis of the Government Census of 1890* (New York, 1893), xxxv–xxxvi.

24. Ibid., xl.

25. Leonard Woolsey Bacon, *A History of American Christianity* (New York, 1897), 403–4.

26. Ibid., 405.

27. William Warren Sweet, *The Story of Religions in America* (New York, 1930), 411.

28. Winthrop Hudson, *The Great Tradition of the American Churches* (New York, 1953).

29. Ibid., 258–59. See also his discussion in Hudson, *Religion in America* (New York, 1965), 81–82.

30. See especially Sidney Mead, *The Lively Experiment: The Shaping of Christianity in America* (New York, 1963); *The Nation with the Soul of a Church* (New York, 1975); *The Old Religion in the Brave New World. Reflections on the Relation Between Christendom and the Republic* (Berkeley, 1977).

31. H. Richard Niebuhr, *The Social Sources of Denominationalism* (New York, 1929).

32. Will Herberg, *Protestant, Catholic, Jew. An Essay in American Religious Sociology* (Garden City, 1955). See discussion in Mark Silk, "Notes on the Judeo-Christian Tradition in America," *American Quarterly* 36 (Spring 1984): 74–77.

33. For example, see Martin Marty, *Pilgrims in Their Own Land. 500 Years of Religion in America* (Boston, 1984); Sydney E. Ahlstrom, *A Religious History of the American People* (New Haven, 1972); Edwin S. Gaustad, *Dis-*

sent in American Religion (Chicago, 1973); Catherine L. Albanese, *America. Religions and Religion* (Belmont, Calif., 1981).

CHAPTER ONE

1. "The Rise and Progress of the Mormon Faith and People," *Southern Literary Messenger*, 10 (Sept. 1844), 527.

2. Quoted in Klaus J. Hansen, *Quest for Empire. The Political Kingdom of God and the Council of Fifty in Mormon History* (East Lansing, Mich., 1967), 25. Thomas J. Yates, "Count Tolstoy and 'The American Religion'," *The Improvement Era* 42 (1939): 94.

3. William Mulder and A. Russell Mortensen, eds., *Among the Mormons. Historic Accounts by Contemporary Observers* (Lincoln, 1958), vi.

4. The persistence and repetitiveness of the enormous amount of anti-Mormon literature are themselves an indication of just how much uncertainty the subject provoked. I shall not attempt to list individual titles. For a discussion of one aspect of the anti-Mormon literature, see Charles N. Cannon, "The Awesome Power of Sex: The Polemical Campaign Against Mormon Polygamy," *Pacific Historical Review* 43 (Feb. 1974): 61–82.

5. Quoted in Hansen, *Quest for Empire*, 117. Also see letter from Joseph Smith, *Times and Seasons* July 1840.

6. For a narrative of how the stronger language developed, see Robert B. Flanders, *Nauvoo: Kingdom on the Mississippi* (Urbana, 1965), 283; and Norman F. Furniss, The *Mormon Conflict, 1850–59* (New Haven, 1960). Two documents often cited as evidence of Mormon disloyalty are Parley Pratt, *A Voice of Warning and Instruction to All People, Containing a Declaration of Faith and Doctrine of the Church of the Latter-day Saints, Commonly Called Mormons* (New York, 1837); and Sidney Rigdon's 1838 Fourth of July oration delivered at Far West, Caldwell County, Missouri. The text of the letter is reprinted in *Brigham Young University Studies* 14 (Summer 1974): 518–27. For Orson Pratt's attitude on leaving Nauvoo, see B(righam) H(enry) Roberts, *History of the Church of Jesus Christ of Latter-day Saints* (Salt Lake City, 1960), 7:515–19.

7. For the most interesting recent example, see Richard L. Bushman, *Joseph Smith and the Origins of Mormonism* (Urbana, 1984). Non-Mormons have also begun to make thoughtful contributions to the notion of Mormon exceptionalism. Jan Shipps, *Mormonism. The Story of a New Religious Tradition* (Urbana, 1985) is a provocative contribution to this genre and a useful corrective to my emphasis.

8. John C. Bennett, *The History of the Saints; or, an Exposé of Joe Smith and Mormonism* (Boston, 1842), 257.

9. Thomas W. Young, *Mormonism. Its Origin, Doctrines, and Dangers* (Ann Arbor, 1900).

10. For balanced accounts of the sexual lives of Mormons, consult Leonard J. Arrington and Davis Bitton, *The Mormon Experience. A History of the Latter-day Saints* (New York, 1979); and Lawrence Foster, *Religion and Sexuality. Three American Communal Experiments in the Nineteenth Century* (New York, 1981).

11. Foster, *Religion and Sexuality*, 240.

12. Quoted in Flanders, *Nauvoo*, 331. For a scholarly version of the same argument, see Ephraim E. Erickson, *The Psychological and Ethical Aspects of Mormon Group Life* (Chicago, 1922), 30.

13. From the *Quincy Whig*, Oct. 17, 1840. Quoted in Cecil A. Snider, "Development of Attitudes in Sectarian Conflict: A Study of Mormonism in Illinois in Contemporary Newspaper Sources," M.A. thesis, University of Iowa, 1933, p. 12.

14. A. Leland Jamison, "Religions on the Christian Perimeter," in James Ward Smith and Jamison, eds., *The Shaping of American Religion* (Princeton, 1961), 215. Also see Klaus J. Hansen, *Mormonism and the American Experience* (Chicago, 1981), esp. p. 82.

15. Oscar Osburn Winther, ed., *The Private Papers and Diary of Thomas Leiper Kane. A Friend to the Mormons* (San Francisco, 1937), 34.

16. Claudia L. Bushman, ed., *Mormon Sisters: Women in Early Utah* (Cambridge, Mass., 1976).

17. For the best discussion, see Hansen, *Quest for Empire*; and Hansen, "The Political Kingdom of God as a Cause for Mormon-Gentile Conflict," *Brigham Young University Studies* 2 (Spring-Summer 1960), 241–60. Also useful is James Keith Melville, "The Political Ideas of Brigham Young," Ph.D. dissertation, University of Utah, 1956.

18. After trouble in Missouri, one Mormon, R. B. Thompson, wrote to the First Presidency some revealing comments about how Mormons destroyed "benevolent and philanthrophic feelings which have been manifested towards us as a people." In seeking to redress their grievances in Missouri, they condemned not merely the "Democracy of Missouri," but "the whole Union, which was by no means united against the Mormons." They applied the label "Demagogue" to Thomas Hart Benson for not answering a letter he had probably not received. See Roberts, *History of the Church*, 3: 351–52. An editorial in the *Warsaw Signal* (Aug. 1844) complained that Mormons made no effort to become a component part of the community. They set themselves up as a separate people and branded others, with no effort to differentiate, as Gentiles. Brigham Young ignored all of this and told Horace Greeley that he could think of no explanation for the hatred manifested toward his people other "than is afforded by the crucifixion of Christ and the kindred treatment of God's ministers, prophets and saints in all ages." See Interview, *New York Daily Tribune*, Aug. 20, 1859.

19. Quoted in Donna Hill, *Joesph Smith. The First Mormon* (Garden City, N.Y., 1977), 52. For background, see Dean C. Jesse, "The Early Accounts of Joseph Smith's First Vision," *Brigham Young University Studies* 9 (Spring

1969): 275–94. One historian notes that Smith's words about these early per-secutions have not been verified by any contemporary source; see Hansen, *Mormonism and the American Experience*, 23.

20. Roberts, *History of the Church*, 5: 157; Hill, *Joseph Smith*, 343, 392. One can follow many similar statements in the early volumes of Roberts and in the Mormon newspaper, *Times and Seasons*.

21. Luther P. Gerlach and Virginia H. Hine, *People, Power, and Change: Movements of Social Transformation* (Indianapolis, 1970), chap. 7.

22. Mulder and Mortensen, *Among the Mormons*, 129.

23. Ibid., 367.

24. Ibid., 171.

25. Arrington and Bitton, *The Mormon Experience*, 69.

26. Georg Simmel, "The Sociology of Secrecy and of Secret Societies," *American Journal of Sociology* 11 (Jan. 1906), 441–98.

27. Roberts, *History of the Church*, 7: 174.

28. See Alma R. Blair, "The Reorganized Church of Jesus Christ of Lat-ter Day Saints: Moderate Mormons," in F. Mark McKiernan, Alma R. Blair, Paul M. Edwards, *The Restoration Movement: Essays in Mormon History* (Lawrence, Kansas, 1973).

29. For elaboration of my views about empirical claims and American reli-gion, see Moore, *In Search of White Crows. Spiritualism, Parapsychology, and American Culture* (New York, 1977). The best discussion of the theological appeal of Mormonism is in Arrington and Bitton, *The Mormon Experience*, 20–43.

30. John Lofland and Rodney Stark, "Becoming a World Saver: A Theory of Conversion to a Deviant Perspective," *American Sociological Review* 30 (Dec. 1965): 862.

31. Mario S. DePillis, "The Social Sources of Mormonism," *Church His-tory* 37 (March 1968): 50–79.

32. Mark Leone, *Roots of Modern Mormonism* (Cambridge, Mass., 1979). For a more balanced view on the counter-cultural thrust of early Mormon-ism, see Hansen, *Mormonism and the American Experience*, 52–54 and *passim*.

33. Leone, *Roots of Mormonism*, 146.

34. Arrington and Bitton, *The Mormon Experience*, 184. Also see Gustave O. Larson, *The "Americanization" of Utah for Statehood* (San Marino, 1971).

35. A column syndicated in January, 1979.

36. Edward Thorndike, "The Origins of Superior Men," *Scientific Monthly* 56 (May 1943): 424–33.

CHAPTER TWO

1. Preface to John Tracy Ellis, *American Catholicism* (Chicago, 1969), ix.

2. Philip Gleason, "Coming to Terms with American Catholic History," *Societas* 3 (Autumn 1973): 305.

3. Thomas T. McAvoy, *A History of the Catholic Church in the United States* (Notre Dame, 1969); McAvoy, *The Americanist Heresy in Roman Catholicism, 1895–1900* (Notre Dame, 1963). For a similar perspective, see John Tracy Ellis, *American Catholicism* (Chicago, 1969); Andrew M. Greeley, *The Catholic Experience. An Interpretation of the History of American Catholicism* (Garden City, N.Y., 1967); James Hennesey, *American Catholics. A History of the Roman Catholic Community in the United States* (New York, 1981).

4. Greeley, *The American Catholic. A Social Portrait* (New York, 1977), 16, 21. Also see Daniel Bell, "Ethnicity and Social Change," in Nathan Glazer and Daniel P. Moynihan, eds., *Ethnicity: Theory and Experience* (Cambridge, Mass., 1975), 171; Peter K. Eisinger, "Ethnicity as a Strategic Option: An Emerging View," *Public Administration Review* 38 (Jan./Feb. 1978): 89–93.

5. David J. O'Brien, *The Renewal of American Catholicism* (New York, 1972), 15, 144. For an acute appraisal of changing fashions, see Philip Gleason, "The Crisis of Americanization" in Gleason, ed., *Contemporary Catholicism in the United States* (Notre Dame, 1969), 3–31; and Gleason, "American Identity and Americanization," *Harvard Encyclopedia of American Ethnic Groups* (Cambridge, Mass., 1980), 31–58.

6. O'Brien, "American Catholicism and the Diaspora," *Cross Currents* (Summer 1966), 307–23. See also O'Brien, *American Catholics and Social Reform: The New Deal Years* (New York, 1968).

7. *Anti-Catholicism in America, 1841–1851. Three Sermons* (New York, 1977), 35–38. Also see the Rev. Edward Beecher, *The Papal Conspiracy Exposed, and Protestantism Defended, in the Light of Reason, History and Scripture* (Boston, 1855).

8. James F. Connelly, *The Visit of Archbishop Gaetano Bedini to the United States, June 1853–February 1854* (Rome, 1960), 195–96.

9. Orestes Brownson, "Mission of America," *Brownson's Quarterly Review*, N.Y. series, 1 (Oct. 1856): 411–12, 435.

10. Letter from Brownson to Isaac Hecker, June 1, 1855, in Joseph F. Gower and Richard M. Leliaert, eds., *The Brownson-Hecker Correspondence* (Notre Dame, 1979), 182.

11. Brownson, "Mission of America," 414.

12. Concord (Mass.) *Freeman*, Oct. 25, 1844. Quoted in Francis D. Nichol, *The Midnight Cry* (Takoma Park, 1944), 298.

13. Letter from Hughes to Brownson, Aug. 29, 1856, Orestes Brownson papers, Notre Dame. Also letter from Brownson to Hughes, Sept. 1, 1856. A similar public clash occurred in June 1861. See Henry F. Brownson, *Orestes A. Brownson's Latter Life from 1856 to 1876* (Detroit, 1900), 413–14.

14. Vincent P. Lannie, *Public Money and Parochial Education. Bishop Hughes, Governor Seward, and the New York School Controversy* (Cleveland, 1968), viii. According to Thomas T. McAvoy, "the policy of Hughes set

back the progress of the Irish immigrant at least a generation." McAvoy, "The Formation of the Catholic Minority in the United States, 1820–1860," *Review of Politics* 10 (Jan. 1948): 13–34. Also see McAvoy, "Orestes A. Brownson and Archbishop John Hughes in 1860," *Review of Politics* 24 (Jan. 1962), 19–47.

15. Greeley, *Catholic Experience*, 125.

16. Brownson to Hecker, Aug. 5, 1857, in Gower and Leliaert, *Brownson-Hecker Correspondence*, 194. Henry F. Brownson, *Orestes A. Brownson's Middle Life from 1845 to 1855* (Detroit, 1899), 582–83.

17. Brownson, "A Few Words on Native Americanism," *Brownson's Quarterly Review* 3rd series 2 (July 1854): 341.

18. Lawrence Kehoe, ed., *Complete Works of the Most Rev. John Hughes* (New York, 1866), 1: 436. On Hughes's response to the Young Ireland movement, see "Reflections and Suggestions in Regard to What Is Called the Catholic Press in the United States," Kehoe, *Complete Works*, 2: 686–701; Josephine Phelan, *The Ardent Exile. The Life and Times of Thomas Darcy McGee* (Toronto, 1951), 98–99.

19. *Harvard Encyclopedia on Ethnic Groups*, 308, The New York City Common Council voted to end the allotment of public funds to ecclesiastical schools in 1824. However, in 1840, the Whig governor, William Seward, reopened the issue. See John Webb Pratt, *Religion, Politics, and Diversity. The Church-State Theme in New York History* (Ithaca, 1967), 158–203. Also Carl F. Kaestle, *The Evolution of an Urban School System, New York City 1750–1850* (Cambridge, Mass., 1973). The early history of public education in Chicago has been treated less fully than the case of New York City, but see James W. Sanders, *The Education of an Urban Minority. Catholics in Chicago, 1833–1965* (New York, 1977), 18–39. For a Catholic view of what happened in Boston, see Robert H. Lord et al., *History of the Archdiocese of Boston* (New York, 1944), 2: 574–623.

20. Kehoe, *Complete Works*, 1: 41–297. For an introduction to some of the issues at stake see Timothy L. Smith, "Protestant Schooling and American Nationality, 1800–1850," *Journal of American History* 53 (March 1967): 679–95.

21. Lannie, *Public Money and Parochial Education*, 247–58. Also see Diane Ravitch, *The Great School Wars. New York City, 1805–1873. A History of the Public Schools as a Battlefield of Social Change* (New York, 1974), 45.

22. Lannie, *Public Money and Parochial Education*, 250.

23. "Letter of John Hughes in Reply to General Cass," *The Metropolitan* 2 (July 1854), 363.

24. Kehoe, *Complete Works*, 1: 232.

25. *Ibid.* In this wording Hughes was very close to Brownson. See Brownson, "The Church and the Constitution," *Brownson's Quarterly Review* New York Series 2 (Oct. 1857), 458.

26. Letter from Brownson to Hecker, Aug. 25, 1870, in Gower and Leliaert, *Brownson-Hecker Correspondence*, 291. "Instead of regarding the Church as having advantages here which she has nowhere else, I think she has here a more subtle and powerful enemy to combat than in any of the old monarchial nations of the world." In 1859, Brownson had written: "We believe American society... is better organized, and organized more in accordance with the needs of Catholic Society, than is any other society on the face of the globe." *Brownson's Quarterly Review*, New York Series 4 (July 1859), 340.

27. Robert D. Cross, *The Emergence of Liberal Catholicism in America* (Cambridge, Mass. 1958), 22–50.

28. As quoted in Donald L. Kinzer, *An Episode in Anti-Catholicism: The American Protective Association* (Seattle, 1964), 32.

29. Edward McSweeney, "American Catholics and the Propagation of the Faith," *American Ecclesiastical Review* 20 (March 1899): 242–43.

30. "Address to the Congress by Hon. Morgan J. O'Brien," in *Progress of the Catholic Church in America and the Great Columbian Catholic Congress of 1893* (Chicago, 1897) 2: 18. See especially Thomas D'Arcy McGee, *The Catholic History of North America* (Boston, 1855), 109–10.

31. John Gilmary Shea, "Puritanism in New England," *American Catholic Quarterly Review* 9 (Jan. 1884): 81, 90.

32. James A. Corcoran, "Martin Luther and His American Worshipers," *American Catholic Quarterly Review* 9 (July 1884): 551.

33. Frederick J. Zwierlein, *The Life and Letters of Bishop McQuaid* (Rochester, 1927), 2: 467–68. Also see Augustus J. Thebaud, *Forty Years in the United States of America, 1839–1885* (New York, 1904), esp. 33–34, 62–63, 137.

34. S.B.A. Harper, "The Relation of the Church and the Constitution of the United States," *American Catholic Quarterly Review* 2 (Oct. 1877): 704. Hecker stated his position in his *The Church and the Age. An Exposition of the Catholic Church in View of the Needs and Aspirations of the Present Age* (New York, 1887).

35. Harper, "Relations of the Church and the Constitution," 719–21. Peter K. Guilday, *A History of the Councils of Baltimore, 1791–1884* (New York, 1932), 246–47. Emphasis, rather than fundamental disagreement over political principle, usually distinguished the line about American institutions taken in Isaac Hecker's *The Catholic World* from the one in the more conservative *American Ecclesiastical Review*.

36. See, for example, "The Catholic Element in the History of the United States," *The Metropolitan* 5 (Oct. 1857) 526.

37. For this reason conservative attacks on American public education could be suspiciously based on liberal principles protesting unwarranted state interference and control. The complaint was despotism. Parents, not the State, should control the education of children. "Compulsory education is

the first door opened to the State by which it may enter upon the general contour of our domestic affairs; it is the first step towards the imposition of the intolerable yoke of paternalism so galling to the intelligent Europeans; it is the beginning of that process of absorption by the State of all individual and corporate rights and powers, making for the complete centralization and abject worship by its citizens of the State. The whole tendency of this movement is un-American and as Americans we oppose it." Dennis T. O'Sullivan, "Is It Opportune?" *American Ecclesiastical Review* 6 (April 1892): 311.

38. "The Chapter 'De Fide Catholic' in the Third Plenary Council of Baltimore," *American Ecclesiastical Review* 16 (Feb. 1897): 152.

39. As quoted in Colman J. Barry, *The Catholic Church and German Americans* (Milwaukee, 1953), 212.

40. Zwierlein, *Life and Letters*, 3: 242.

41. Quoted in O'Brien, *Renewal of American Catholicism*, 144.

42. Gerald P. Fogarty, *The Vatican and the Americanist Crisis: Denis J. O'Connell, American Agent in Rome, 1885–1903* (Rome, 1974), 143, 211.

43. Zwierlein, *Life and Letters*, 3: 175.

44. Cross, *Liberal Catholicism*, 175.

45. Robert Emmett Curran, *Michael Augustine Corrigan and the Shaping of Conservative Catholicism in America, 1878–1902* (New York, 1978), 224.

46. For one nativist attack on Ireland, see James M. King, *Facing the Twentieth Century. Our Country: Its Power and Peril* (New York, 1899), 475–76.

47. For Corrigan's reaction to Cahenslyism, see Curran, *Michael Augustine Corrigan*, 324. For a general discussion of German Catholics, see Philip Gleason, *The Conservative Reformers. German-American Catholics and the Social Order* (Notre Dame, 1968).

48. Hennesey, *American Catholics*, 195.

49. A. H. Walburg, *The Question of Nationality in Its Relation to the Catholic Church in the United States* (St. Louis, 1889), 40. See also Walburg, *German Language and Literature* (Columbus, 1897).

50. Walburg, *The Question of Nationality*, 40.

51. Ibid., 13, 28–29.

52. Ibid., 61,18.

53. Preuss, "Americanizing the Immigrant," *Fortnightly Review* (St. Louis) 25 (May 15, 1918): 156–59, as quoted in Richard M. Linkh, *American Catholicism and European Immigrants, 1900–1924* (New York, 1975), 22–23.

54. Barry, *Catholic Church and German Americans*, 249.

55. The number of books on ethnic Catholic communities is expanding rapidly. For recent examples, see Jay P. Dolan, *The Immigrant Church. New York's Irish and German Catholics, 1815–1865* (Baltimore, 1975); Joseph John Parot, *Polish Catholics in Chicago 1850–1920. A Religious History* (DeKalb, 1981); Richard M. Linkh, *American Catholicism and European Immigrants, 1900–1924* (New York, 1975); Harold J. Abramson, *Ethnic Diversity in Cath-*

olic America (New York, 1973). The inspiration for much of this scholarship was Nathan Glazer and Daniel Patrick Moynihan, *Beyond the Melting Pot: The Negroes, Puerto Ricans, Jews, Italians, and Irish of New York City* (Cambridge, Mass., 1963).

56. For a discussion of status and economic matters, see Andrew M. Greeley, *The American Catholic. A Social Portrait* (New York, 1977).

57. O'Brien, *Renewal of American Catholicism*, 74–75,109–10, 151.

58. Mel Piehl, *Breaking Bread. The Catholic Worker and the Origin of Catholic Radicalism in America* (Philadelphia, 1982).

59. But see, David Noel Doyle, *Irish Americans, Native Rights and National Empires. The Structure, Attitudes and Division of the Catholic Minority in the Decade of Expansion, 1890–1901* (New York, 1976), 198–207, 263–71. American Catholics sometimes did criticize the racist ideas used to justify American expansion.

60. Philip Gleason, *The Conservative Reformers*, 216–20.

61. H. Richard Niebuhr, *The Kingdom of God in America* (Hamden, Conn. 1956), 17. Niebuhr was in part quoting from André Siegfried, *America Comes of Age* (New York, 1927).

62. Doyle, *Irish Americans*, 8–9.

CHAPTER THREE

1. Irving Howe, *World of Our Fathers. The Journey of the East European Jews to America and the Life They Found and Made* (New York, 1976), 71.

2. C. Bezalel Sherman, *The Jew Within American Society. A Study in Ethnic Individuality* (Detroit, 1961), 123.

3. Louis Hartz, *The Liberal Tradition in America. An Interpretation of American Political Thought Since the Revolution* (New York, 1955).

4. Marshall Sklare, ed., *The Jew in American Society* (New York, 1974), 53–55.

5. Abraham Cahan, *The Rise of David Levinsky* (New York, 1960; first published 1917), 96. For a discussion of Cahan, see Howe, *World of Our Fathers*; also Allen Guttmann, *The Jewish Writer in America. Assimilation and the Crisis of Identity* (New York, 1971).

6. Bridenbaugh, "The Great Mutation," *American Historical Review* 68 (Jan. 1963), 322–23.

7. I have not tried to document historical points that are not in dispute. For the best surveys see Nathan Glazer, *American Judaism* (Chicago, 1972); Joseph L. Blau, *Judaism in America. From Curiosity to Third Faith* (Chicago, 1976); Oscar Handlin, *Adventure in Freedom: Three Hundred Years of Jewish Life in America* (New York, 1954); Max I. Dimont, *The Jews in America. The Roots, History, and Destiny of American Jews* (New York, 1978); Moses Rischin, *The Promised City. New York Jews, 1870–1914* (Cambridge, Mass., 1962); Salo W. Baron, *Steeled by Adversity. Essays and Addresses on American Jewish Life* (Philadelphia 1971).

8. Quoted in Glazer, *American Judaism*, 35.

9. Abraham Moise, "An Address Delivered Before the Reformed Society of Israelites on Its Second Anniversary, Nov., 1826, quoted in Joseph L. Blau and Salo W. Baron, eds., *The Jews of the United States, 1790–1840. A Documentary History*, (New York, 1963), 2:658.

10. Quoted in Theodore Friedman and Robert Gordis, eds., *Jewish Life in America* (New York, 1955), 110.

11. Dimont, *The Jews in America*, 121.

12. For the best account of Conservative Judaism, see Marshall Sklare, *Conservative Judaism. An American Religious Movement* (New York, 1972).

13. For evidence of this, see Michael R. Marrus, *The Politics of Assimilation. A Study of the French Jewish Community at the Time of the Dreyfus Affair* (Oxford, 1971), 120–21.

14. On anti-Semitism in the United States, see especially John Higham, *Send These to Me. Jews and Other Immigrants in Urban America* (New York, 1975).

15. Sklare, *The Jew in American Society*, 33.

16. Howe, *World of Our Fathers*. Howe's most sustained discussion of religion runs from page 190 to page 200.

17. Howe, *World of Our Fathers*, 120.

18. Howe, *World of Our Fathers*, 306.

19. Howe, *World of Our Fathers*, 190. See the discussion in C. Bezalel Sherman, "Secularism and Religion in the Jewish Labor Movement," in Friedman and Gordis, *Jewish Life*, 109–27.

20. Sherry Gorelick, *City College and the Jewish Poor. Education in New York, 1880–1924* (New York, 1982).

21. Seymour Martin Lipset and Everett Carll Ladd, "Jewish Academics in the United States," in Sklare, *The Jew in American Society*, 287.

22. Quoted in Barbara Miller Solomon, *Ancestors and Immigrants. A Changing New England Tradition* (Cambridge, Mass., 1956), 19.

23. Stephan Thernstrom, *The Other Bostonians: Poverty and Progress in the American Metropolis, 1800–1970* (Cambridge, Mass., 1973), ch. 7.

24. Higham, *Send These to Me*, esp. 138–73.

25. Marcia Graham Synnott, *The Half-Opened Door. Discrimination and Admissions at Harvard, Yale, and Princeton, 1900–1970* (Westport, Conn.,1979).

26. For thoughtful discussions of the problems of minority Jewish consciousness and the need for group belonging, see the works of Kurt Lewin: for example, "Psycho-Sociological Problems of a Minority Group," *Character and Personality* 3 (March 1935): 175–87; "Bringing Up the Jewish Child," *The Monorah Journal* 28 (Winter 1940): 29–45; "Jewish Education and Reality," *Jewish Education* 15 (May 1944): 125–29; "Self-Hatred Among Jews," *Contemporary Jewish Record* 4 (1941): 219–232.

27. Arnold M. Eisen, *The Chosen People in America. A Study in Jewish Religious Ideology* (Bloomington, 1983), 8.

28. Higham, *Send These to Me*, 205.

29. Joshua A. Fishman et al., *Language Loyalty in the United States: The Maintenance and Perpetuation of Non-English Mother Tongues by American Ethnic and Religious Groups* (The Hague, 1966), 73; Higham, *Send These to Me*, 196-246.

30. Walter Laqueur, *A History of Zionism* (New York, 1972), 180.

31. Eisen, *The Chosen People*, provides an excellent discussion of efforts by American rabbis to deal with the difficult concept of "chosenness." Also see "The State of Jewish Belief: A Symposium," *Commentary* 42 (Aug. 1966): 71-160.

32. For a reflection of this point, see Daniel Bell, "A Parable of Alienation," *Jewish Frontier* 13 (Nov. 1946): 12-19.

33. Sidney Goldstein and Calvin Goldscheider, "Jewish Religiosity.Ideological and Ritualistic Dimensions," in Sklare, *The Jew in American Society*, 209-11. *Encyclopaedia Judaica*, (Jerusalem, 1971), 5: 905.

34. Eisen, *The Chosen People*, 41.

35. Ibid., 135.

CHAPTER FOUR

1. For a fuller discussion, see R. Laurence Moore, "The Occult Connection? Mormonism, Christian Science, and Spiritualism," in Howard Kerr and Charles L. Crow, eds., *The Occult in America. New Historical Perspectives* (Urbana, 1983), 135-61.

2. Francis Edward Marsten, *The Mask of Christian Science* (New York, 1909), 6.

3. The best biography of Eddy remains the officially sanctioned three volumes of Robert Peel, *Mary Baker Eddy* (New York, 1966-77). The best discussions of Christian Science and American religion are Stephen Gottschalk, *The Emergence of Christian Science in American Religious Life* (Berkeley, 1973) and J. Stillson Judah, *The History and Philosophy of the Metaphysical Movements in America* (Philadelphia, 1967). For a psychobiography, see Julius Silberger, *Mary Baker Eddy An Interpretive Biography of the Founder of Christian Science* (Boston, 1980).

4. Eddy, *Retrospection and Introspection* (Boston, 1891), 47.

5. The claim that Eddy in fact plagiarized from Quimby was most forcefully made by Horatio W. Dresser. See Dresser, ed., *The Quimby Manuscripts Showing the Discovery of Spiritual Healing and the Origin of Christian Science* (New York, 1921). For Eddy's story, see *Science and Health with a Key to the Scripture*, 6th ed. (Boston, 1883), 3-4.

6. Eddy, *Science and Health with a Key to the Scriptures*, 119th edition (Boston, 1900), 1.

7. In addition to the OED, see A. P. Sinnett, *The Occult World* (London, 1881) and Edward A. Tiryakian, ed., *On the Margin of the Visible. Sociology, the Esoteric, and the Occult* (New York, 1974).

8. Sinnett, *Occult World*, 1.

9. This charge, made by Richard Kennedy, was printed in a series of muckraking attacks written for *McClure's Magazine* by Georgine Milmine. See 29 (Aug. 1907): 448. The articles appeared between January 1907 and June 1908.

10. Eddy, *Retrospection and Introspection*, 96. Eddy, *Science and Health* (Lynn, 1878), 156.

11. See the introduction to Arthur Cory, *Christian Science Instruction* (Los Gatos, 1950).

12. Eddy, *Science and Health*, 3rd ed. (Lynn, 1881), 2:42.

13. Eddy used the term Metaphysical Science to distinguish her system both from materialistic science and from occult science. See *Retrospection and Introspection*, 96.

14. For example, to make plain the hitherto unknown "inner" sense of the words of the Bible, Eddy added a glossary of spiritual meanings (a Key to the Scripture) to the sixth and subsequent editions of *Science and Health*. The connection between her glossary and Swedenborg's *A Dictionary of Correspondences, Representatives, and Significatives, Derived from the Word of the Lord* (first printed in Boston in 1841) is clear.

15. Robert Peel, *Christian Science. Its Encounter with American Culture* (New York, 1958), 83–86.

16. Eddy, *Science and Health*, (Lynn, 1878), 2:47.

17. Eddy, *Science and Health with Key to Scriptures*, 119th ed. (Boston, 1900), 282.

18. Milmine, *McClure's Magazine* 29 (Sept. 1907): 579; 29 (July 1907): 346.

19. Adam Herbert Dickey, *Memoirs of Mary Baker Eddy* (Brookline, 1927). A church-approved version of Eddy's last years, also written by a member of the household, makes no mention of malicious animal magnetism; see the Rev. Irving C. Tomlinson, *Twelve Years with Mary Baker Eddy, Recollections and Experiences* (Boston, 1945).

20. Dickey, *Memoirs*, 44–45, 47–49, 123.

21. Swami Abhedananda, *Christian Science and Vedanta* (New York, 1902), 1. Also see Wendell Thomas, *Hinduism Invades America* (New York, 1930) and Raymond J. Cunningham, "The Impact of Christian Science on the American Churches, 1880–1910," *American Historical Review* 72 (April 1967): 885–905.

22. When Evans published his book in 1886, the *Christian Science Journal* (August 1886) reproved Evans for having forced Christianity "into the farcical grooves of Occultism."

23. Sydney E. Ahlstrom, *A Religious History of the American People* (New Haven, 1972), 1019. See also Judah, *Metaphysical Movements in America*.

24. Ahlstrom, *Religious History*, 1020.

25. In both the nineteenth and twentiety centuries, the influence of occult systems was also felt in areas of high culture. Viola Sachs, *The Game of Cre-*

ation (Paris, 1982). Many young "modernists" who revolutionized the arts
were well versed in Theosophy. See Sherrye Cohn, "Arthur Dove and Theosophy: Visions of a Transcendental Reality," *Arts Magazine* (Oct. 1983), 86–
91.

26. Tiryakian, *Margin of the Visible*, 6.

27. Charles Y. Glock, "The Role of Deprivation in the Origin and Evolution of Religious Groups," Robert Lee and Martin E. Marty, eds., *Religion
and Social Conflict*, (New York, 1964), 29.

28. John Elward Brown, *In the Cult Kingdom. Mormonism, Eddyism, Rus-
sellism* (Siloam Springs, Ark., 1918), 95. In addition to *Retrospection and
Introspection*, see Calvin A. Frye, *Visions of Mary Baker Eddy* (Rumford, R.I.,
1935).

29. For a discussion of mediums, see Moore, *In Search of White Crows*,
102–29.

CHAPTER FIVE

1. In popular expressions of millennialism, it is not always easy to distinguish a pre- and a post-millennial position. Postmillennialists expected the
return of Christ only after a thousand-year period of earthly peace. For this
reason, they are often characterized as optimistic about the chances for
worldly progress without direct divine intervention, and melioristic and
gradualistic in their attitude toward reform. In fact, antebellum postmillen-
nials just as commonly expected cataclysmic upheaval and rupture in the near
future. In their perfectionism, they were neither more nor less optimistic
than their premillennial counterparts. Premillennials did believe that things
would get much worse before they got better and their longed-for Kingdom
was technically a spiritual one. However, the difference between human and
spiritual was commonly lost in visionary prophecies. As did many of their
postmillennial counterparts, premillennialists expected a sudden and imminent entry into the golden age. In its general view of historical development,
premillennialism is not such a distant relative of certain popular forms of
Marxism.

2. Nathan Hatch, *The Sacred Cause of Liberty. Republican Thought and the
Millennium in Revolutionary New England* (New Haven, 1977), 141. John
E. Smylie, "National Ethos and the Church," *Theology Today* 20 (Oct. 1963):
315.

3. Ernest Lee Tuveson, *Redeemer Nation. The Idea of America's Millennial
Role* (Chicago, 1968).

4. Robert Mapes Anderson, *Vision of the Disinherited. The Making of
American Pentecostalism* (New York, 1979); Timothy P. Weber, *Living in
the Shadow of the Second Coming. American Premillennialism. 1875–1925*
(New York, 1979); Ernest Sandeen, *The Roots of Fundamentalism. British
and American Millenarianism, 1800–1930* (Chicago, 1970).

5. Constant H. Jacquest, ed., *Yearbook of American and Canadian Churches, 1984* (Nashville, 1984). See also Vinson Synan, *The Holiness-Pentecostal Movement in the United States* (Grand Rapids, 1971).

6. Weber, *Second Coming,* 32–33.

7. The almost unbelievable publishing success of Hal Lindsey's *The Late Great Planet Earth* (1970) should by itself dispel the notion that Christian premillennialism has lost its audience. By 1981 Lindsey's book had sold 18 million copies throughout the world.

8. J. F. C. Harrison, *The Second Coming. Popular Millenarianism, 1780–1850* (New Brunswick, 1979), 224. Also see Clarke Garrett, *Respectable Folly: Millenarians and the French Revolution in France and England* (Baltimore, 1975); Christopher Hill, *The World Turned Upside Down. Radical Ideas During the English Revolution* (London, 1972); Stephen A. Marini, *Radical Sects of Revolutionary New England* (Cambridge, Mass., 1982).

9. Harrison, *The Second Coming,* 202. Also see Jonathan M. Butler, "Adventism and the American Experience," in Edwin Gaustad, ed., *The Rise of Adventism. Religion and Society in Mid-Nineteenth-Century America* (New York, 1974); and Francis D. Nichol, *The Midnight Cry. A Defense of the Character and Conduct of William Miller and the Millerites* (Takoma Park, 1944). I am also indebted to Ronald Graybill's unpublished paper "The Abolitionist-Millerite Connection."

10. Gerder Lerner, *The Grimké Sisters from South Carolina: Rebels Against Slavery* (Boston, 1967), 306.

11. Ibid., 308.

12. Leon Festinger et al., *When Prophecy Fails* (Minneapolis, 1956).

13. Butler, "Adventism," 194.

14. Reinhold Niebuhr, *Moral Man and Immoral Society. A Study in Ethics and Politics* (New York, 1932).

15. Uriah Smith, *The United States in the Light of Prophecy, or, An Exposition of Rev. 13: 11–17* (Battle Creek, 1872); Smith, *The Marvel of Nations. Our Country: Its Past, Present, and Future, and What the Scriptures Say of It* (Battle Creek, 1886); Smith, *Daniel and the Revelation. The Response of History to the Voice of Prophecy* (Battle Creek, 1897). For Miller's views, see Joshua V. Himes, *Views of the Prophecies and Prophetic Chronology, Selected from Manuscripts of William Miller, with a Memoir of His Life* (Boston, 1842) and William Miller, *Evidence from Scripture and History of the Second Coming of Christ, about the Year 1843* (Boston, 1842).

16. Smith, *United States in the Light of Prophecy,* 77–84; Smith, *The Marvel of Nations,* 136–37.

17. Ronald L. Numbers, *Prophetess of Health. A Study of Ellen G. White* (New York, 1976); Richard W. Schwartz, *John Harvey Kellogg* (Nashville, 1970).

18. White, "Our Duty to the Poor," *The Present Truth* 18 (Nov. 19, 1861); White, *Welfare Ministry. Instruction in Christian Neighborhood Service* (Washington, D. C., 1952), 15, 174–75, 202, 258.

19. Butler, "Adventism," 200–01.

20. Eric J. Hobsbawm, *Social Bandits and Primitive Rebels. Studies in Archaic Forms of Social Movements in the 19th and 20th Centuries* (Glencoe, 1959), esp. 6, 58–59, 63–64, 106–7. Also see Sylvia L. Thrupp, ed. *Millennial Dreams in Action. Essays in Comparative Study* (The Hague, 1962).

21. Books with useful historical material include James A. Beckford, *The Trumpet of Prophecy. A Sociological Study of Jehovah's Witnesses* (New York, 1975); Alan Rogerson, *Millions Now Living Will Never Die. A Study of Jehovah's Witnesses* (London, 1969); William J. Whalen, *Armageddon Around the Corner. A Report on Jehovah's Witnesses* (New York, 1962); Herbert Hewitt Stroup, *The Jehovah's Witnesses* (New York, 1945).

22. Whalen, *Armageddon*, 19. David Manwaring, *Render Unto Caesar. The Flag Salute Controversy* (Chicago, 1962) and Philip E. Jacob and Mulford Q. Sibley, *Conscription of Conscience. The American State and the Conscientious Objector 1940–47* (Ithaca, 1952).

23. Beckford, *Trumpet of Prophecy*, 86.

24. See discussion in George M. Marsden, *Fundamentalism and American Culture. The Shaping of Twentieth-Century Evangelicalism: 1870–1925* (New York, 1980), 146. Shirley Jackson Case, *The Millennial Hope. A Phase of War-Time Thinking* (Chicago, 1918) and Harris Franklin Rall, *Modern Premillennialism and the Christian Hope* (New York, 1920).

25. Frank Bartelman, *What Really Happened at Azusa Street* (Northridge, Calif., 1962), 32–34. (Originally published in 1925 as *How Pentecost Came to Los Angeles*).

26. James R. Green, *Grass-Roots Socialism. Radical Movements in the Southwest, 1895–1943* (Baton Rouge, 1978), 172–73.

27. A. P. Sexton, "The Last Days," *Pentecostal Holiness Advocate*, July 5, 1917.

28. Charles Fox Parham, *A Voice Crying in the Wilderness* (Baxton Springs, Kansas, 1944), 59, 118 (first published in 1902). Also see Sarah E. Parham, *The Life of Charles F. Parham. Founder of the Apostolic Faith Movement* (Joplin, Mo., 1930).

29. Parham, *Charles F. Parham*, 274. Rev. George Floyd Taylor, *The Second Coming of Jesus* (Franklin Springs, Ga., 1950, first published in 1916).

30. Quoted in Marsden, *Fundamentalism and American Culture*, 206.

31. Anderson, *Vision of the Disinherited*, 222.

32. Carl Brumbeck, *What Meaneath This? A Pentecostal Answer to a Pentecostal Question* (Springfield, Mo., 1947), 314–15.

33. Liston Pope, *Millhands and Preachers. A Study of Gastonia* (New Haven, 1942).

34. Editorial, *Church of God Evangel*, Dec. 30, 1963.

35. Aimee Semple McPherson, *America Awake* (Los Angeles, n.d.), 29–32.

36. Princeton Religion Research Center, *Religion in America, 1982* (Princeton, 1982), esp. 128–9.

37. For samples, see Sarah Parham, *Life of Charles Parham*; Ethel E. Goss, *The Winds of God. The Story of the Early Pentecostal Days, 1901–1914, in the Life of Howard A. Goss* (New York, 1958); Ambrose Jessup Tomlinson, *Diary of A. J. Tomlinson* (Queen's Village, N.Y., 1949–55); Aimee Semple McPherson, *This Is That. Personal Experiences, Sermons, and Writings* (Los Angeles, 1923).

38. For a forceful reminder of how little ambivalence contradictory religious positions can provoke, I am indebted to the comments of Timothy Weber.

39. David Edwin Harrell, Jr., *All Things Are Possible. The Healing and Charismatic Revivals in Modern America* (Bloomington, 1975), 227.

40. Arthur Ernest Paris, *Black Pentecostalism. Southern Religion in an Urban World* (Amherst, 1982), 3–4.

41. Marsden, *Fundamentalism and American Culture*, viii.

42. See the related discussion in Leo P. Ribuffo, *The Old Christian Right. The Protestant Far Right from the Depression to the Cold War* (Philadelphia, 1983), 105.

CHAPTER SIX

1. James Edwards Adams, *Preus of Missouri: A Report on the Great Lutheran Civil War* (New York, 1977); Milton L. Rudnick, *Fundamentalism and the Missouri Synod. A Historical Study of Their Interaction and Mutual Influence* (Saint Louis, 1966); Timothy L. Smith, *Called Unto Holiness. The Story of the Nazarenes* (Kansas City, 1962); David Edwin Harrell, *A Social History of the Disciples of Christ* (Nashville, 1966–73).

2. Timothy L. Smith, "Protestants Falwell Does Not Represent," *New York Times*, Oct. 22, 1980; Neil Jumonville, "Diversity Among Evangelicals," *New York Times*, May 12, 1981.

3. Ernest Sandeen, *The Roots of Fundamentalism: British and American Millenarianism 1800–1930* (Chicago, 1970); George M. Marsden, *Fundamentalism and American Culture. The Shaping of Twentieth-Century Evangelicalism: 1870–1925* (New York, 1980); also see the exchange between Sandeen and Marsden in the *Christian Scholar's Review* 1 (Winter 1971): 141–51 and (Spring 1971): 227–33.

4. For background, see Anne C. Loveland, *Southern Evangelicals and the Social Order, 1800–1860* (Baton Rouge, 1980); Donald Mathews, *Religion in the Old South* (Chicago, 1977); and John R. McKivigan, *The War Against Proslavery Religion: Abolitionism and the Northern Churches 1830–1865* (Ithaca, 1984).

5. Robert E. Hooper, *Crying in the Wilderness: A Biography of David Lipscomb* (Nashville, 1979); David Lipscomb, *Civil Government. Its Origin, Mis-*

sion, and Destiny and a Christian's Relation to It (Nashville, 1957); David Edwin Harrell, Jr., *Quest for a Christian America. The Disciples of Christ and American Society to 1866* (Nashville, 1966); David Edwin Harrell, Jr., *The Social Sources of Division in the Disciples of Christ, 1865–1900* (Nashville, 1973); Nathan O. Hatch, "The Christian Movement and the Demand for a Theology of the People," *Journal of American History* 67 (Dec. 1980): 545–67.

6. Harrell, *Social Sources of Division*, 23, 26–29, 225; Lipscomb, *Civil Government*, 24, 128, 133, 140; Alexander Campbell, "The Destiny of Our Country," *Popular Lectures and Addresses* (Philadelphia, 1863), 170.

7. "Evangelicals Turning to Politics Fear Moral Slide Imperils Nation," *New York Times*, Aug. 19, 1980.

8. "What Time Is It?" *The Prophetic Times* (June–July, 1871), 94.

9. Marsden, *Fundamentalism and American Culture*, 80–85; Marsden, "Fundamentalism as an American Phenomenon. A Comparison with English Evangelicalism," *Church History* 46 (June 1977): 215–32.

10. "Lying Figures," *The Truth or Testimony for Christ* 9 (1882): 536; William G. McLoughlin, Jr., *Billy Sunday Was His Real Name* (Chicago, 1955); Marsden, *Fundamentalism and American Culture*, 135.

11. Ralph Lord Roy, *Apostles of Discord. A Study of Organized Bigotry and Disruption on the Fringes of Protestantism* (Boston, 1953). For other books on schismatic figures, see Stewart G. Cole, *The History of Fundamentalism* (New York, 1931) and Charles Allyn Russell, *Voices of American Fundamentalism. Seven Biographical Studies* (Philadelphia, 1976).

12. Winrod's attacks on most American politicians tended to merge in the 1930s, as did the gloomy forecasts of many other premillenarians, with a strong patriotism; in the July 1939 issue of *The Defender* (the "Americanism Issue"), he wrote: "During the days of international unrest and great uncertainty, we must have faith that America has neither abandoned God, nor been abandoned by God. The same Divine hand that watched over the founders of this Republic, that guided them in the framing of our Constitution, is still with us to give strength and guidance today."

13. *Moody's Bible Institute Monthly*, Dec., 1963.

14. J. Franklyn Norris, *Inside History of the First Baptist Church, Fort Worth, and Temple Baptist Church, Detroit. Life Story of Dr. J. Frank Norris*, 224. For bibliographical information on Norris, also see, C. Allyn Russell, "J. Frank Norris: Violent Fundamentalist," *Southwestern Historical Quarterly* 75 (Jan. 1972): 271–302; Clovis Gwin Morris, "He Changed Things: The Life and Thought of J. Frank Norris" (Ph.D. dissertation, Texas Tech, 1973).

15. Editorial, *The Searchlight*, Sept. 17, 1948.

16. This suggestion is of course tongue in cheek; but were it possible to transcribe the Fundamentalist critique of modernism into secular language,

the result could easily resemble Lasch's jeremiad, *The Culture of Narcissism. American Life in an Age of Diminishing Expectations* (New York, 1978).

17. Stewart Cole, "The Psychology of the Fundamentalist Movement," Ph.D. dissertation, University of Chicago, 1929, pp. 61–62.

18. Robert Elwood Wenger, "Social Thought in American Fundamentalism 1918–1933," Ph.D. dissertation, University of Nebraska, 1973, 57–72.

19. Liberals did not dare to raise questions about science until the outbreak of World War II. The following two quotations from *The Christian Century* in 1930 were typical of the liberal stance in the first part of the twentieth century: "Science will increasingly serve human interests. . .A Scientific age when it arrives will insistently turn attention toward inclusive meanings of life. The world-embracing social consciousness that has already appeared in science, education, philanthropy, and religion will be deepened by the advances of science, invention, and enterprise"; "Our faiths divide us, our science brings us together. It is a great gain for our modern world that science in all lands compels us to think the same thoughts."

20. "Interview with Timothy L. Smith," *Christianity Today* 21 (Nov. 19, 1976): 24. Nineteenth-century premillennialists often worried about their intellectual respectability as the following editorial, written in 1864 in *The Prophetic Times* suggests: "To those especially who are located (in America) where but little attention is given to God's revelations concerning the future, who are left to utter their convictions comparatively alone, and who are met with taunts and ridicule . . . it is a matter of real refreshing, to find so many men of learning, position, and force in the world (in England) thus employing their gifts and talents to awaken the Church to the fact, that there is a reality in these doctrines, however they may have been here and there disfigured by fanaticism."

21. Rev. W. H. Daniels, *Moody: His Words, Work, and Workers* (New York, 1877); R. A. Torrey, *Why God Used D. L. Moody* (New York, 1925).

22. Norris's extensive papers furnish the richest source of information on his life. They are housed on 27 microfilm reels at the Baptist Historical Commission in Nashville. Unfortunately, papers prior to 1928 were destroyed in a fire. The original collection of papers is in the Dargan-Carver Library.

23. He fought one of his bitterest battles just two years before his death in 1952. That one resulted in a split between him and G. Beauchamp Vick, who had been one of his closest and most useful associates.

24. Telegram to the Temple Baptist Church, April 28, 1947, Norris Papers. Another telegram printed on the front page of his newspaper, *The Searchlight*, March 11, 1949, provides a typical self-estimate: "We have highest officials our friends . . . Luncheon today as guest of Texas delegation including Senators Tom Connally and Lyndon Johnson, Speaker Sam Rayburn and Congressman Lucas. Whitehouse Friday to see Big Boss. . . Have

luncheon Thursday with top industrialist and Sam Rayburn and Tom Connally. Interesting to bring top industrialists and leading Democrats together."

25. Letter to Luther Holcomb, Sept. 27, 1929; quoted in Clovis Morris, "He Changed Things," 355.

26. For the best study of modernism, see William R. Hutchison's superb *The Modernist Impulse in American Protestantism* (Cambridge, 1976).

27. Part Three of Marsden's *Fundamentalism and American Culture* provides the best account. Also see Roland Tenus Nelson, "Fundamentalism and the Northern Baptist Convention," Ph.D. dissertation, Chicago, 1964.

28. John R. Rice, *The Evangelist, His God-Given Place, Work, Importance; His Critics, His Rewards, His Dangers* (Murfeesburo, Tenn., 1968), 180.

29. Harry Emerson Fosdick, *The Living of These Days, An Autobiography* (New York, 1956), 162.

30. Princeton Religion Research Center, *Religion in America 1982*, 31–32.

31. For various estimates, see Richard Quebedeaux, *The Young Evangelicals. Revolution in Orthodoxy* (New York, 1974), 47; Dean M. Kelley, *Why Conservative Churches Are Growing. A Study in Sociology of Religion* (New York, 1972); "Evangelicals Turning to Politics," *New York Times*, Aug. 19, 1980. Predictably, the most separatist-minded of the Fundamentalists provided the gloomiest assessments of strength. George Dollar restricted the number of "real" Fundamentalists, those Christians with a "war psychology" who had no use for Billy Graham, the Moody Bible Institute, or the NAE, to four million; see Dollar, *A History of Fundamentalism in America* (Greenville, S.C., 1973). Dollar is a professor of church history at Bob Jones University.

32. Princeton, *Religion in America*, 73–74. *Christianity Today* 6 (Nov. 10, 1961): 11.

33. "Poll Finds Americans Split on Creation Idea," *New York Times*, Aug. 29, 1982.

34. Joel A. Carpenter, "Fundamentalist Institutions and the Rise of Evangelical Protestantism, 1929–1942," *Church History* 49 (March 1980): 62–75; William G. McLoughlin, *Billy Graham. Revivalist in a Secular Age* (New York, 1960), 21–22; Louis Gasper, *The Fundamentalist Movement* (The Hague, 1963); Rudnick, *Fundamentalism and the Missouri Synod*.

35. Quebedeaux, *The Young Evangelicals*; David F. Wells and John D. Woodbridge, eds., *The Evangelicals. What They Believe, Who They Are, Where They Are Changing* (Nashville, 1975).

36. David F. Wells, "The Reformation: Will History Repeat Itself?", *Christianity Today* 19 (Oct. 25, 1974): 8.

37. David Moberg, "Fundamentalists and Evangelicals in Society," in Wells and Woodbridge, *The Evangelicals*, 160.

38. Princeton, *Religion in America*, 89; "Poll Finds Evangelicals Aren't United Voting Bloc," *New York Times*, Sept. 7, 1980.

39. Martin E. Marty, "Tensions Within Contemporary Evangelicalism: A Critical Appraisal," Wells and Woodbridge, *The Evangelicals*, 176.

40. Moberg, "Fundamentalists and Evangelicals," 162–63.

41. Mark Hatfield, *Between a Rock and a Hard Place* (Waco, 1976), 94.

42. Patricia U. Bonomi, "'Stewards of the Mysteries of God.' Clerical Authority and the Great Awakening in the Middle Colonies," in Gerald Grieson, ed., *Professions and Professional Ideologies in America* (Chapel Hill, 1983).

CHAPTER SEVEN

1. W. E. B. DuBois, *The Souls of Black Folk* (New York, 1969; first published in 1903), 276.

2. Nathan Glazer and Daniel Patrick Moynihan, *Beyond the Melting Pot. The Negroes, Puerto Ricans, Jews, Italians, and Irish of New York City* (Cambridge, Mass., 1970), xix–xx. Glazer's long note on these pages suggests how his thought evolved between the first edition of the book which had been published in 1963 and the second.

3. E. Franklin Frazier, *The Negro Church in America* (New York, 1974; first published in 1963), esp. chap. 1.

4. Lawrence W. Levine, *Black Culture and Black Consciousness. Afro-American Folk Thought from Slavery to Freedom* (New York, 1977); Eugene Genovese, *Roll Jordan Roll. The World the Slaves Made* (New York, 1974).

5. Melville Herskovits, *The Myth of the Negro Past* (Boston, 1958; first published 1941).

6. Thomas Sowell, *Ethnic America. A History* (New York, 1981), 208–15.

7. Lawrence Jones, "The Organized Church: Its Historic Significance and Changing Role in Contemporary Black Experience," in Harry A. Johnson, ed., *Negotiating the Mainstream. A Survey of the Afro-American Experience* (Chicago, 1978), 114.

8. The most balanced summary of the subject is Albert J. Raboteau, *Slave Religion. The "Invisible Institution" in the Antebellum South* (New York, 1978).

9. Herskovits, *Myth of Negro Past*. Raboteau's book, again, provides the best summary of the debate over African survivals, but see also Leonard E. Barrett, *Soul Force. African Heritage in Afro-American Religion* (Garden City, N.Y., 1974) and Jon Butler, "The Dark Ages of American Occultism, 1760–1848," in Howard Kerr and Charles Crow, eds., *The Occult in America. New Historical Perspectives* (Urbana, 1983).

10. August Meier et al., eds., *Black Protest Thought in the Twentieth Century* (Indianapolis, 1971). For a provocative discussion of the Uncle Tom myth, see Wilson Jeremiah Moses, *Black Messiahs and Uncle Toms. Social and Literary Manipulations of a Religious Myth* (University Park, Penn., 1982), 49–66.

11. John Steinbeck vented the problem for white intellectuals when he said: "I am constantly amazed at the qualities we expect in Negroes. No race has ever offered another such high regard. We expect Negroes to be wiser than we are, more tolerant than we are, braver, more dignified than we, more self-controlled and self-disciplined. . . In a word, while maintaining that Negroes are inferior to us, by our unquestioning faith in them we prove our conviction that they are superior in many fields, even fields we are presumed to be trained and conditioned in and they are not." Quoted in C. Eric Lincoln, *The Black Muslims in America* (Boston, 1961), 136.

12. For accounts, see Frazier, *The Negro Church*; Carter G. Woodson, *The History of the Negro Church* (Washington, 1921); Carol V. R. George, *Segregated Sabbaths. Richard Allen and the Emergence of Independent Black Churches 1760–1840* (New York, 1973). Also Allen's autobiography, *The Life Experience and Gospel Labors of the Rt. Rev. Richard Allen* (reprinted New York, 1960).

13. Benjamin Quarles, *Black Abolitionists* (New York, 1969), 68.

14. Quoted in Moses, *Black Messiahs*, 45. For the best account of the responses of black ministers to colonization proposals, see Leonard I. Sweet, *Black Images of America, 1784–1870* (New York, 1976), esp. chap. 4.

15. Leon F. Litwack, *Been in the Storm So Long. The Aftermath of Slavery* (New York, 1979), 539.

16. Sweet, *Black Images*, 64.

17. Ibid., 25.

18. Walter L. Williams, *Black Americans and the Evangelization of Africa, 1817–1900* (Madison,1982), 89–94 and passim.

19. Edward W. Blyden, *Christianity, Islam, and the Negro Race* (London, 1888), 17.

20. Edwin S. Redkey, *Black Exodus: Black Nationalist and Back-to Africa Movements, 1890–1910* (New Haven, 1969), 35–36. Redkey's book is good not only on Turner but on the whole subject of the development of black nationalism. See also M. M. Ponton, *Life and Times of Henry M. Turner* (New York, 1970; first published in 1917).

21. The prevailing view appears to be that of Frazier who wrote rather gently that "on the whole, the Negro's church was not a threat to white domination and aided the Negro to become accommodated to an inferior status."*The Negro Church*, 51. Joseph R. Washington, Jr. has contributed a considerably less generous assessment in *Black Religion. The Negro and Christianity in the United States* (Boston, 1964). Also see C. Eric Lincoln, *The Black Church Since Frazier* (New York, 1974).

22. Levine, *Black Culture*, 140.

23. Jones, "The Organized Church," 123.

24. John Bracey et al., eds. *Black Nationalism in America* (Indianapolis, 1970), 127.

25. For the prototype of much that followed, see Carlo Ginzburg, *The Cheese and the Worms: The Cosmos of a Sixteenth Century Miller* (Baltimore, 1980).

26. Blyden, *Christianity, Islam*, 44.

27. Benjamin Elijah Mays and Joseph William Nicholson, *The Negro's Church* (New York, 1933), 7; Hart Nelsen et al., eds., *The Black Church in America* (New York, 1971), 10.

28. Peter Kolchin, "Reevaluating the Antebellum Slave Community: A Comparative Perspective," *Journal of American History* 70 (Dec. 1983): 579–601.

29. For example, see Mays and Nicholson, *The Negro's Church*, 224–25. For a somewhat different view, see Lincoln, *The Black Church Since Frazier*, 122.

30. Gayraud S. Wilmore, *Black Religion and Black Radicalism.* (Garden City, N.Y., 1972), 222.

31. Washington, *Black Religion*, 52–78.

32. Frazier, *The Negro Church*, 80–85.

33. In *The Souls of Black Folk* (p. 45), DuBois commented: "It is a particular sensation, this double consciousness, this sense of always looking at one's self through the eyes of others, of measuring one's soul by the tape of a world that looks on in amused contempt and pity."

34. Payne, for example, referred to black spiritual songs as "Corn-field Ditties" and in characterizing the services in many black churches as loud, rude, and extravagant, he declared: "These meetings must always be more damaging physically, morally, and religiously than beneficial. How needful it is to have an intelligent ministry to teach these people who hold to this ignorant mode of worship the true method of serving God." Bishop Daniel Alexander Payne, *Recollections of Seventy Years* (New York, 1968; first published in 1888), 94, 256.

35. DuBois noted that when a conference of "friends of the Negro" met at Lake Mohonk at the turn of the century to discuss the problems of the Negro, not a Negro was present. Alain Locke, ed., *The New Negro. An Interpretation* (New York, 1968; first published in 1925), 412.

36. See Johnson, "Harlem: the Culture Capital," in Locke, ed., *The New Negro*, 301–11.

37. Randall K. Burkett, *Black Redemption; Churchmen Speak for the Garvey Movement* (Philadelphia, 1978); Burkett, *Garveyism as a Religious Movement* (Metuchen, N.J., 1978). In addition to Burkett, see Moses's more critical account in *Black Messiahs*, 132–41.

38. For background see Arthur Huff Fauset, *Black Gods of the Metropolis. Negro Religious Cults of the Urban North* (New York, 1974; first published, 1944); Sara Harris, *Father Divine. Holy Husband* (Garden City, N.Y., 1953); Ivan H. Light, *Ethnic Enterprise in America; Business and Welfare among Chinese, Japanese, and Blacks* (Berkeley, 1962); Robert Weisbrot, *Father Divine and the Struggle for Racial Equality* (Urbana, 1983).

39. The best accounts are Lincoln, *The Black Muslims*; E. U. Essien-Udom, *Black Nationalism: A Search for an Identity In America* (Chicago, 1962); Yvonne Yazbeck Haddad, "Muslims in the United States," in Marjorie Kelly, ed., *Islam. The Religious and Political Life of a World Community* (New York, 1984); and Earle Waugh et al., eds., *The Muslim Community in North America* (Edmonton, Alberta, 1983). Also see the comments in C. Eric Lincoln, *Race, Religion, and the Continuing American Dilemma* (New York, 1984), 154–69.

40. Washington, *Black Religion*, 125.

41. On the subject of black nationalism, aside from what has been cited, see Essien-Udom, *Black Nationalism*.

42. A number of the writers who contributed to Hart Nelsen et al., *The Black Church* noted this fact. See the contributions by Clifton Brown, Gary Marx, and Ronald Johnstone.

43. For a controversial discussion of black responses to paternalism, see Sowell, *Ethnic America*, chap. 8.

44. Lincoln, *Black Church Since Frazier*, 179.

45. James H. Cone, *A Black Theology of Liberation* (Philadelphia, 1970). See also Cone, *Black Theology and Black Power* (New York, 1969). Albert B. Cleage, Jr., *The Black Messiah* (New York, 1969); Cleage, *Black Christian Nationalism* (New York, 1972); Gayraud S. Wilmore, *Black Religion and Black Radicalism*; "The Black Church," *The Black Scholar* 2 (Dec. 1970).

46. Watts, "Caucuses and Caucasians," in C. Eric Lincoln, *The Black Experience in Religion* (Garden City, N.Y., 1974), 25. See also Washington, *Black Religion*, 31.

47. Cited by Herskovits, *Myth of the Negro Past*, 31.

48. Bracey, *Black Nationalism*, 233–34.

49. Harold Cruse, *The Crisis of the Negro Intellectual* (New York, 1967), 147–70.

50. Quoted in Robert G. Weisbord and Arthur Stein, *Bittersweet Encounter. The Afro-American and the American Jew* (Westport, Conn., 1970), 97. For background see Nat Hentoff, ed., *Black Anti-Semitism and Jewish Racism* (New York, 1969).

POSTSCRIPT

1. Bellah, "Civil Religion in America," in William G. McLoughlin and Robert N. Bellah, eds., *Religion in America* (Boston, 1968), 3–23. First published in *Daedalus* (Winter, 1967).

2. The work of Will Herberg, Sidney Mead, and William McLoughlin has been especially persuasive and influential. For discussions of the issues see Russell E. Richey and Donald Jones, eds., *American Civil Religion* (New York, 1974); John F. Wilson, *Public Religion in American Culture* (Philadelphia, 1979); Gail Gehrig, *American Civil Religion: An Assessment* (1979).

3. See especially the essays by Roger Chartier and Carlo Ginzburg in Steve Kaplan, ed., *Understanding Popular Culture. Europe from the Middle Ages to the Nineteenth Century* (Berlin, 1984).

4. Robert Bellah, *The Broken Covenant: American Civil Religion in a Time of Trial* (New York, 1975).

5. Will Herberg, *Protestant, Catholic, Jew. An Essay in American Religious Sociology* (Garden City, N.Y., 1955) 99.

6. Gordon Allport and Michael Ross, "Personal Religious Orientation and Prejudice," *Journal of Personality and Social Psychology* 5 (April 1967): 432–42. Charles Y. Glock and R. Stark, *Christian Beliefs and Anti-Semitism* (New York, 1966).

7. Edwin S. Gaustad, "America's Institutions of Faith: A Statistical Postscript," in McLoughlin and Bellah, *Religion in America*, 111–33.

8. Andrew Greeley, *The Denominational Society. A Sociological Approach to Religion in America* (Glenview, Ill., 1972).

Index

237

Printed in the United States
1665

9 780195 051889